Selected Lyrics

Selected Lyrics

THEOPHILE GAUTIER

TRANSLATED BY NORMAN R. SHAPIRO

YALE UNIVERSITY PRESS ■ NEW HAVEN & LONDON

A MARGELLOS
WORLD REPUBLIC OF LETTERS BOOK

The Margellos World Republic of Letters is dedicated to making literary works from around the globe available in English through translation. It brings to the English-speaking world the work of leading poets, novelists, essayists, philosophers, and playwrights from Europe, Latin America, Africa, Asia, and the Middle East to stimulate international discourse and creative exchange.

Publication of this book has been aided by a grant from the Thomas and Catharine McMahon Fund of Wesleyan University, established through the generosity of the late Joseph McMahon.

Yale University Press books may be purchased in quantity for educational, business, or promotional use. For information, please e-mail sales.press@yale.edu (U.S. office) or sales@yaleup.co.uk (U.K. office).

Set in Electra type by Keystone Typesetting, Inc.
Printed in the United States of America by Sheridan Books, Ann Arbor, Michigan.

The Library of Congress has cataloged the hardcover edition as follows:
Gautier, Théophile, 1811–1872.
   [Selections. English. 2011]
   Selected lyrics / Théophile Gautier ; translated by Norman R. Shapiro.
      p. cm. — (A Margellos world republic of letters book)
   Includes bibliographical references.
   ISBN 978-0-300-16433-6 (cloth : alk. paper) 1. Gautier, Théophile, 1811–1872—
Translations into English. I. Shapiro, Norman R. II. Title.
   PQ2258.A2 2011
   841'.7—dc22   2010022695

ISBN 978-0-300-18155-5 (pbk.)

A catalogue record for this book is available from the British Library.

10 9 8 7 6 5 4 3 2 1

For poet John Hollander,
the godfather of this collection,
in friendship and admiration

CONTENTS

Several years ago poet John Hollander suggested that I might like to consider translating the nineteenth-century French author Théophile Gautier. Not his macabre, often lurid prose tales, typical of early Romantic fare and rather well known to Anglophone readers through a variety of translations over the years, but a sampling from his large body of verse, lesser known especially outside of France. Indeed, even the French often know Gautier the poet less than he deserves, recalling little more than the garish crimson waistcoat he flaunted at the tempestuous premiere of Victor Hugo's *Hernani* in 1830; and many of his countrymen are even unaware of the generally (though not universally) accepted role attributed to him as a bridge between the personal effusiveness of the Romantics and the striking plasticity of the so-called Parnassian school. And this even though many, as students, might well have memorized at least the final capstone stanza of his poem "Art," the *ars poetica* of the "Art for Art's Sake" inspiration.

I followed John Hollander's suggestion. These translations are the result. Rather than present them in the traditional, approximately chronological order—often difficult to ascertain with precision for Gautier—I have chosen to make the mature *Emaux et Camées*, in its entirety, the centerpiece of my collection and to proceed in more or less reverse chronology with less extensive selections from the works leading up to it, especially the vigorously exotic *España*, a blend of both Romantic local color and Parnassian visuality. A more critical, "scholarly" presentation would, to my mind, go beyond the scope of this sampling, the essential purpose of which is to acquaint the English-speaking reader with aesthetic texts, not academic explications.

As I have often said, the joy of literary translation for me lies in facing, and one hopes meeting, the challenge—or challenges—that the original work presents. Those presented by Gautier's have been many, not only in content and form, but especially in that far less definable and too often elusive element, the "tone." I have even chosen to up the inherent artistic challenge by closely adopting—adapting?— Gautier's forms into English, and hewing to his rhymes and meters, though not, certainly, by trudging line-for-line through his texts or by attempting to graft my lines onto the exact syllable-count of his multi-ruled syllabic French prosody. While I render his eight-syllable lines of *Emaux et Camées* into English equivalents, I avoid a similar correspondence for his alexandrines, in *España* and much of his earlier verse, for example. To have opted otherwise would, no doubt, have given me more "breathing room" to spread out in, but it would also have resulted in the plodding twelve-syllable line that formal English poetry, since Pope, generally tries to avoid. As for the "tone," I have used an idiom—lexicon as well as syntax—consistent, I think, with Gautier's own, albeit across the linguistic and cultural divide.

Translator colleagues will appreciate the effort that has gone into trying to meet the challenges mentioned. Casual readers probably will not. Which is, in fact—ironically—a great compliment, since we translators always hope that we have made it all look easy. With all that, I have done my best to explain, in copious notes, the large number of historic, geographic, literary, and artistic allusions that Gautier seems to have taken pleasure in working into his poems. Sometimes one even suspects his motives just a little . . .

That said, it is always a pleasure, once the "pièce de résistance" has been cooked up and served, to offer the "dessert": our appreciation to those who have inspired our work and helped it along its way.

My very special thanks go to poet and friend John Hollander, whose confidence resulted in this collection's conception; to colleague Jeffrey Mehlman, for his informative and elegant appreciation of the newborn; and, no less, to my research assistant *cum* computer guru and amanuensis extraordinaire, French Wall, for expert midwifery, electronic and otherwise, during the lengthy labor. I continue, likewise, to be grateful to Wesleyan University for its ongoing support of my several endeavors, as well as to Rosalind Eastaway and Linda Cummings for a spate of editorial chores. As ever, I am indebted to dear friends Evelyn Singer Simha and Caldwell Titcomb for their invaluable encouragement; to Allan and the late, much-lamented Sylvia Kliman for moral support throughout. Likewise, to Sean, for putting up with me.

For their often needed and much appreciated good cheer, I thank Tim Smith, Max Binder, and Chase Carpenter, denizens of Adams House in Harvard University, where, through the generosity of co-masters Judy and Sean Palfrey, Sophia Chaknis, David Seley, and the company of other good friends, much of this work took shape at the dining hall's "corner table." And, for a variety of interest, kind words, and generous actions, my thanks to friends Odile Ayral-Clause, Ames Brown, Jim Kates, Christine Lalande, Joyce Lowrie, Catherine Ostrow, Joseph Phillips, Jeffrey Rider, Louisa Solano, and Daniel Wuenschel.

Never forgotten is the spirit of my late mother, who long ago transmitted to me, viva voce if not through the genes, her love of poetry, and who, I feel, is still doing so.

INTRODUCTION

The significance of Théophile Gautier's verse is perhaps best grasped in terms of a division splitting French poetry of the nineteenth century virtually down the middle: on the one hand, Victor Hugo, a poetry of Progress, moralistically mindful of the imperative to promote the Good; on the other, Charles Baudelaire, an aesthetic already decadent in its refusal to think beyond the compulsion to relieve tedium. The two, as Paul Valéry (and later Walter Benjamin) suggested, were in a situation of perfect "complementarity"—or incompatibility. Yet it was Gautier's odd fate to serve as a kind of hinge between them. For he was, in 1830, Hugo's lieutenant at the near riot occasioned by the first performance of the poet's *Hernani* and, in 1857, the esteemed dedicatee of Baudelaire's masterwork, *Les Fleurs du mal.* Gautier, that is, occupies a "considerable place," as André Gide, who was no fan, put it, in the history of French poetry, and it may be assumed that coming to terms with his achievement is to accede to a new dimension of understanding of French poetry itself.

Norman Shapiro has been idiosyncratically coming to terms with French poetry for many years now. We owe him extraordinary versions of all of Jean de La Fontaine, but also of Baudelaire and much of Paul Verlaine and Jacques Prévert. He has given us a major anthology of French Renaissance poetry as well as a thousand-page collection of poetry in French by women poets. It is almost as though he had decided that a poem would not be understood until it was literally re-created in a foreign medium—English. Or that poetry demanded translation as a kind of fulfillment. Or perhaps it is a tragic presentiment that with the waning of literary culture—what some have called the "graphosphere"—in France, a refuge of some sort is needed to redeem what all too often seems on the brink of implosion. (Otherwise put: wherefore the gleam of Gautier's *émail*—that is, enamel—in an age of disposable e-mail?) One is tempted to imagine Norman Shapiro carrying out, line by line, the quietly redemptive "task of the translator," as Benjamin called it, in his perch in Cambridge.

Shapiro is not the first Cantabrigian to have taken momentously to Gautier. In 1873 Henry James penned the first of five texts on the poet, and his brother William quickly decided it was his "best performance," "quite as good as Gautier himself." It was soon the talk of the town, James's father wrote him. James got things just right: Gautier, he wrote, "knew the French color-box as well as if he had ground the pigments, and it may really be said of him that he did grind a great many of them."[1] This is the painterly Gautier, the man for whom the external world famously existed. It was the Gautier whose nuances in a stanza on Venice were evoked by Oscar Wilde, in *The Picture of Dorian Gray*, as a "floating down the green water-ways of the pink and pearl city, [while] seated on a black gondola with silver prow and trailing curtains." Beyond that, one senses, in James on Gautier, the novelist engaging his own ambivalent fascination for the French-pagan attachment to irresistible surfaces, "sublime good looks," and "thick-coming fancies."[2] It is as though James, in Gautier, were discovering his calling as a novelist, or at least the plot of *The Ambassadors*.

Might Gautier not offer as well the very medium within which a great translator might discover—or rediscover—the mythic basis of his calling? It has been said that the bliss of the translator is to be able to write great novels without having to worry about plot. Transpose that

---

[1] Henry James, *Literary Criticism: French Writers* (New York: Library of America, 1984), 421.

[2] Ibid., 367, 368.

notion to poetry, and one might say that the bliss of the translator is to be able to write great poems without having to be bothered with inspiration. The point is worth registering to the extent that Gautier, a poet of surfaces and horizontal affinities, had all but done away with depth of thought (i.e., the pedagogical heresy) or elevation of sentiment (i.e., the humanitarian heresy). His, as Baudelaire intuited, was a poetry of "horizontal" and not "vertical" correspondences.[3] And horizontal correspondence is the very medium in which the translator does his "carrying over."

Consider the "pantheistic madrigal" "Hidden Affinities" as the translator's breviary:

> In temple wall of times long past—
> Three thousand Attic years, blue-skied—
> Have stood two marble blocks, joined fast,
> Dreaming their white dreams, side by side.

White is, of course, the color of marble, but it is also the blankness of a dream with no other content than its relation—of hidden affinity— with another dream that would translate it. And one wonders whether the white of the famous "Symphony in White Major"—

> As all that sight-numbing array,
> Joined with the flesh of pearl-shell white,
> Lets us feast on the lush display:
> Orgies of northland white delight

—already so anticipatory of Stéphane Mallarmé's poem of a swan dying white on wintry white, is not as much about the semantic emptiness of sheer syntactical relation as about the multiple nuances of whiteness it is taken to convey.

---

[3] The point has been elaborated by Michel Brix in his introduction to Théophile Gautier, *Œuvres poétiques complètes* (Paris: Bartillat, 2004), xxxix.

But no doubt Gautier's great poem of translation is "Obelisks' Longings." The subject is "brother" obelisks: one, hauled from Egypt and placed on the Place de la Concorde, alongside a Seine ("gutters' black sewer vile") that seems no more than a cruel parody of "Father Nile," mourning lost Egypt with "tears of granite"; the other, still in Luxor, feeling equally estranged as it keeps watch:

> Light deadened through a film of lead
> Nile's sluggish waves monotonous
> Glow in a dull sun overhead,
> Billow with hippopotamus.

The poem seems to yearn for the reciprocity or "restitution," as George Steiner put it, of translation. It is a dimension that perhaps puts it a step ahead of Baudelaire's poem of Parisian exile, "The Swan" (memorably translated into German by Benjamin, into English by Shapiro), and already on its way to a paradoxical fulfillment of sorts— "fragments of a vessel to be glued together," in Benjamin's phrase—as sheer difference in the beating wing of Mallarmé's dying swan.

I have, of course, neglected the almost kaleidoscopic craft of these translations, no doubt because superior craft is frequently invoked as a put-down in the case of the acrobatic Gautier. But this introduction would be remiss if it did not attend to the special constraint Shapiro has labored under and overcome. For Gautier, in his *ars poetica*, made a point of denying the translator all wiggle room:

> All false constraints begone!
> But, Muse, to walk aright,
>> Best don
> A cothurn firm and tight.

When the shoe (or cothurn) is that tight, offering that little wiggle room, it is difficult indeed for the signifier, to use Claude Lévi-Strauss's coinage, to *float* enough to pull off the small miracle of a successful translation. That Shapiro manages to do so as often as he does is a subject of wonder that will leave many a reader entranced.

But then again, the dream of a Gautier (or a "Théofield Gautier," as she called him) "quite as good as Gautier himself," the subject of Mary James's letter of 1873 to her son Henry, is a dream that has been dreamt before in Cambridge. After James, who, perhaps out of panic, judged Baudelaire "an altogether inferior poet to Gautier," came Ezra Pound, whose short list—in his *ABC of Reading*—of nineteenth-century French poets to be studied begins with Gautier, and then T. S. Eliot, a number of whose quatrains of the 1920s are plainly the work of a devoted reader of *Emaux et Camées*. Which is to say that this volume takes its place in a very American tradition even as it mines deeply one of the crucial treasures of a very French one. That it does so, on both fronts, as auspiciously as it does is a matter that will command the gratitude of both readers of poetry and students of translation for years to come.

Jeffrey Mehlman

EMAUX ET CAMEES

1852 – 1872

PREFACE

Pendant les guerres de l'empire,
Gœthe, au bruit du canon brutal,
Fit *le Divan occidental,*
Fraîche oasis où l'art respire.

Pour Nisami quittant Shakspeare,
Il se parfuma de çantal,
Et sur un mètre oriental
Nota le chant qu'Hudhud soupire.

Comme Gœthe sur son divan
A Weimar s'isolait des choses
Et d'Hafiz effeuillait les roses,

Sans prendre garde à l'ouragan
Qui fouettait mes vitres fermées,
Moi, j'ai fait *Emaux et Camées.*

PREFACE

Goethe wrote *West's Divan* as men[1]
Waged war to cannons' blare and boom:
A cool oasis in the gloom,
Where stifled art might breathe again.

And spurning even Shakespeare's pen,
For Nisami's, praised Hudhud, whom[2]
He sang to measures' spice-perfume:
O Oriental denizen!

Like Weimar's divaned Goethe, lying
Safe from the times' atrocities,
Plucking rose-petals of Hafiz,[3]

I scorned the wind-whipped storm, come flying
Against my windowpanes one day,
And fashioned *Emaux et Camées.*

AFFINITES SECRETES

Madrigal panthéiste

Dans le fronton d'un temple antique,
Deux blocs de marbre ont, trois mille ans,
Sur le fond bleu du ciel attique
Juxtaposé leurs rêves blancs;

Dans la même nacre figées,
Larmes des flots pleurant Vénus,
Deux perles au gouffre plongées
Se sont dit des mots inconnus;

Au frais Généralife écloses,
Sous le jet d'eau toujours en pleurs;
Du temps de Boabdil, deux roses
Ensemble ont fait jaser leurs fleurs;

Sur les coupoles de Venise
Deux ramiers blancs aux pieds rosés,
Au nid où l'amour s'éternise
Un soir de mai se sont posés.

Marbre, perle, rose, colombe,
Tout se dissout, tout se détruit;
La perle fond, le marbre tombe,
La fleur se fane et l'oiseau fuit.

HIDDEN AFFINITIES

Pantheistic Madrigal

In temple wall of times long past—
Three thousand Attic years, blue-skied—
Have stood two marble blocks, joined fast,
Dreaming their white dreams, side by side.

Sharing the same light-mottled shell,
Two pearls in ocean's deep-most reach—
Tears mourning Venus's farewell—[4]
Spoke words uncommon, each to each.

In cool Generalife's clime,
Beneath its ever-spouting jet,
Two roses of Boabdil's time[5]
Chatted in friendly tête-à-tête.

Atop Venice's domes, one night
In month of May, there, two ring-doves—
White, pink of feet—chanced to alight,
Nesting, to share their lives and loves.

Marble, pearl, ring-dove, rose... These must,
Each one, soon all be dead or dying;
The pearl melts, marble falls to dust;
The rose fades, wilts; the bird goes flying...

En se quittant, chaque parcelle
S'en va dans le creuset profond
Grossir la pâte universelle
Faite des formes que Dieu fond.

Par de lentes métamorphoses,
Les marbres blancs en blanches chairs,
Les fleurs roses en lèvres roses
Se refont dans des corps divers.

Les ramiers de nouveau roucoulent
Au cœur de deux jeunes amants,
Et les perles en dents se moulent
Pour l'écrin des rires charmants.

De là naissent ces sympathies
Aux impérieuses douceurs,
Par qui les âmes averties
Partout se reconnaissent sœurs.

Docile à l'appel d'un arome,
D'un rayon ou d'une couleur,
L'atome vole vers l'atome
Comme l'abeille vers la fleur.

L'on se souvient des rêveries
Sur le fronton ou dans la mer,
Des conversations fleuries
Près de la fontaine au flot clair,

Dissolving, every jot of matter
Rejoins the crucible that, through
All time, contains, mixes the batter
That God molds, melts, and shapes anew.

In gentle metamorphosis
White marble turns to fair white flesh;
Rose blooms to lips of pink: such, this
Parade of forms transformed afresh.

Again the ring-doves coo their love
In two young lovers' hearts; the while,
Are pearls reborn as teeth, whereof,
Like jewels encased, shine laughter's smile;

Whence form those kindred sympathies
That, not to be denied, control
The sweet, boundless affinities
One senses for a sister soul.

Heeding a scent's call willingly—
A ray of light's, a color's power—
Atom to atom flies, like bee
Straight in its flight unto the flower.

Then one recalls the dreams one dared
To dream by temple walls; or in
The sea; or chats two flowers had shared
By fountain's waters crystalline.

Des baisers et des frissons d'ailes
Sur les dômes aux boules d'or,
Et les molécules fidèles
Se cherchent et s'aiment encor.

L'amour oublié se réveille,
Le passé vaguement renaît,
La fleur sur la bouche vermeille
Se respire et se reconnaît.

Dans la nacre où le rire brille,
La perle revoit sa blancheur;
Sur une peau de jeune fille,
Le marbre ému sent sa fraîcheur.

Le ramier trouve une voix douce,
Echo de son gémissement,
Toute résistance s'émousse,
Et l'inconnu devient l'amant.

Vous devant qui je brûle et tremble,
Quel flot, quel fronton, quel rosier,
Quel dôme nous connut ensemble,
Perle ou marbre, fleur ou ramier?

Kisses and fluttering wings, above
Golden-balled domes, will chirr and trill
As molecules, true to their love,
Seek out each other, loving still.

Love, once forgotten, all but dead,
Awakes... Vague pasts stir from afar.
The flowers, on lips of scarlet red,
Breathe in their scent, sense who they are.[6]

In mottled shell now laughter peels
Again; pearls gleam white, as before.
On maid's white flesh cool marble feels
The thrill of shining flesh once more.

The ring-dove, echoing his moan,
Warbles again his gentle voice;
Resistance weakens; once unknown
Strangers turn lovers and rejoice.

And you, for whom I tremble, burning,
What temple wall, rosebush, or dome,
What waters, pearls, ring-doves, returning,
Knew us first in our kindred home?

LE POEME DE LA FEMME

Marbre de Paros

Un jour, au doux rêveur qui l'aime,
En train de montrer ses trésors,
Elle voulut lire un poème,
Le poème de son beau corps.

D'abord, superbe et triomphante
Elle vint en grand apparat,
Traînant avec des airs d'infante
Un flot de velours nacarat :

Telle qu'au rebord de sa loge
Elle brille aux Italiens
Ecoutant passer son éloge
Dans les chants des musiciens.

Ensuite, en sa verve d'artiste,
Laissant tomber l'épais velours,
Dans un nuage de batiste
Elle ébaucha ses fiers contours.

Glissant de l'épaule à la hanche,
La chemise aux plis nonchalants,
Comme une tourterelle blanche
Vint s'abattre sur ses pieds blancs.

THE POEM OF WOMAN

Paros Marble

One day, she set out to recite—
Displaying charms of flesh and dress—
A poem for her love's delight:
Poem writ of her loveliness.

First she appeared in splendid clothes—
Regal her mien, haughty her mood—
Trailing behind, in princess-pose,
A velvet wake, nacarat-hued:[7]

At her *Italiens* box, see her
Leaning, in radiant brilliance, thus,
As, in their airs, doting *chanteurs*
Extol her presence glorious![8]

Then, with an artiste's elegance,
She would let fall her velvet cape
In batiste cloud, and strike a stance,
Proud to reveal her comely shape;

Slipping demurely from above,
Shoulders to hips, with casual pleat
And fold, her blouse—white turtledove—
Fell round the whiteness of her feet.

Pour Apelle ou pour Cléomène,
Elle semblait, marbre de chair,
En Vénus Anadyomène
Poser nue au bord de la mer.

De grosses perles de Venise
Roulaient au lieu de gouttes d'eau,
Grains laiteux qu'un rayon irise,
Sur le frais satin de sa peau.

Oh! quelles ravissantes choses,
Dans sa divine nudité,
Avec les strophes de ses poses,
Chantait cet hymne de beauté!

Comme les flots baisant le sable
Sous la lune aux tremblants rayons,
Sa grâce était intarissable
En molles ondulations.

Mais bientôt, lasse d'art antique,
De Phidias et de Vénus,
Dans une autre stance plastique
Elle groupe ses charmes nus.

Sur un tapis de Cachemire,
C'est la sultane du sérail,
Riant au miroir qui l'admire
Avec un rire de corail;

For Apelles, Cleomenes,
Marbled of flesh, she seemed to be
Venus Anadyomenes,
Posing unclad beside the sea.[9]

Venetian pearls swirled large and bright,
Instead of droplets, on her flesh;
Mild-white beads, mottling in the light,
Over her skin, smooth, satin-fresh.

Oh! Nudity divine! What sights
To charm the eye's gaze passion-smitten!
Each pose, a stanza; fancy's flights
Sung in this hymn to beauty written!

As billows plant their kiss upon
The sand, beneath the quivering moon,
Endless, her grace rolled on and on,
Wave after wave, delight-bestrewn.

But soon, viewing Antiquity—
Phidias, Venus too!—askance,
She groups in naked artistry
Her charms in yet another stance:

Sultana of the harem, she
Lay on a Kashmir carpet while
Her glass looked back admiringly,
Laughing in a pink coral smile;

La Géorgienne indolente,
Avec son souple narguilhé,
Etalant sa hanche opulente,
Un pied sous l'autre replié.

Et comme l'odalisque d'Ingres,
De ses reins cambrant les rondeurs,
En dépit des vertus malingres,
En dépit des maigres pudeurs!

Paresseuse odalisque, arrière!
Voici le tableau dans son jour,
Le diamant dans sa lumière;
Voici la beauté dans l'amour!

Sa tête penche et se renverse;
Haletante, dressant les seins,
Aux bras du rêve qui la berce,
Elle tombe sur ses coussins.

Ses paupières battent des ailes
Sur leurs globes d'argent bruni,
Et l'on voit monter ses prunelles
Dans la nacre de l'infini.

D'un linceul de point d'Angleterre
Que l'on recouvre sa beauté :
L'extase l'a prise à la terre;
Elle est morte de volupté!

With supple hookah at her lips,
The Georgian maiden, opulent
Of flesh, lies lazing on lush hips,
One foot behind the other bent;

Like Ingres's odalisque outspanned—
Rounded her curves and svelte—despite
Her virtues' vague discomfort, and
Despite her lures, immodest quite![10]

You, idle odalisque, away!
Here, the real portrait looming true,
The diamond in her bright array;
Beauty in love's light, shining through!

Head to one side, thrown back, she sprawls,
Bosom erect, in to-and-fro's—
Breathless—with cradling arms, and falls
Into her cushions' sweet repose.

Beating their wings before her eyes
Of silvered brown, her lids we see
Fluttering, as her pupils rise
Through opal-pearled infinity.

Her body's loveliness is worth
Its shroud of English lace outspread;
Ecstasy wrenched her from the earth;
In fleshly bliss now she lies dead![11]

Que les violettes de Parme,
Au lieu des tristes fleurs des morts
Où chaque perle est une larme,
Pleurent en bouquets sur son corps!

Et que mollement on la pose
Sur son lit, tombeau blanc et doux,
Où le poète, à la nuit close,
Ira prier à deux genoux.

Instead of death's dour flowers, weeping,
Whose every droplet is a tear,
Let Parma violets mourn her, heaping
Somber bouquets about her bier.

Gently, let her be laid upon
Her bed, tomb soft and white; and there,
The poet, as night awaits the dawn,
On bended knee, will pause in prayer.

ETUDE DE MAINS

I

Impéria

Chez un sculpteur, moulée en plâtre,
J'ai vu l'autre jour une main
D'Aspasie ou de Cléopâtre,
Pur fragment d'un chef-d'œuvre humain;

Sous le baiser neigeux saisie
Comme un lis par l'aube argenté,
Comme une blanche poésie
S'épanouissait sa beauté.

Dans l'éclat de sa pâleur mate
Elle étalait sur le velours
Son élégance délicate
Et ses doigts fins aux anneaux lourds.

Une cambrure florentine,
Avec un bel air de fierté,
Faisait, en ligne serpentine,
Onduler son pouce écarté.

A-t-elle joué dans les boucles
Des cheveux lustrés de don Juan,
Ou sur son caftan d'escarboucles
Peigné la barbe du sultan,

STUDY IN HANDS

I

Imperia

I saw a plaster hand, on view
In sculptor's studio, set apart...
Aspasia's? Cleopatra's?... Who?[12]
This fragment's human work of art?

Like lily silvered by the dawn,
Frozen in kiss of snow, its light
Loveliness dazzled me, and shone
In poetry of purest white.

Though pallid, wan, yet striking, it
Spread over velvet, graceful, slender
Fingers—delicate, exquisite—
Decked thick with rings of weighty splendor.

Thumb high, in serpentine-like pose,
Arched in a svelte and shapely line,
It lay, fine set, like one of those
Hands held with proud air Florentine.

Did it comb out the sultan's beard
On jeweled caftan? Or, with twirls
And twistings, when Don Juan appeared,
Play in his lustrous, glistening curls?

Et tenu, courtisane ou reine,
Entre ses doigts si bien sculptés,
Le sceptre de la souveraine
Ou le sceptre des voluptés?

Elle a dû, nerveuse et mignonne,
Souvent s'appuyer sur le col
Et sur la croupe de lionne
De sa chimère prise au vol.

Impériales fantaisies,
Amour des somptuosités;
Voluptueuses frénésies,
Rêves d'impossibilités,

Romans extravagants, poèmes
De haschisch et de vin du Rhin,
Courses folles dans les bohèmes
Sur le dos des coursiers sans frein;

On voit tout cela dans les lignes
De cette paume, livre blanc
Où Vénus a tracé des signes
Que l'amour ne lit qu'en tremblant.

A courtesan's? A queen's? Did this[13]
Wrought hand a scepter wield? Which one?
The paragon of fleshly bliss?
Sovereignty's beauteous paragon?

Doubtless, by little starts and fits,
It lit, poised, in its fluttering,
On the she-lion croup of its
Chimera-dream, caught on the wing;

The Empire's fantasies; bombastic
Love of fantastic, sumptuous schemes;
Voluptuous frenzies orgiastic;
Impossible and futile dreams;

Wild tales; poetic escapades
Of hashish, Rhine-wine sorcery;
Dashing Bohemian cavalcades
On steeds unbridled, coursing free...

Such are the things the eye divines
In that white book, by Venus written:
Blank palm where she has traced the signs
One reads, a-tremble, terror-smitten.

II

Lacenaire

Pour contraste, la main coupée
De Lacenaire l'assassin,
Dans des baumes puissants trempée,
Posait auprès, sur un coussin.

Curiosité dépravée
J'ai touché, malgré mes dégoûts,
Du supplice encor mal lavée
Cette chair froide au duvet roux.

Momifiée et toute jaune
Comme la main d'un pharaon,
Elle allonge ses doigts de faune
Crispés par la tentation.

Un prurit d'or et de chair vive
Semble titiller de ses doigts
L'immobilité convulsive,
Et les tordre comme autrefois.

Tous les vices avec leurs griffes
Ont, dans les plis de cette peau,
Tracé d'affreux hiéroglyphes,
Lus couramment par le bourreau.

II

Lacenaire

Close by, in contrast, lying there,
Encushioned, was the severed hand—
Pungent-embalmed—of Lacenaire,
Assassin and scourge of the land;

Curio most depraved! But, though
Repulsed, I reached and touched it, still
Barely cleansed of its horrors! Oh!
That flesh, red-downed and deathly chill!

Sallow hand, like a mummy's wrought,
All yellowed, laid-out pharaoh-wise,
Spreading its faun-like fingers, taut,
As if to seize its tempting prize;

Exuding from their tips, an itching
Lusting for living flesh and gold,
About to writhe, convulsed, and twitching
Before their victims, as of old.

Vice clawed vile hieroglyph designs
Of heinous wrongs—most foul, most fell—
In all its wrinkles, all its lines,
Signs that the executioner knew well!

On y voit les œuvres mauvaises
Ecrites en fauves sillons,
Et les brûlures des fournaises
Où bouillent les corruptions;

Les débauches dans les Caprées
Des tripots et des lupanars,
De vin et de sang diaprées,
Comme l'ennui des vieux Césars!

En même temps molle et féroce,
Sa forme a pour l'observateur
Je ne sais quelle grâce atroce,
La grâce du gladiateur!

Criminelle aristocratie,
Par la varlope ou le marteau
Sa pulpe n'est pas endurcie,
Car son outil fut un couteau,

Saints calus du travail honnête,
On y cherche en vain votre sceau.
Vrai meurtrier et faux poète,
Il fut le Manfred du ruisseau!

One sees its scabrous deeds large writ
In the palm's bestial creases, and
The boiling cauldron scalding it
With every crime at sin's command;

Capri's debauches libertine,
Of fleshpot brothels orgy-rife
Stained through with blot of blood and wine
Like the old Caesar's blasé life.[14]

At once both soft and savage, its
Shape shows a curious elegance,
A fearsome grace that counterfeits
The gladiator's graceful stance!

Crime's aristocracy! No plane,
No hammer's labors ever made
Its flesh tough time and time again!
Its only tool, the dagger-blade...

Work's honest calluses! For you
We look in vain, no sign we see:
Evil's false poet, butcher true—
A Manfred of the gutter, he![15]

VARIATIONS SUR LE CARNAVAL DE VENISE

I

Dans la rue

Il est un vieil air populaire
Par tous les violons raclé,
Aux abois des chiens en colère
Par tous les orgues nasillé.

Les tabatières à musique
L'ont sur leur répertoire inscrit;
Pour les serins il est classique,
Et ma grand'mère, enfant, l'apprit.

Sur cet air, pistons, clarinettes
Dans les bals aux poudreux berceaux,
Font sauter commis et grisettes,
Et de leurs nids fuir les oiseaux.

La guinguette, sous sa tonnelle
De houblon et de chèvrefeuil,
Fête, en braillant la ritournelle,
Le gai dimanche et l'argenteuil.

L'aveugle au basson qui pleurniche
L'écorche en se trompant de doigts;
La sébile aux dents, son caniche
Près du lui le grogne à mi-voix.

VARIATIONS ON THE CARNIVAL OF VENICE

I

In the Street

A popular old song there is,
Scratched out on every violin;
Hand-organs twang; each dog growls his
Dismay thereat, day out day in.

Musical snuffbox reliquary,
Year after year, forgets it not;
Classic canary tune; the very
One grandmamma learned as a tot.[16]

To trumpet's blast and clarinets'—
In dusty dancehall arbor-fest—
Bookkeepers dance with brash coquettes
And birds wake, fleeing from their nest.

And the same blaring melody,
In hops-decked bowers of sweet woodbine,
Fetes Sundays and their revelry
With the joys of a village wine.

Blind man sobs it on his bassoon,
Squeaking most of the notes all wrong;
Near him, his dog—not quite in tune! —
Plate in his mouth, whimpers along.

Et les petites guitaristes,
Maigres sous leurs minces tartans,
Le glapissent de leurs voix tristes
Aux tables des cafés chantants.

Paganini, le fantastique,
Un soir, comme avec un crochet,
A ramassé le thème antique
Du bout de son divin archet,

Et, brodant la gaze fanée
Que l'oripeau rougit encor,
Fait sur la phrase dédaignée
Courir ses arabesques d'or.

II

Sur les lagunes

Tra la, tra la, la, la, la laire!
Qui ne connaît pas ce motif?
A nos mamans il a su plaire,
Tendre et gai, moqueur et plaintif :

L'air du Carnaval de Venise,
Sur les canaux jadis chanté
Et qu'un soupir de folle brise
Dans le ballet a transporté!

Guitarist maidens in ill-fitting
Tartan plaids — scrawny-figured — raise
Sad, wailing voices to it, sitting
Tabled in cabaret-cafés.

One night, wild Paganini, there,
Upon a crochet's tail — or so
To speak! — hooked up that ancient air
With the tip of his heavenly bow.[17]

Embroidering the wilted, faded
Muslin, still reddish, tattered, he
Crochet'd the tune, disdained and jaded,
With arabesques' gold filigree.[18]

II

On the Lagunes

Tra la, tra la, la, la, la laire!
Who cannot know that tune? Sad, gay,
Delicate, mocking, debonair...
Our mammas loved it in their day:

That "Carnival of Venice," sung
On the canals in bygone days,
The breeze's sigh, blown mad among
The dance steps of the old ballets!

Il me semble, quand on le joue,
Voir glisser dans son bleu sillon
Une gondole avec sa proue
Faite en manche de violon.

Sur une gamme chromatique,
Le sein de perles ruisselant,
La Vénus de l'Adriatique
Sort de l'eau son corps rose et blanc.

Les dômes sur l'azur des ondes,
Suivant la phrase au pur contour,
S'enflent comme des gorges rondes
Que soulève un soupir d'amour.

L'esquif aborde et me dépose,
Jetant son amarre au pilier,
Devant une façade rose,
Sur le marbre d'un escalier.

Avec ses palais, ses gondoles,
Ses marcarades sur la mer,
Ses doux chagrins, ses gaîtés folles,
Tout Venise vit dans cet air.

Une frêle corde qui vibre
Refait sur un pizzicato,
Comme autrefois joyeuse et libre,
La ville de Canaletto!

When it is played I seem to see
A gondola gliding erect
On its blue wake, effortlessly,
Plying its high prow, fiddle-necked.

Against the melody chromatic,
Venus, her breast with droplets pearled,
Rises up from the Adriatic,
Her body pink and white unfurled.

Like sigh of love the bosom raising,
The domes, against the waters' blue,
Trace the pure contour of the phrasing,
Swelling full, as round breasts will do.

I land as my skiff touches ground
By a façade of pink; and there,
A pillar chaining it around,
Next to a rising marble stair...

Gondolas, palaces, her nights
Of seaborne revels, sweet chagrin...
Venice, with all her wild delights,
Sings us that song and lives therein.

A pizzicato plucked upon
A fragile string... And, with that ditty,
Shines the free air that gaily shone
On Canaletto's timeless city![19]

III

Carnaval

Venise pour le bal s'habille.
De paillettes tout étoilé,
Scintille, fourmille et babille
Le carnaval bariolé.

Arlequin, nègre par son masque,
Serpent par ses mille couleurs,
Rosse d'une note fantasque
Cassandre son souffre-douleurs.

Battant de l'aile avec sa manche
Comme un pingouin sur un écueil,
Le blanc Pierrot, par une blanche,
Passe la tête et cligne l'œil.

Le Docteur bolonais rabâche
Avec la basse aux sons traînés;
Polichinelle, qui se fâche,
Se trouve une croche pour nez.

Heurtant Trivelin qui se mouche
Avec un trille extravagant,
A Colombine Scaramouche
Rend son éventail ou son gant.

III

Carnival

Venice is dressing for the ball.
In Carnival's glitter displayed—
A-swarm, a-prattle... Glistening, all
The city's gaudy escapade.

Harlequin, black of mask, of hues[20]
Variegated, serpentine,
Thwacks dupe Cassandra's back... And whose
Fantasy feeds his cruel design.

Flapping a wing, like, on a floe,
A penguin in long-sleeve disguise,
Powder-faced lady—pale Pierrot—
Peeks from behind and blinks her eyes.

Bologna's doctor patters his
Endless drawled basso do-re-mi;
Old Pulcinella—Punch, that is—
Hook-nosed, stands quivering angrily.

As Trivelin blows his nose with much
Trilled fanfare, Scaramouche—do tell!—
Returns a glove, or fan, or such
To Colombine, fair demoiselle.

Sur une cadence se glisse
Un domino ne laissant voir
Qu'un malin regard en coulisse
Aux paupières de satin noir.

Ah! fine barbe de dentelle,
Que fait voler un souffle pur,
Cet arpège m'a dit : C'est elle!
Malgré tes réseaux, j'en suis sûr,

Et j'ai reconnu, rose et fraîche,
Sous l'affreux profil de carton,
Sa lèvre au fin duvet de pêche,
Et la mouche de son menton.

IV

Clair de lune sentimental

A travers la folle risée
Que Saint-Marc renvoie au Lido,
Une gamme monte en fusée,
Comme au clair de lune un jet d'eau…

A l'air qui jase d'un ton bouffe
Et secoue au vent ses grelots,
Un regret, ramier qu'on étouffe,
Par instant mêle ses sanglots.

A domino, jogged in the dance,
Slips from the brow where it lay set,
Shows naught but a sly look askance,
Behind its black satin lorgnette.

Ah! The fine lace beard wafting free,
Fluttering on a guiltless sigh:
Arpeggio that told me: "'Tis she!"
Much though your wiles would gull my eye;

Yes, she it was! I recognized,
Behind that ugly mask, her skin—
Lip pink with peach down, undisguised—
And beauty spot dotting her chin.

IV

Sentimental Moonlight

Above the wild hilarity—
San Marco's to the Lido—I
Hear a scale gusting suddenly
Like water-jet in moonlight sky...

In the gay, prattling wind above
The tinkling air, contrariwise,
A sad lament at times—ring-dove,
Perhaps?—gasps low its sobs, its sighs.

Au loin, dans la brume sonore,
Comme un rêve presque effacé,
J'ai revu, pâle et triste encore,
Mon vieil amour de l'an passé.

Mon âme en pleurs s'est souvenue
De l'avril, où, guettant au bois
La violette à sa venue,
Sous l'herbe nous mêlions nos doigts...

Cette note de chanterelle,
Vibrant comme l'harmonica,
C'est la voix enfantine et grêle,
Flèche d'argent qui me piqua.

Le son en est si faux, si tendre,
Si moqueur, si doux, si cruel,
Si froid, si brûlant, qu'à l'entendre
On ressent un plaisir mortel,

Et que mon cœur, comme la voûte
Dont l'eau pleure dans un bassin,
Laisse tomber goutte par goutte
Ses larmes rouges dans mon sein.

Jovial et mélancolique,
Ah! vieux thème du carnaval,
Où le rire aux larmes réplique,
Que ton charme m'a fait de mal!

Far off, in mists' deep-echoing gloom,
Still have I that pale sadness seen
Of last year's love, gone to its doom,
Done, like a dream all but swept clean.

My soul in tears, recalls the day
In April when, eager to find
Spring's earliest violet, we two lay
Deep in the grass, our hands entwined.

So high among the rest, so young...
Like a harmonica's, that thin,
Frail, piping voice that pricked and stung...[21]
That silver dart that did me in.

Tender, cruel, hot, cold, out of key...
Blend of so many an opposite,
That its sweet, mocking sound gives me
Such joy that I would die of it,

And that my heart, like arched vault weeping
Into a pool below, recessed,
Lets fall its droplets—red tears, seeping,
One at a time, into my breast.

Carnival-tune... Now sad, now jolly...
Ageless, this theme of yours! But oh!
Laughter and tears, gay melancholy—
How you have wrought your charm, my woe!

SYMPHONIE EN BLANC MAJEUR

De leur col blanc courbant les lignes,
On voit dans les contes du Nord,
Sur le vieux Rhin, des femmes-cygnes
Nager en chantant près du bord,

Ou, suspendant à quelque branche
Le plumage qui les revêt,
Faire luire leur peau plus blanche
Que la neige de leur duvet.

De ces femmes il en est une,
Qui chez nous descend quelquefois,
Blanche comme le clair de lune
Sur les glaciers dans les cieux froids;

Conviant la vue enivrée
De sa boréale fraîcheur
A des régals de chair nacrée,
A des débauches de blancheur!

Son sein, neige moulée en globe,
Contre les camélias blancs
Et le blanc satin de sa robe
Soutient des combats insolents.

SYMPHONY IN WHITE MAJOR

White-necked in gently curving line,
In the old folktales of the North,
Swan-ladies on the timeless Rhine
Sing by the shore, glide back and forth.

Or, hanging from a nearby bough
The feathers of their bright white gown,
Shine in a skin all whiter now
Than the snow-plumage of their down.

Of these belles, one especially
Is there who will betimes draw nigh,[22]
White as the moonlight sparkling free
Against the glacier-gleaming sky,

As all that sight-numbing array,
Joined with the flesh of pearl-shell white,
Lets us feast on the lush display:
Orgies of northland white delight.

Globe of round-molded snow, her breast
With both her robe's white satin vies
And white camellias, bosom-pressed,
Challenging them in surly wise.

Dans ces grandes batailles blanches,
Satins et fleurs ont le dessous,
Et, sans demander leurs revanches,
Jaunissent comme des jaloux.

Sur les blancheurs de son épaule,
Paros au grain éblouissant,
Comme dans une nuit du pôle,
Un givre invisible descend.

De quel mica de neige vierge,
De quelle moelle de roseau,
De quelle hostie et de quel cierge
A-t-on fait le blanc de sa peau?

A-t-on pris la goutte lactée
Tachant l'azur du ciel d'hiver,
Le lis à la pulpe argentée,
La blanche écume de la mer;

Le marbre blanc, chair froide et pâle,
Où vivent les divinités;
L'argent mat, la laiteuse opale
Qu'irisent de vagues clartés;

L'ivoire, où ses mains ont des ailes,
Et, comme des papillons blancs,
Sur la pointe des notes frêles
Suspendent leurs baisers tremblants;

In these combats of whiteness, lo!
Satin and flower will bested be;
And seeking no revenge, will grow
Yellowed, in jaundiced jealousy.

Upon her shoulder's whiteness, fine
As Paros dazzling-grained, there lies[23]
A skim of frost's scarce-seen design,
As when night's shades dim Polar skies.

What virgin flake metallic, not
Yet tainted? Marrow from within
A reed? The host? A candle?... What
Composed the whiteness of her skin?

Was it the milk-white drops astride
The winter sky's azure blue dome?
Silver-pulped lily? Or the tide
Rolling beneath a froth-white foam?

White marble? Cold, pale flesh, wherein
Dwell the divinities of White?
Silver unburnished? Opaline
Glimmers flecked with brief bursts of light?

Ivory keys, where winged hands go flying—
White butterflies!—flitting at will,
Lighting on fragile notes, and plying
Kisses with fluttering, trembling trill?

L'hermine vierge de souillure,
Qui pour abriter leurs frissons,
Ouate de sa blanche fourrure
Les épaules et les blasons;

Le vif-argent aux fleurs fantasques
Dont les vitraux sont ramagés;
Les blanches dentelles des vasques,
Pleurs de l'ondine en l'air figés;

L'aubépine de mai qui plie
Sous les blancs frimas de ses fleurs;
L'albâtre où la mélancolie
Aime à retrouver ses pâleurs;

Le duvet blanc de la colombe,
Neigeant sur les toits du manoir,
Et la stalactite qui tombe,
Larme blanche de l'antre noir?

Des Groenlands et des Norvèges
Vient-elle avec Séraphita?
Est-ce la Madone des neiges,
Un sphinx blanc que l'hiver sculpta,

Sphinx enterré par l'avalanche,
Gardien des glaciers étoilés,
Et qui, sous sa poitrine blanche,
Cache de blancs secrets gelés?

Ermine unblemished, virgin fur
Wrapped round, in pure white panoply,
Against the quivering chill of her
Shoulders, in blazoned finery?

Weird-bloomed quicksilver branches, limned
On windowpanes, a-gleam, a-glare?
Pools trimmed in whitest lace, undimmed?
A nymph's tears, frozen, hovering there?

May's honeysuckle, bowing low
Beneath the weight of flowered frost?
Sad alabaster's yearning woe,
Seeking its whiteness, once feared lost?

Dove's feathers, white down that appears
To snow on manor rooftops? Or
The ice stalactite dripping tears
Of white on the dark cavern's floor?

In Séraphita's company,[24]
Hails she from Greenland's, Norway's lands?
Madonna of the snows, is she
A white sphinx carved by winter's hands?

A sphinx buried in vast snow-slides
And who, beneath their star-strewn crest—
Guardian of the glaciers—hides
White secrets in her frozen breast?

Sous la glace où calme il repose,
Oh! qui pourra fondre ce cœur!
Oh! qui pourra mettre un ton rose
Dans cette implacable blancheur!

Oh! To that ice-bound heart, who will
Impart a tinge of pink, befitting?
Oh! Who will melt it, calm and chill,
In all that whiteness unremitting?

COQUETTERIE POSTHUME

Quand je mourrai, que l'on me mette,
Avant de clouer mon cercueil,
Un peu de rouge à la pommette,
Un peu de noir au bord de l'œil.

Car je veux dans ma bière close,
Comme le soir de son aveu,
Rester éternellement rose
Avec du kh'ol sous mon œil bleu.

Pas de suaire en toile fine,
Mais drapez-moi dans les plis blancs
De ma robe de mousseline,
De ma robe à treize volants.

C'est ma parure préférée;
Je la portais quand je lui plus.
Son premier regard l'a sacrée,
Et depuis je ne la mis plus.

Posez-moi, sans jaune immortelle,
Sans coussin de larmes brodé,
Sur mon oreiller de dentelle
De ma chevelure inondé.

POSTHUMOUS COQUETTISHNESS

When in the coffin, dead I lie,
Before they nail it, let them spread
A bit of black about my eye,
About my cheek, a bit of red.

For, in the bier, I wish to be
Forever rouged, as I was then,
The night he swore his love to me,
My blue eye rimmed with kohl again.

For me no shroud of fabric fine!
Wrap me in robe of muslin, rather:
That white and pleated robe of mine,
That white one, all a-flounce, a-gather.

Of all my gowns the favorite.
I wore it when my beauty shone,
Pleasing him. Holy relic, it
Remained too sacred to put on!

No cushioned tomb's tear-woven grace,
Gold *immortelles* strewn here and there;
Lay me out on my pillow's lace,
Drowned in my flood of flowing hair;

Cet oreiller, dans les nuits folles,
A vu dormir nos fronts unis,
Et sous le drap noir des gondoles
Compté nos baisers infinis.

Entre mes mains de cire pâle,
Que la prière réunit,
Tournez ce chapelet d'opale,
Par le pape à Rome bénit :

Je l'égrènerai dans la couche
D'où nul encor ne s'est levé;
Sa bouche en a dit sur ma bouche
Chaque *Pater* et chaque *Ave*.

The pillow that, each frenzied night,
Saw our brows joined in gentle slumber;
And, draped in gondolas' dark light,
Counted our kisses, past all number.

Betwixt my wax-pale palms, clasped in
A silent prayer, together pressed,
Twist round this chaplet opaline
That once, in Rome, the Pope had blessed:

And I shall tell my beads divine,
Encouched whence none might rise to flee:
Where my love's lips spoke prayers on mine:
Paters and *Aves*, solemnly...

DIAMANT DU CŒUR

Tout amoureux, de sa maîtresse,
Sur son cœur ou dans son tiroir,
Possède un gage qui'il caresse
Aux jours de regret ou d'espoir.

L'un d'une chevelure noire,
Par un sourire encouragé,
A pris une boucle que moire
Un reflet bleu d'aile de geai.

L'autre a, sur un cou blanc qui ploie,
Coupé par derrière un flocon
Retors et fin comme la soie
Que l'on dévide du cocon.

Un troisième, au fond d'une boîte,
Reliquaire du souvenir,
Cache un gant blanc, de forme étroite,
Où nulle main ne peut tenir.

Cet autre, pour s'en faire un charme,
Dans un sachet, d'un chiffre orné,
Coud des violettes de Parme,
Frais cadeau qu'on reprend fané.

DIAMOND OF THE HEART

Mistresses' lovers all possess
Some token, safely kept, or worn
Over their heart, that they caress
In hopeful days or days forlorn.

One, by a smile encouraged, took
A lock, a curl, whose shimmering
Reflection has that blue-black look
That glistens from the jay's jet wing.

Another, filching from a slender
Nape, head bowed, clipped its treasure: this
Fine, twisted tuft, like strands of tender
Silk, carded from the chrysalis.

Lover the third chooses to bury
A white glove in a chest, where it
Lies, dainty in its reliquary,
Too small for human hand to fit.

Another sews—lest he forget–
In satchel monogram-brocaded,
Nosegay of Parma violet,
Picked fresh but now grown withered, faded.

Celui-ci baise la pantoufle
Que Cendrillon perdit un soir;
Et celui-ci conserve un souffle
Dans la barbe d'un masque noir.

Moi, je n'ai ni boucle lustrée,
Ni gant, ni bouquet, ni soulier,
Mais je garde, empreinte adorée
Une larme sur un papier :

Pure rosée, unique goutte,
D'un ciel d'azur tombée un jour,
Joyau sans prix, perle dissoute
Dans la coupe de mon amour!

Et, pour moi, cette obscure tache
Reluit comme un écrin d'Ophyr,
Et du vélin bleu se détache,
Diamant éclos d'un saphir.

Cette larme, qui fait ma joie,
Roula, trésor inespéré,
Sur un de mes vers qu'elle noie,
D'un œil qui n'a jamais pleuré!

This one kisses the slipper fair
That Cinderella lost that night.
This one would keep breath's very air
In his black mask's beard if he might.

Myself, I have no fine bouquet,
No slipper, lustrous lock, or glove;
But I worship, long as I may,
The tear-stained paper of my love.[25]

One dewdrop, pure, from azure sky
Fallen one day into my draught;
Priceless gem, pearl dissolved in my
Cup of love, waiting to be quaffed...[26]

For me, that spot—rich jewel-case
From lush Ophir, sparkles among[27]
The vellum blue, spreading its grace
Like diamond from a sapphire sprung.

That tear, source of my dearest pleasure—
Her tear, my joy forevermore—
Rained on my verse, unhoped-for treasure,
From eyes that never wept before.

PREMIER SOURIRE DU PRINTEMPS

Tandis qu'à leurs œuvres perverses
Les hommes courent haletants,
Mars qui rit, malgré les averses,
Prépare en secret le printemps.

Pour les petites pâquerettes,
Sournoisement lorsque tout dort,
Il repasse des collerettes
Et cisèle des boutons d'or.

Dans le verger et dans la vigne,
Il s'en va, furtif perruquier,
Avec une houppe de cygne,
Poudrer à frimas l'amandier.

La nature au lit se repose;
Lui descend au jardin désert,
Et lace les boutons de rose
Dans leur corset de velours vert.

Tout en composant des solfèges,
Qu'aux merles il siffle à mi-voix,
Il sème aux prés les perce-neiges
Et les violettes aux bois.

SPRING'S FIRST SMILE

As mankind, breathless, perseveres
In tasks of vain frivolity,
March, laughing through her shower-tears,
Prepares spring's coming, secretly.

As everything still sleeps in sweet
Repose, for daisies he makes bold,
Pressing their little collars, neat,
And chiseling button-buds of gold.

Like a wigmaker on the sly,
He flours his powder-frost upon
Almond tree, vine; then, by and by,
Wafts white the air with tuft of swan.

He comes, visits the garden, now
Barren, as nature lies a-bed;
Corsets the buds on rosebush bough,
Laced up, girt soft, green-velveted.

Teaching the blackbirds gentle trills
And tremolos, the woods he sows
With violet, and the fields he fills
With snowdrops, poking through the snows.

Sur le cresson de la fontaine
Où le cerf boit, l'oreille au guet,
De sa main cachée il égrène
Les grelots d'argent du muguet.

Sous l'herbe, pour que tu la cueilles,
Il met la fraise au teint vermeil,
Et te tresse un chapeau de feuilles
Pour te garantir du soleil.

Puis, lorsque sa besogne est faite,
Et que son règne va finir,
Au seuil d'avril tournant la tête,
Il dit : « Printemps, tu peux venir! »

On cress-strewn fount, where sips the deer,
Ear cocked, with hidden hand he tells
His silvered beads, bright, tinkling clear:
His lily-of-the-valley bells.

He hides strawberries on the ground,
Crimson, for you to pick, each one,
And weaves a hat of leaves, tressed round,
To shield you from the warming sun.

And when his tasks are done, and when
His reign is ending, beckoning,
Standing on April's threshold, then
Says he: "Now may you join us, spring."

CONTRALTO

On voit dans le Musée antique,
Sur un lit de marbre sculpté,
Une statue énigmatique
D'une inquiétante beauté.

Est-ce un jeune homme? est-ce une femme,
Une déesse, ou bien un dieu?
L'amour, ayant peur d'être infâme,
Hésite et suspend son aveu.

Dans sa pose malicieuse,
Elle s'étend, le dos tourné
Devant la foule curieuse,
Sur son coussin capitonné.

Pour faire sa beauté maudite,
Chaque sexe apporta son don.
Tout homme dit : C'est Aphrodite!
Toute femme : C'est Cupidon!

Sexe douteux, grâce certaine,
On dirait ce corps indécis
Fondu, dans l'eau de la fontaine,
Sous les baisers de Salmacis.

CONTRALTO

Antiquity's museum shows,
On sculpted marble bed, a thing
Of beauty rare but puzzling pose:
Statue fair but disquieting.

A young man or a woman? He
Or she? A god? A goddess? Love,
Lest it commit an infamy,
Unsure, suspends judgment thereof.

With impish pose and countenance,
Back turned, upon a cushioned mat
It sprawls, as the crowds gape askance,
Not sure what they are looking at.

Each sex bestows, as it sees fit,
Its gift of beauty, oddly cursed:
"Fair Aphrodite," men dub it;
"Cupid!" say women, roles reversed!

Its beauty, clear; its sex, obscure;
Such that one would declare that this
Must be a water-nymph for sure,
Spawned of the kiss of Salmacis.[28]

Chimère ardente, effort suprême
De l'art et de la volupté,
Monstre charmant, comme je t'aime
Avec ta multiple beauté!

Bien qu'on défende ton approche,
Sous la draperie aux plis droits
Dont le bout à ton pied s'accroche,
Mes yeux ont plongé bien des fois.

Rêve de poète et d'artiste,
Tu m'as bien des nuits occupé,
Et mon caprice qui persiste
Ne convient pas qu'il s'est trompé.

Mais seulement il se transpose,
Et, passant de la forme au son,
Trouve dans sa métamorphose
La jeune fille et le garçon.

Que tu me plais, ô timbre étrange!
Son double, homme et femme à la fois,
Contralto, bizarre mélange,
Hermaphrodite de la voix!

C'est Roméo, c'est Juliette,
Chantant avec un seul gosier;
Le pigeon rauque et la fauvette
Perchés sur le même rosier;

Chimera, whom great efforts bore,
Of sheer voluptuous artistry;
Delightful monster! I adore
Your beauteous multiplicity!

Protected from the looks of those
Venturing close with gaze untoward,
And draped unto your very toes,
Yet oft my eyes plunge netherward.

Many a night my thoughts are stirred
By you, poet's and artist's dream;
Nor ever has my fancy erred
In its caprice, strange though you seem.

Merely has it your parts transposed,
From shape to sound; the voice within
Has been no less metamorphosed:
Both masculine and feminine.

O curious timbre! Tone bizarre!
You are my pleasure, my delight:
Contralto, double-sexed, you are
The voice's true hermaphrodite!

Romeo and his Juliet
Singing both from one throat together;
Hoarse pigeon, warbling *alouette*,
On rosebush poised, feather to feather;

C'est la châtelaine qui raille
Son beau page parlant d'amour;
L'amant au pied de la muraille,
La dame au balcon de sa tour;

La papillon, blanche étincelle,
Qu'en ses détours et ses ébats
Poursuit un papillon fidèle,
L'un volant haut et l'autre bas;

L'ange qui descend et qui monte
Sur l'escalier d'or voltigeant;
La cloche mêlant dans sa fonte
La voix d'airain, la voix d'argent;

La mélodie et l'harmonie,
Le chant et l'accompagnement;
A la grâce la force unie,
La maîtresse embrassant l'amant!

Sur le pli de sa jupe assise,
Ce soir, ce sera Cendrillon
Causant près du feu qu'elle attise
Avec son ami le grillon;

Demain le valeureux Arsace
A son courroux donnant l'essor,
Ou Tancrède avec sa cuirasse,
Son épée et son casque d'or;

Chatelaine and her page: tableau
Of her scorn for his woeful love;
Lady and lover: he below,
She on the balcony above;

The butterfly, white spark, who—flitting
Zigzag of light against the sky—
Pursues with passion unremitting
His faithful mate, now low, now high...

The angel who, on fluttering wings,
The golden staircase climbs, descends;
The bell, whose metal bellowings
Its voice of brass and silver blends;

The melody and harmony;
Treble air sung above the bass;
Grace and strength joined in unity:
Lover in mistress's embrace.

This evening it will be the patter
'Twixt Cinderella—of mean attire!—[29]
And cricket-friend chattering at her
As she sits stirring up the fire.

Tomorrow, Arsace the bold,
Venting his rage; or debonair
Tancred, helmeted all in gold,
Dagger and shield raised in the air;

Desdemona chantant le Saule,
Zerline bernant Mazetto,
Ou Malcolm le plaid sur l'épaule;
C'est toi que j'aime, ô contralto!

Nature charmante et bizarre
Que Dieu d'un double attrait para,
Toi qui pourrais, comme Gulnare,
Etre le Kaled d'un Lara,

Et dont la voix, dans sa caresse,
Réveillant de cœur endormi,
Mêle aux soupirs de la maîtresse
L'accent plus mâle de l'ami!

"Willow," by Desdemona sung,
Mazetto gulled Zerlina-wise,
Malcolm, with tartan shoulder-hung;
Contralto, you, my joy, my prize![30]

Nature both charming and bizarre,
By God to twofold pleasure bred,
You, who could be—like fair Gulnare?—
Sire Lara's boy-girl page Kaled,

And whose voice cooing its caress,
Rousing the sleeping heart, will blend
With mistress's sighs of distress
The manly accent of the friend![31]

CÆRULEI OCULI

Une femme mystérieuse,
Dont la beauté trouble mes sens,
Se tient debout, silencieuse,
Au bord des flots retentissants.

Ses yeux, où le ciel se reflète,
Mêlent à leur azur amer,
Qu'étoile une humide paillette,
Les teintes glauques de la mer.

Dans les langueurs de leurs prunelles,
Une grâce triste sourit;
Les pleurs mouillent les étincelles
Et la lumière s'attendrit;

Et leurs cils comme des mouettes
Qui rasent le flot aplani,
Palpitent, ailes inquiètes,
Sur leur azur indéfini.

Comme dans l'eau bleue et profonde,
Où dort plus d'un trésor coulé,
On y découvre à travers l'onde
La coupe du roi de Thulé.

CÆRULEI OCULI

A woman of dark mystery,
Of sense-distressing beauty, stands
Before me, silent utterly,
Beside the waves' brash-echoing sands.

Her eyes blend with the bitter blue
Of azure skies—wet with a glint's
Sequin-like twinkle—a dullish hue
Of glaucous ocean's sea-green tints.

Their sparks flare, moist with teardrops, while
Their pupils ever languid grow,
And, with a sad grace flash a smile
On the light's brooding afterglow.

Their lashes seem like gulls a-wing,
Flitting above the tide, that skim
Its smooth expanse, and fluttering
Before their azure gaze, lit dim.

In the blue waves where, sunken, sleeps
Many a treasure, moldering,
One glimpses there, amid the deeps,
The goblet rare of Thule's king.[32]

Sous leur transparence verdâtre,
Brille parmi le goëmon,
L'autre perle de Cléopâtre
Près de l'anneau de Salomon.

La couronne au gouffre lancée
Dans la ballade de Schiller,
Sans qu'un plongeur l'ait ramassée,
Y jette encor son reflet clair.

Un pouvoir magique m'entraîne
Vers l'abîme de ce regard,
Comme au sein des eaux la sirène
Attirait Harald Harfagar.

Mon âme, avec la violence
D'un irrésistible désir,
Au milieu du gouffre s'élance
Vers l'ombre impossible à saisir.

Montrant son sein, cachant sa queue,
La sirène amoureusement
Fait ondoyer sa blancheur bleue
Sous l'émail vert du flot dormant.

L'eau s'enfle comme une poitrine
Aux soupirs de la passion;
Le vent, dans sa conque marine,
Murmure une incantation.

Nestled amid the seaweed's swirl,
Through glance transparent, greenish-eyed,
Shines Cleopatra's other pearl,[33]
With Solomon's ring, side by side.[34]

The crown in Schiller's ballad sung,[35]
That none went diving after when
Into the chasm it was flung,
Casts bright reflections once again.

A magic force draws, lures me on
Toward those eyes' pit crepuscular,
As the sea-siren, once upon
A time, lured Harald Harfagar.[36]

My soul, seared with resistless fires,
Would leap across the chasm's breach
To seize the object it desires:
The shadow it can never reach.

Baring her breast, hiding her tail,
The siren sways a blue-white sheen,
Seductively, beneath the pale,
Calm-sleeping sea's enameled green.

Bosom-like, then, the water swells
As passion's sighs moan through the air;
And the winds, in her great conch shell's
Nautilus chambers, drone a prayer.

« Oh! viens dans ma couche de nacre,
Mes bras d'onde t'enlaceront;
Les flots, perdant leur saveur âcre,
Sur ta bouche, en miel couleront.

« Laissant bruire sur nos têtes,
La mer qui ne peut s'apaiser,
Nous boirons l'oubli des tempêtes
Dans la coupe de mon baiser. »

Ainsi parle la voix humide
De ce regard céruléen,
Et mon cœur, sous l'onde perfide,
Se noie et consomme l'hymen.

"Come to my pearled couch! Round your waist
My sea-arms shall enlace your hips;
The waves will lose their acrid taste
And flow like honey on your lips.

"As the sea roars on, limitless,
Above our heads in the abyss,
We shall quaff storm's forgetfulness
In the cup of my tender kiss."

So spoke the watery voice to me
With gaze cerulean, fascinated;
My heart, in the waves' perfidy,
Drowns, as the act is consummated...

RONDALLA

Enfant aux airs d'impératrice,
Colombe aux regards de faucon,
Tu me hais, mais c'est mon caprice,
De me planter sous ton balcon.

Là, je veux, le pied sur la borne,
Pinçant les nerfs, tapant le bois,
Faire luire à ton carreau morne
Ta lampe et ton front à la fois.

Je défends à toute guitare
De bourdonner aux alentours.
Ta rue est à moi : — je la barre
Pour y chanter seul mes amours,

Et je coupe les deux oreilles
Au premier racleur de jambon
Qui devant la chambre où tu veilles
Braille un couplet mauvais ou bon.

Dans sa gaîne mon couteau bouge;
Allons, qui veut de l'incarnat?
A son jabot qui veut du rouge
Pour faire un bouton de grenat?

RONDALLA

Child, empress-aired... Dove, with a leer
Of falcon's eye! How you hate me!
Yet I obey my whim and, here—
Staunch—stand beneath your balcony.

Feet on the milestone, with each string
I pluck, each wooden tap, I vow,
At your grim window, I would bring
Light to your lamp and to your brow.

No other's but my own guitar
Will I permit to strum its love.
Your street belongs to me! I bar
All gallants from the use thereof;[37]

And the first "ham-bone scraper" who
Wails as you lie awake, a-bed—
Fair tune or foul—will have his two
Ears separated from his head![38]

Restless, restive my dagger grows
And longs to be unscabbarded!
What churls would see their fine jabots
Pearled with a rosebud's crimson red?

Le sang dans les veines s'ennuie,
Car il est fait pour se montrer;
Le temps est noir, gare la pluie!
Poltrons, hâtez-vous de rentrer.

Sortez, vaillants! sortez, bravaches!
L'avant-bras couvert du manteau,
Que sur vos faces de gavaches
J'écrive des croix au couteau!

Qu'ils s'avancent! seuls ou par bande,
De pied ferme je les attends.
A ta gloire il faut que je fende
Les naseaux de ces capitans.

Au ruisseau qui gêne ta marche
Et pourrait salir tes pieds blancs,
Corps du Christ! je veux faire une arche
Avec les côtes des galants.

Pour te prouver combien je t'aime,
Dis, je tuerai qui tu voudras :
J'attaquerai Satan lui-même,
Si pour linceul j'ai tes deux draps.

Porte sourde!—Fenêtre aveugle!
Tu dois pourtant ouïr ma voix;
Comme un taureau blessé je beugle,
Des chiens excitant les abois!

Blood, born to leap forth from the veins,
Languishes, swells impatient, stirs...
The skies grow dark, beware the rains!
Be off, you lily-livered curs.

Come, valiant braves! Come, knave scapegraces!
With forearm cloak-enwrapped, let me
Carve on your scurvy wretches' faces
Crosses to mark your infamy!

Let them come all at once, or each
By each! Here will I lay them low
And, for your glory, gladly breach
Their haughty nostrils with one blow![39]

When foul stream would besmirch your toes
Of white with waters dank and dark,
'Sblood! I would take the ribs of those
Suitors of yours and build an ark.

To prove my love for you, would I
Kill whom you wish, then taunt, unbowed,
Satan himself, could I but lie
Clothed in your bed-sheets for my shroud...

Door shut! Window unlit! Yet you
Must hear my voice! Like wounded bull,
I bellow my hullabaloo
That makes dogs bark their gullets-full!

Au moins plante un clou dans ta porte :
Un clou pour accrocher mon cœur.
A quoi sert que je le remporte
Fou de rage, mort de langueur ?

At least, drive in your door a nail
For me to hang my heart upon.
Why keep it, when, in love's travail,
I die, enraged and woebegone?

NOSTALGIES D'OBELISQUES

I

L'Obélisque de Paris

Sur cette place je m'ennuie,
Obélisque dépareillé;
Neige, givre, bruine et pluie
Glacent mon flanc déjà rouillé;

Et ma vieille aiguille, rougie
Aux fournaises d'un ciel de feu,
Prend des pâleurs de nostalgie
Dans cet air qui n'est jamais bleu.

Devant les colosses moroses
Et les pylônes de Luxor,
Près de mon frère aux teintes roses
Que ne suis-je debout encor,

Plongeant dans l'azur immuable
Mon pyramidion vermeil
Et de mon ombre, sur le sable,
Ecrivant les pas du soleil!

Rhamsès, un jour mon bloc superbe,
Où l'éternité s'ébréchait,
Roula fauché comme un brin d'herbe,
Et Paris s'en fit un hochet.

OBELISKS' LONGINGS

I

The Paris Obelisk

Flanks rusting in this dismal square,
Frozen with rain, snow, mists, and frost,
Obelisk—once a stately pair!—
I languish now, alone and lost;

And my slim shaft that once had shone
Red in the brazier-sky of old,
Wears a nostalgic pallor, grown
Ashen in this air, gray and cold.

Mid Luxor's pylons grim once set—
Colossal monuments—how will
I understand that I stand yet
Not by my brother, pink-hued still?

My sun-glazed pyramidion[40]
Once pierced the timeless azure; and
My shadow, pacing ever on,
Traced out the hours circling the sand!

Ramses, one day was my proud mass
Hauled round, breaching eternity,
Sickled down like a blade of grass—
And Paris made a toy of me.

La sentinelle granitique,
Gardienne des énormités,
Se dresse entre un faux temple antique
Et la chambre des députés.

Sur l'échafaud de Louis seize,
Monolithe au sens aboli,
On a mis mon secret, qui pèse
Le poids de cinq mille ans d'oubli.

Les moineaux francs souillent ma tête,
Où s'abattaient dans leur essor
L'ibis rose et le gypaëte
Au blanc plumage, aux serres d'or.

La Seine, noir égout des rues,
Fleuve immonde fait de ruisseaux,
Salit mon pied, que dans ses crues
Baisait le Nil, père des eaux,

Le Nil, géant à barbe blanche
Coiffé de lotus et de joncs,
Versant de son urne qui penche
Des crocodiles pour goujons!

Les chars d'or étoilés de nacre
Des grands pharaons d'autrefois
Rasaient mon bloc heurté du fiacre
Emportant le dernier des rois.

A granite sentinel the while,
Standing ground midst her travesties—
A temple, pseudo-antique style,
And the Chamber of Deputies.

My cryptic monolith they placed
By Louis Seize's guillotine:[41]
Five thousand years forthwith erased:
Meaningless now, forgot, swept clean...

The Westworld's sparrows foul my head[42]
Where once would perch, midst noble flight,
The ibis pink, the vulture spread—
Gold-taloned, vast-winged, plumed in white.

Their Seine—gutters' black sewer vile—
Rings my feet round in filth; the very
Feet that the swells of Father Nile
Would kiss in homage tributary;

Nile, white-beard giant lotus-tressed,
With urn-poured waters opulent:
No minnows of the paltriest,
But crocodiles magnificent!

The tumbrel carting off the last
Of kings smashed flush against my base,
That Pharaohs' chariots of the past
Scarce grazed, gold-pearled, in stately pace.

Jadis, devant ma pierre antique,
Le pschent au front, les prêtres saints
Promenaient la bari mystique
Aux emblèmes dorés et peints;

Mais aujourd'hui, pilier profane
Entre deux fontaines campé,
Je vois passer la courtisane
Se renversant dans son coupé.

Je vois, de janvier à décembre,
La procession des bourgeois,
Les Solons qui vont à la chambre,
Et les Arthurs qui vont au bois.

Oh! dans cent ans quels laids squelettes
Fera ce peuple impie et fou,
Qui se couche sans bandelettes
Dans des cercueils que ferme un clou,

Et n'a pas même d'hypogées
A l'abri des corruptions,
Dortoirs où, par siècles rangées,
Plongent les générations!

Sol sacré des hiéroglyphes
Et des secrets sacerdotaux,
Où les sphinx s'aiguisent les griffes
Sur les angles des piédestaux;

Time was, the sacred priests would guide—
Brows double-crowned—before my stone,
The mystic bari-barque, a-glide,
Gilded with emblems all their own.[43]

But here, now mere pillar profane,
A shameless courtesan I see,
Landau-riding, 'twixt fountains twain,
Poised languidly, seductively.

Year in, year out, with never a pause,
I see parade those good bourgeois;
Now Solons off to write their laws,
Dandies off to woods' tra-la-la...[44]

These impious fools, hundred years hence,
Will be but ugly bones, and lie,
Swath-less, in the impermanence
Of their nail-shut sarcophagi,

Without vast temple vaults to keep
Them free of flesh's degradations—
Great chambers wrought for centuries' sleep
Plumbed deep for endless generations!

Holy soil of the hieroglyphic;
Of priestly secrets, where sphinx paws
Rub on their pedestals pontific
To sharpen to a point their claws;

Où sous le pied sonne la crypte,
Où l'épervier couve son nid,
Je te pleure, ô ma vieille Egypte,
Avec des larmes de granit!

II

L'Obélisque de Luxor

Je veille, unique sentinelle
De ce grand palais dévasté,
Dans la solitude éternelle,
En face de l'immensité.

A l'horizon que rien ne borne,
Stérile, muet, infini,
Le désert sous le soleil morne,
Déroule son linceul jauni.

Au-dessus de la terre nue,
Le ciel, autre désert d'azur,
Où jamais ne flotte une nue,
S'étale implacablement pur.

Le Nil, dont l'eau morte s'étame
D'une pellicule de plomb,
Luit, ridé par l'hippopotame,
Sous un jour mat tombant d'aplomb;

Where, low, an echoing crypt one hears;
Where sparrow hawk cradles its nest...
I mourn you, Egypt mine, with tears
Of granite shed, wrenched from my breast!

II

The Luxor Obelisk

Sentinel-like, I stand before
This palace ground, laid waste, and face
In solitude, forevermore,
The vast immensity of space.

Toward the horizon limitless,
Outstretched beneath sun's cheerless heat,
The desert, in mute barrenness,
Unfurls its jaundiced winding-sheet.

Above the naked land, the sky—
Other desert of azure, where
Never the merest cloud floats by—
Starkly pure, overspreads the air.

Light deadened through a film of lead,
Nile's sluggish waves monotonous
Glow in a dull sun overhead,
Billow with hippopotamus;

Et les crocodiles rapaces,
Sur le sable en feu des îlots,
Demi-cuits dans leurs carapaces,
Se pâment avec des sanglots.

Immobile sur son pied grêle,
L'ibis, le bec dans son jabot,
Déchiffre au bout de quelque stèle
Le cartouche sacré de Thot.

L'hyène rit, le chacal miaule,
et, traçant des cercles dans l'air,
L'épervier affamé piaule,
Noire virgule du ciel clair.

Mais ces bruits de la solitude
Sont couverts par le bâillement
Des sphinx, lassés de l'attitude
Qu'ils gardent immuablement.

Produit des blancs reflets du sable
Et du soleil toujours brillant,
Nul ennui ne t'est comparable,
Spleen lumineux de l'Orient!

C'est toi qui faisais crier : Grâce!
A la satiété des rois
Tombant vaincus sur leur terrasse,
Et tu m'écrases de ton poids.

And the rapacious crocodiles,
Sob-swooning on the riverside's
Blazing sand of its modest isles,
Bake in their carapaceous hides.

Ibis, perched on a monument,
Stands on his frail leg, still and stiff,
Pecking his breast, and most intent
On puzzling out Thot's cartouche-glyph.[45]

Hyena laughs and jackal squawks
As, comma-shaped, his wings outspanned,
Hungry peeps trace the sparrow hawk's
Black circles high above the land.

But sounds of solitude like those
Are covered by the yawns untold
Of sphinxes, wearying of the pose
That, changeless, they must ever hold.

Born of sand's glittering grains; born, too,
Of a sun's sheer bedazzlement,
No ennui can compare to you,
O *spleen* spawned of the Orient![46]

You it was who made kings cry "Peace!"
Prostrate on terrace emptiness;
And I, seeking ennui's surcease,
Stand conquered, crushed by you no less.

Ici jamais le vent n'essuie
Une larme à l'œil sec des cieux.
Et le temps fatigué s'appuie
Sur les palais silencieux.

Pas un accident ne dérange
La face de l'éternité;
L'Egypte, en ce monde où tout change,
Trône sur l'immobilité.

Pour compagnons et pour amies,
Quand l'ennui me prend par accès,
J'ai les fellahs et les momies
Contemporaines de Rhamsès;

Je regarde un pilier qui penche,
Un vieux colosse sans profil
Et les canges à voile blanche
Montant ou descendant le Nil.

Que je voudrais comme mon frère,
Dans ce grand Paris transporté,
Auprès de lui, pour me distraire,
Sur une place être planté!

Là-bas, il voit à ses sculptures
S'arrêter un peuple vivant,
Hiératiques écritures,
Que l'idée épelle en rêvant.

Here, never does the cool breeze flick
A tear from heaven's dry, tearless eye;
And time, fatigued, hangs weighty, thick,
As palace walls stand mutely by.

No accident will disarrange
Eternity's motionless face;
And Egypt, in this world of change,
Enthroned, reigns over changeless space.

When boredom takes its toll of me—
Friendless and womanless, alone—
Fellahs have I for company
And mummies Ramses must have known;[47]

I see a pillar—listing shaft,
Ancient colossus—its profile
In ruins... White-sailed cangia-craft,
Upstream and down, plying the Nile.[48]

Oh, how I wish that, like my brother,
I were set in that Paris square,
To know the joys, one with the other,
Of that great town spread round him there!

For he sees people—living!—come
Gaze at his carvings' priestly writ,
Setting their marveling minds to plumb
The hieratic sense of it.

Les fontaines juxtaposées
Sur la poudre de son granit
Jettent leurs brumes irisées;
Il est vermeil, il rajeunit!

Des veines roses de Syène
Comme moi cependant il sort,
Mais je reste à ma place ancienne,
Il est vivant et je suis mort!

The fountains cast their rainbow spray
Over his granite dust. In truth,
Their droplets' mottle-hued array
Bestow on him the glow of youth.

He and I came to life within
Aswan's pink veins, together bred;[49]
But I am yet where I have been:
He is alive, and I am dead!

VIEUX DE LA VIEILLE

15 décembre

Par l'ennui chassé de ma chambre,
J'errais le long du boulevard :
Il faisait un temps de décembre,
Vent froid, fine pluie et brouillard;

Et là je vis, spectacle étrange,
Echappés du sombre séjour,
Sous la bruine et dans la fange,
Passer des spectres en plein jour.

Pourtant c'est la nuit que les ombres,
Par un clair de lune allemand,
Dans les vieilles tours en décombres,
Reviennent ordinairement;

C'est la nuit que les Elfes sortent
Avec leur robe humide au bord,
Et sous les nénuphars emportent
Leur valseur de fatigue mort;

C'est la nuit qu'a lieu la revue
Dans la ballade de Zedlitz,
Où l'Empereur, ombre entrevue,
Compte les ombres d'Austerlitz.

VETERANS OF THE OLD GUARD

15 December

Chased from my room by boredom, I
Strolled the boulevard; and everywhere
A fine rain from the wind-chilled sky
Hung in December's mist-filled air.

And there appeared—curious, surely—
Specters from phantom-realm, who could
Be seen—in mist and mire, obscurely—
Despite daylight's unlikelihood!

For nighttime is the part of day—
By German moonlight, usually!—
When shades, in towers rotting away,
Return from their captivity;

Night, when the Elf-world's dreaded Willies—[50]
Robes moist—rise from their watery vaults
And drag beneath the water lilies
The dancer, near dead from his waltz;

Night, when in Zedlitz's ballade,[51]
The emperor counts, as befits
His shade, the fallen *camarades*,
Shades of the dead at Austerlitz.

Mais des spectres près du Gymnase,
A deux pas des Variétés,
Sans brume ou linceul qui les gaze,
Des spectres mouillés et crottés!

Avec ses dents jaunes de tartre,
Son crâne de mousse verdi,
A Paris, boulevard Montmartre,
Mob se montrant en plein midi!

La chose vaut qu'on la regarde :
Trois fantômes de vieux grognards,
En uniformes de l'ex-garde,
Avec deux ombres de hussards!

On eût dit la lithographie
Où, dessinés par un rayon,
Les morts, que Raffet déifie,
Passent, criant : Napoléon!

Ce n'était pas les morts qu'éveille
Le son du nocturne tambour,
Mais bien quelques *vieux de la vieille*
Qui célébraient le grand retour.

Depuis la suprême bataille,
L'un a maigri, l'autre a grossi;
L'habit jadis fait à leur taille,
Est trop grand ou trop rétréci.

But specters, here, a mere stone's throw
From the Gymnase, the Variétés,[52]
Muddied and wet?... Not *comme il faut*,
Shrouded and mist-clad! And by day?

Paris? Montmartre? Unlikely scene,
Like sprite-queen Mab, here, at high noon,[53]
Teeth yellow-scaled, skull mossy green,
Showing herself sunlight-bestrewn!

A spectacle well worth the while:
Three of yesteryear's regulars—
Grumbling phantoms in old-guard style—
Joined by two shades of bold hussars.

That Raffet lithograph one might,
Indeed, have thought this scene; the one
Where the dead, sketched in beams of light,
Pass by and cry "Napoleon!"[54]

No corpses these, roused by the drum
For their nocturnal brief sojourn;
But veterans of the old guard, come
To celebrate his grand return.[55]

Since the great battle each has grown
Thinner or fatter; and, for all,
The uniforms, for each one sewn,
Are, some, too big and, some, too small.

Nobles lambeaux, défroque épique,
Saints haillons, qu'étoile une croix,
Dans leur ridicule héroïque
Plus beaux que des manteaux de rois!

Un plumet énervé palpite
Sur leur kolbach fauve et pelé;
Près des trous de balle, la mite
A rongé leur dolman criblé;

Leur culotte de peau trop large
Fait mille plis sur leur fémur;
Leur sabre rouillé, lourde charge,
Creuse le sol et bat le mur;

Ou bien un embonpoint grotesque,
Avec grand'peine boutonné,
Fait un poussah dont on rit presque,
Du vieux héros tout chevronné.

Ne les raillez pas, camarade;
Saluez plutôt chapeau bas
Ces Achilles d'une Iliade
Qu'Homère n'inventerait pas.

Respectez leur tête chenue!
Sur leur front par vingt cieux bronzé,
La cicatrice continue
Le sillon que l'âge a creusé.

Laughable, their heroic airs
And cross-emblazoned posturings;
Noble rags, epic tatters, theirs,
Yet fairer far than many a king's!

Plumes sag over their weather-beaten
Colbacks, with bearskin all but bare;
Their capes—all bullet-holed, worm-eaten
Dolmans—are quite the worse for wear.

Leather culottes, grown much too wide,
Make myriad folds against their thighs;
Blades, rusted, sway from side to side,
Drag on the ground in weighty wise.

Or else, such their avoirdupois
That buttons fail, and one appears
With paunch like those squat tumbler-toys';[56]
Heroes, met now with japes and jeers!

Doff your hat, comrade! Best you had
Not mock these staunch Achilles, spent
Of strength in their own *Iliad*,
One that no Homer would invent.

Respect their hoary heads! For, on
Their score of sun-bronzed countries' skin,
Ever their scars will mark anon
The furrows age has traced therein.

Leur peau, bizarrement noircie,
Dit l'Egypte aux soleils brûlants;
Et les neiges de la Russie
Poudrent encor leurs cheveux blancs.

Si leurs mains tremblent, c'est sans doute
Du froid de la Bérésina;
Et s'ils boitent, c'est que la route
Est longue du Caire à Wilna;

S'ils sont perclus, c'est qu'à la guerre
Les drapeaux étaient leurs seuls draps;
Et si leur manche ne va guère,
C'est qu'un boulet a pris leur bras.

Ne nous moquons pas de ces hommes
Qu'en riant le gamin poursuit;
Ils furent le jour dont nous sommes
Le soir et peut-être la nuit.

Quand on oublie, ils se souviennent!
Lancier rouge et grenadier bleu,
Au pied de la colonne, ils viennent
Comme à l'autel de leur seul dieu.

Là, fiers de leur longue souffrance,
Reconnaissants des maux subis,
Ils sentent le cœur de la France
Battre sous leurs pauvres habits.

That skin, bizarrely darkened, glows
With burning sun of Egypt's sands;
And, on their heads, bespattered snows
Spread white, bespeak rude Russia's lands.

Their hands shake? Berezina's chill
Undoubtedly the reason was;[57]
They limp? The trudge from Cairo till
They camped at Vilna was the cause.

Frozen and stiff? In their campaign,
Flags' cloth, the only clothes they wore;
Useless their sleeve? In cannon-rain
An arm blown off was arm no more.

Let us not mock them nastily,
Whom taunting urchins chase, incite:
They were the day whose twilight, we;
Or even less, the shades of night.

We may forget; they never do:
Here, to this column-altar come—
Old lancers red, grenadiers blue—
They pay their god encomium.[58]

Proud of their suffering, harsh and long,
Recalling all the scars they bear,
They feel the heart of France pound strong
Beneath the tatters they now wear.

Aussi les pleurs trempent le rire
En voyant ce saint carnaval,
Cette mascarade d'empire
Passer comme un matin de bal;

Et l'aigle de la grande armée
Dans le ciel qu'emplit son essor,
Du fond d'une gloire enflammée,
Etend sur eux ses ailes d'or!

Thus do tears damp the laughter spawned
By their sainted pretense displayed,
This Empire make-believe, now dawned
Like festive daylight mascarade.

And the Great Army's eagle-flight,
Soaring the skies to realms untold,
From depths of glory, flaming bright,
Spreads over them its wings of gold.

TRISTESSE EN MER

Les mouettes volent et jouent;
Et les blancs coursiers de la mer,
Cabrés sur les vagues, secouent
Leurs crins échevelés dans l'air.

Le jour tombe; une fine pluie
Eteint les fournaises du soir,
Et le steam-boat crachant la suie
Rabat son long panache noir.

Plus pâle que le ciel livide
Je vais au pays du charbon
Du brouillard et du suicide;
—Pour se tuer le temps est bon.

Mon désir avide se noie
Dans le gouffre amer qui blanchit;
Le vaisseau danse, l'eau tournoie,
Le vent de plus en plus fraîchit.

Oh! Je me sens l'âme navrée;
L'Océan gonfle, en soupirant,
Sa poitrine désespérée,
Comme un ami qui me comprend.

SADNESS AT SEA

The seagulls, playing, fly about;
And the white stallions of the sea,
Backs arched over the waves, shake out
Their tousled, windswept manes, blown free.

Down sinks the sun; night is afoot...
Rain quells day's oven-heat, as looms
Our paddleboat, spewing its soot,
Laying out smoke in long black plumes.

More pallid than the sallow sky,
Toward land of coal, of fog—and land
Of suicide!—my course I ply...
Fine night to die by one's own hand![59]

My passionate desire is drowned,
Sunk to the bitter, whitening deeps;
Cold blows the wind. Water swirls round
And round... Boat dances, prances, leaps...

Oh! How my soul distresses me!
And Ocean, with a sigh, will swell
Her breast forlorn, in sympathy,
Like a dear friend who knows me well.

Allons, peines d'amour perdues,
Espoirs lassés, illusions
Du socle idéal descendues,
Un saut dans les moites sillons!

A la mer, souffrances passées,
Qui revenez toujours, pressant
Vos blessures cicatrisées
Pour leur faire pleurer du sang!

A la mer, spectres de mes rêves,
Regrets aux mortelles pâleurs
Dans un cœur rouge ayant sept glaives,
Comme la Mère des douleurs.

Chaque fantôme plonge et lutte
Quelques instants avec le flot
Qui sur lui ferme sa volute
Et l'engloutit dans un sanglot.

Lest de l'âme, pesant bagage,
Trésors misérables et chers,
Sombrez, et dans votre naufrage
Je vais vous suivre au fond des mers!

Bleuâtre, enflé, méconnaissable,
Bercé par le flot qui bruit,
Sur l'humide oreiller du sable
Je dormirai bien cette nuit!

Come, all you lovesick woes, now ended;
Tired hopes, vain dream-illusions too,
From pedestals ideal descended...
Into the furrowing waves with you!

Into the sea, past suffering,
Wounds living yet! Into the flood!
Scars that you press, still festering,
To make them weep their tears of blood!

Into the sea, dream-specters mine,
Death-pale regrets, in red heart rent
By seven blades, like our divine
Mother of sorrows, heaven-sent.[60]

Each phantom fights a moment, swirls
Against the waves—a-toss, a-bob—
That fold it, struggling in their furls,
Swallow it down with but a sob.

Soul's ballast, hanging weightily—
You, treasures dear and worthless too!—
Go sinking to the deepmost sea,
And thither shall I follow you!

Face bloated, bluish, featureless,
Rocked by the roaring waves, my head,
Pillowed on wet sands' gentleness...
Deep shall I sleep in this night's bed!...

...Mais une femme dans sa mante
Sur le pont assise à l'écart,
Une femme jeune et charmante
Lève vers moi son long regard.

Dans ce regard, à ma détresse
La Sympathie aux bras ouverts
Parle et sourit, sœur ou maîtresse.
Salut, yeux bleus! bonsoir, flots verts!

Les mouettes volent et jouent;
Et les blancs coursiers de la mer,
Cabrés sur les vagues, secouent
Leurs crins échevelés dans l'air.

But there, on deck, sitting askance,
A fair, young woman, cloaked, will cast
Her gaze upon me; soulful glance,
Deep-eyed, that seems to last and last...

And in that glance, arms beckoning me,
A Kindred Soul speaks to my plight
And smiles... Sister? Or mistress, she?...
Blue eyes, good day! Green waves, good night!

The seagulls, playing, fly about;
And the white stallions of the sea,
Backs arched over the waves, shake out
Their tousled, windswept manes, blown free.

A UNE ROBE ROSE

Que tu me plais dans cette robe
Qui te déshabille si bien,
Faisant jaillir ta gorge en globe,
Montrant tout nu ton bras païen!

Frêle comme une aile d'abeille,
Frais comme un cœur de rose-thé,
Son tissu, caresse vermeille,
Voltige autour de ta beauté.

De l'épiderme sur la soie
Glissent des frissons argentés,
Et l'étoffe à la chair renvoie
Ses éclairs roses reflétés.

D'où te vient cette robe étrange
Qui semble faite de ta chair,
Trame vivante qui mélange
Avec ta peau son rose clair?

Est-ce à la rougeur de l'aurore,
A la coquille de Vénus,
Au bouton de sein près d'éclore,
Que sont pris ces tons inconnus?

TO A PINK DRESS

I love you in that dress, scant-gowned,
Showing so fair your bosom's charm,
Jutting your firm breasts high, globes round,
Baring your naked, pagan arm.[61]

Frail wisp of cloth, like wing of bee,
Fresh as a tea-rose heart, that dress—
Scarlet caress—goes fluttering free,
Swirling about your loveliness.

Your skin's pale silver quiverings
Glisten among the silken sash's
Glints, that reflect pink shimmerings
Back to your flesh in little flashes.

Whence comes that strange dress that could be
One with your flesh, enmeshed therein;
Live threads that blend mysteriously
Their bright pinks with your tender skin?

Is it from dawn's reddish rays looming
Over the morn, or from the shell
Of Venus, or breast's bud-tip blooming,
That come these rare tones? Who can tell?

Ou bien l'étoffe est-elle teinte
Dans les roses de ta pudeur?
Non; vingt fois modelée et peinte,
Ta forme connaît sa splendeur.

Jetant le voile qui te pèse,
Réalité que l'art rêva,
Comme la princesse Borghèse
Tu poserais pour Canova.

Et ces plis roses sont les lèvres
De mes désirs inapaisés,
Mettant au corps dont tu les sèvres
Une tunique de baisers.

Or has the cloth the roses' hue
Of modesty, naïve and fresh?
No! Twenty times a model, you
Know well the splendors of your flesh!

Then, letting fall the veil, you would
Let art perceive reality,
And—as Princess Borghese could—
Pose for Canova, nude as she![62]

Those pink folds are the lips whereof
I dream, yearn—unfulfilled—to drape
Your body, that fends off my love,
At length, with a kiss-woven cape.

LE MONDE EST MECHANT

Le monde est méchant, ma petite :
Avec son sourire moqueur
Il dit qu'à ton côté palpite
Une montre en place de cœur.

—Pourtant ton sein ému s'élève
Et s'abaisse comme la mer,
Aux bouillonnements de la sève
Circulant sous ta jeune chair.

Le monde est méchant, ma petite :
Il dit que tes yeux vifs sont morts
Et se meuvent dans leur orbite
A temps égaux et par ressorts.

—Pourtant une larme irisée
Tremble à tes cils, mouvant rideau,
Comme une perle de rosée
Qui n'est pas prise au verre d'eau.

Le monde est méchant, ma petite :
Il dit que tu n'as pas d'esprit,
Et que les vers qu'on te récite
Sont pour toi comme du sanscrit.

PEOPLE ARE NASTY

People are nasty, *ma petite:*
With sneering smile they will recall
That in your breast must surely beat
A watch, and not a heart at all.

—And yet your bosom, like the sea,
Rises and falls, as passion fresh
Bubbles and seethes: sap coursing free
Within your youth's hot-burning flesh.

People are nasty, *ma petite:*
They say your sparkling eyes are dead,
But move, matched in their orbs, complete
With springs wound up inside your head.

—And yet it was no water-glass
That hung a tear of opal guise,
Tremblingly from your lash, alas—
Like fluttering sash—before your eyes.

People are nasty, *ma petite:*
They say your wits are precious few,
And that the poems my lips repeat
In your praise "are all Greek to you."

—Pourtant, sur ta bouche vermeille,
Fleur s'ouvrant et se refermant,
Le rire, intelligente abeille,
Se pose à chaque trait charmant.

C'est que tu m'aimes, ma petite,
Et que tu hais tous ces gens-là.
Quitte-moi;—comme ils diront vite :
Quel cœur et quel esprit elle a!

—And yet on your lips flower-red,
Smiles—like the bee, quick-witted creature—
Opening, closing, laughter-bred,
Light on your every charming feature.

Why so? You love me, *ma petite*,
And hate all of those slanderers.
But leave me? Ah! Then hear them bleat:
"Oh! What a heart, what wits are hers!"

INES DE LAS SIERRAS

A la Petra Camara

Nodier raconte qu'en Espagne
Trois officiers cherchant un soir
Une venta dans la campagne,
Ne trouvèrent qu'un vieux manoir;

Un vrai château d'Anne Radcliffe,
Aux plafonds que le temps ploya,
Aux vitraux rayés par la griffe
Des chauves-souris de Goya,

Aux vastes salles délabrées,
Aux couloirs livrant leur secret,
Architectures effondrées
Où Piranèse se perdrait.

Pendant le souper, que regarde
Une collection d'aïeux
Dans leurs cadres montant la garde,
Un cri répond aux chants joyeux;

D'un long corridor en décombres,
Par la lune bizarrement
Entrecoupé de clairs et d'ombres,
Débusque un fantôme charmant;

INES DE LAS SIERRAS

For Petra Cámara

Nodier tells us that, in Spain,
Three officers one night, by chance,
Sought out a country inn in vain,
And found naught but an ancient manse;

One of those Ann Radcliffe chateaus,[63]
With ceilings sagging, all but gone;
Tracery windows clawed by those
Bats that a Goya might have drawn;

Once-secret passageways, great halls
Lying in ruins, and crisscrossed
By crumbled maze of fallen walls
Where Piranesi could get lost![64]

And, as they sup before the eyes
Of framed ancestral band, intent
On keeping watch, as their songs rise,
A cry covers their merriment.

From a long, rubbled corridor,
Splitting moon's chiaroscuro, there
Looms, in the gloom, standing before
Our revelers, a phantom fair.

Peigne au chignon, basquine aux hanches,
Une femme accourt en dansant,
Dans les bandes noires et blanches
Apparaissant, disparaissant.

Avec une volupté morte,
Cambrant les reins, penchant le cou,
Elle s'arrête sur la porte,
Sinistre et belle à rendre fou.

Sa robe, passée et fripée
Au froid humide des tombeaux,
Fait luire, d'un rayon frappée,
Quelques paillons sur ses lambeaux;

D'un pétale découronnée
A chaque soubresaut nerveux,
Sa rose, jaunie et fanée,
S'effeuille dans ses noirs cheveux.

Une cicatrice, pareille
A celle d'un coup de poignard,
Forme une couture vermeille
Sur sa gorge d'un ton blafard;

Et ses mains pâles et fluettes,
Au nez des soupeurs pleins d'effroi
Entre-choquent les castagnettes,
Comme des dents claquant de froid.

Comb in her chignoned hair, held tight,
She twirls her hips, skirt a-swirl, nearing
The three, through bands of shade and light,
By turns appearing, disappearing...

Neck bent, deathly voluptuous,
Back arched, she strides, stops at the door—
Sinister beauty, sight that thus
Would make men lose their senses for.

Catching a single silver beam,
The sequins of her ragged dress—
Near threadbare—make its tatters gleam
In chill tomb's death-damp cheerlessness

With every quiver of her head,
A petal from her rosebud crown
Falls on her black hair; flower whose red
Has faded now, turned yellow, brown...

A scar—wrought by a dagger-blade,
It seems—a seam incarnadine
Across her breast its mark has made,
Scarlet against its sallow skin;

Striking fear in the diners three,
She clicks and clacks, like teeth a-chatter,
As with pale, bony fingers, she
Taunts them with castanets a-clatter.

Elle danse, morne bacchante,
La cachucha sur un vieil air,
D'une grâce si provocante,
Qu'on la suivrait même en enfer.

Ses cils palpitent sur ses joues
Comme des ailes d'oiseau noir,
Et sa bouche arquée a des moues
A mettre un saint au désespoir.

Quand de sa jupe qui tournoie
Elle soulève le volant,
Sa jambe, sous le bas de soie,
Prend des lueurs de marbre blanc.

Elle se penche jusqu'à terre,
Et sa main, d'un geste coquet,
Comme on fait des fleurs d'un parterre,
Groupe les désirs en bouquet.

Est-ce un fantôme? est-ce une femme?
Un rêve, une réalité,
Qui scintille comme une flamme
Dans un tourbillon de beauté?

Cette apparition fantasque,
C'est l'Espagne du temps passé,
Aux frissons du tambour de basque
S'élançant de son lit glacé,

Dour bacchante, on an ancient air
Her grace casts the cachuca's spell[65]
So temptingly that, then and there,
One would fain follow her to hell.

Her lashes flutter roundabout
Her cheeks, like bird's wing, black of feather;
And her lush lips, curved in a pout,
Could make a saint quite snap his tether!

And when she lifts her skirt knee-high,
As it goes swirling faster, faster,
Her silk-hosed leg suggests a thigh
Glowing like marbled alabaster.

Now she stoops low and, gesturing round
In a most coy, coquettish way,
As one would pluck blooms from the ground,
Lust-flowers fashion her bouquet.

A spectre this? A woman? What?
A glittering reality,
This whirling flame? Or is it but
A dream? A beauteous fantasy?

This sight fantastic is, I vow,
Spain frozen in what once had been,
Springing anew, a-shiver now
In clattering clang of tambourine,

Et brusquement russuscitée
Dans un suprême boléro,
Montrant sous sa jupe argentée
La *divisa* prise au taureau.

La cicatrice qu'elle porte,
C'est le coup de grâce donné
A la génération morte
Par chaque siècle nouveau-né.

J'ai vu ce fantôme au Gymnase,
Où Paris entier l'admira,
Lorsque dans son linceul de gaze,
Parut la Petra Camara,

Impassible et passionnée,
Fermant ses yeux morts de langueur,
Et comme Inès l'assassinée,
Dansant un poignard dans le cœur!

Revived in this bolero, girt
About the thigh with a rosette—[66]
Torero's gift!—as twirls the skirt
In every silvered pirouette.

The scar she bears? The coup de grâce
That every newborn century
Wreaks on the one before, en masse,
Sent to its death and destiny.

At the Gymnase that ghost I saw
When, in her shroud-like gauze—entrancing
Toast of all Paris struck with awe—
Our Petra Cámara stood dancing.

Eyes closed in languorous lethargy—
Like Inès, victim-counterpart,
Passionate yet impassive—she
Danced with a dagger in her heart![67]

ODELETTE ANACREONTIQUE

Pour que je t'aime, ô mon poète,
Ne fais pas fuir par trop d'ardeur
Mon amour, colombe inquiète,
Au ciel rose de la pudeur.

L'oiseau qui marche dans l'allée
S'effraye et part au moindre bruit;
Ma passion est chose ailée
Et s'envole quand on la suit.

Muet comme l'Hermès de marbre,
Sous la charmille pose-toi;
Tu verras bientôt de son arbre
L'oiseau descendre sans effroi.

Tes tempes sentiront près d'elles,
Avec des souffles de fraîcheur,
Une palpitation d'ailes
Dans un tourbillon de blancheur,

Et la colombe apprivoisée
Sur ton épaule s'abattra,
Et son bec à pointe rosée
De ton baiser s'enivrera.

LITTLE ANACREONTIC ODE

If, poet, you would have my love,
Let not your ardor make me flee,
A-tremble, like a frightened dove,
To the pink skies of modesty.

The bird, hopping about, takes wing
At merest rustle, slightest stir:
My passion too—bewingèd thing—
Takes flight when someone follows her.

But if, like marble Hermes, set
In arbor-grove, you quietly
Stand still, soon will she cease to fret,
And you will see her quit her tree.

Your brow, your temples will begin
To revel in the cool delight
Of wings' breath, fluttering within
A dizzying, dazzling whirl of white.

Tamed now, the dove no more demurs,
And on your shoulder lights. And this
Little pink-pointed beak of hers
Will grow drunk on your gentle kiss.

FUMEE

Là-bas, sous les arbres s'abrite
Une chaumière au dos bossu;
Le toit penche, le mur s'effrite,
Le seuil de la porte est moussu.

La fenêtre, un volet la bouche;
Mais du taudis, comme au temps froid
La tiède haleine d'une bouche,
La respiration se voit.

Un tire-bouchon de fumée,
Tournant son mince filet bleu,
De l'âme en ce bouge enfermée
Porte des nouvelles à Dieu.

SMOKE

Over there, trees are sheltering
A hunchbacked hut... A slum, no more...
Roof askew, walls and wainscoting
Falling away... Moss hides the door.

Only one shutter, hanging... But
Seeping over the windowsill,
Like frosted breath, proof that this hut,
This slum, is living, breathing still.

Corkscrew of smoke... A wisp of blue
Escapes the hovel, whose soul it is...
Rises to God himself, and who
Receives the news and makes it his.

APOLLONIE

J'aime ton nom d'Apollonie,
Echo grec du sacré vallon,
Qui, dans sa robuste harmonie,
Te baptise sœur d'Apollon.

Sur la lyre au plectre d'ivoire,
Ce nom splendide et souverain,
Beau comme l'amour et la gloire,
Prend des résonances d'airain.

Classique, il fait plonger les Elfes
Au fond de leur lac allemand,
Et seule la Pythie à Delphes
Pourrait le porter dignement,

Quand relevant sa robe antique
Elle s'assoit au trépied d'or,
Et dans sa pose fatidique
Attend le dieu qui tarde encor.

APOLLONIE

I love your name Apollonie—
Such robust harmony, the sound!
Baptized Apollo's sister, she:
Echo of Greek vale's sacred ground.

When ivory plectrum plucks lyre-strings
To sing that splendid, sovereign name,
With brasses' resonance it rings
In beauty's love and glory's fame.

Classic, it makes Elves delve, a-leap,[68]
Midst German lake; and no one is—
Save Delphi's Pythia—fit to keep
Such a fine name, so much like his,

When, ancient robe tucked up, pose set
On fate's tripod of gold, she will
Sit and await—till doomsday yet!—
The god who keeps her waiting still.[69]

L'AVEUGLE

Un aveugle au coin d'une borne,
Hagard comme au jour un hibou,
Sur son flageolet, d'un air morne,
Tâtonne en se trompant de trou,

Et joue un ancien vaudeville
Qu'il fausse imperturbablement;
Son chien le conduit par la ville,
Spectre diurne à l'œil dormant.

Les jours sur lui passent sans luire;
Sombre, il entend le monde obscur,
Et la vie invisible bruire
Comme un torrent derrière un mur!

Dieu sait quelles chimères noires
Hantent cet opaque cerveau!
Et quels illisibles grimoires
L'idée écrit en ce caveau!

Ainsi dans les puits de Venise,
Un prisonnier à demi fou,
Pendant sa nuit qui s'éternise,
Grave des mots avec un clou.

THE BLIND MAN

A blind man, on the thoroughfare,
Startle-eyed as an owl by day,
Piping a dismal little air,
Taps here and there, loses his way,

Tootles awry his time-old ditty
Undauntedly, as by his side
Lopes his dog, guides him through the city,
Specter diurnal, sleepy-eyed.

Days, stark, wash over him, unlit;
He hears the dark world's constant din
And all that life unseen, as it
Rolls, rushing, like a flood walled in!

God knows what black chimeras haunt
That brain opaque, what lot befalls;
And what dire spells the mind is wont
To scribble on those death-vault walls!

Like prisoner grown half-mad, who, pent,
Rots beneath Venice in her jail
Eternal, and whose hours are spent
Scratching a message with a nail...[70]

Mais peut-être aux heures funèbres,
Quand la mort souffle le flambeau,
L'âme habituée aux ténèbres
Y verra clair dans le tombeau!

But when the torch, in tomb immured,
Dies in the breath of death, maybe
The soul, to shades' gloom long inured,
Will see with deathly clarity!

LIED

Au mois d'avril, la terre est rose,
Comme la jeunesse et l'amour;
Pucelle encore, à peine elle ose
Payer le Printemps de retour.

Au mois de juin, déjà plus pâle
Et le cœur de désir troublé,
Avec l'Eté tout brun de hâle
Elle se cache dans le blé.

Au mois d'août, bacchante enivrée,
Elle offre à l'Automne son sein,
Et roulant sur la peau tigrée,
Fait jaillir le sang du raisin.

En décembre, petite vieille,
Par les frimas poudrée à blanc,
Dans ses rêves elle réveille
L'Hiver auprès d'elle ronflant.

LIED

In April days the earth is pink
As youth and love: a virgin, who
Would scarcely even dare to think
Of paying Spring her proper due.

In June, already less robust—
Heart wracked with her desire's sharp pain—
In Summer's bronze she hides her lust,
Lying concealed amid the grain.

In August, drunken maenad, she
Offers lush breasts to Autumn's use,
As, tiger-striped, cavorting free,
She bleeds grapes of their trellis-juice.[71]

December then... Now old, she has
Grown wizened, powdered white, frost-spread.
Dreaming, she jostles Winter, as
He snores beside her in her bed.

FANTAISIES D'HIVER

I

Le nez rouge, la face blême,
Sur un pupitre de glaçons,
L'Hiver exécute son thème
Dans le quatuor des saisons.

Il chante d'une voix peu sûre
Des airs vieillots et chevrotants;
Son pied glacé bat la mesure
Et la semelle en même temps;

Et comme Hændel, dont la perruque
Perdait sa farine en tremblant,
Il fait envoler de sa nuque
La neige qui la poudre à blanc.

II

Dans le bassin des Tuileries,
Le cygne s'est pris en nageant,
Et les arbres, comme aux féeries,
Sont en filigrane d'argent.

Les vases ont des fleurs de givre,
Sous la charmille aux blancs réseaux;
Et sur la neige on voit se suivre
Les pas étoilés des oiseaux.

WINTER FANTASIES

I

Red-nosed and pallid-faced, before
A stand, ice-hung, with music set,
Winter sings notes marked on the score,
His theme in the seasons' quartet.

In quavering voice he blares and bleats
Old-fashioned airs of long ago.
With his chill, ice-shod sole, he beats
The measured rhythms, timed just so.

Like Handel, who, shaking his head,
Would set his flour-curled wig awry,
He flicks the powdered whiteness, spread
Behind his neck, sweeps, lets it fly.

II

The gliding swan, now ice-bound, stands
In the pool of the Tuileries,[72]
And the trees, like a fairyland's,
Are decked in silvered filigree.

The urned flowers sparkle frosted glints
Beneath the white-pathed arbor-way;
And in the snow one sees the prints—
Star-shaped—of birds' flitting display.

Au piédestal où, court-vêtue,
Vénus coudoyait Phocion,
L'Hiver a posé pour statue
La Frileuse de Clodion.

III

Les femmes passent sous les arbres
En martre, hermine et menu-vair,
Et les déesses, frileux marbres,
Ont pris aussi l'habit d'hiver.

La Vénus Anadyomène
Est en pelisse à capuchon;
Flore, que la brise malmène,
Plonge ses mains dans son manchon.

Et pour la saison, les bergères
De Coysevox et de Coustou,
Trouvant leurs écharpes légères,
Ont des boas autour du cou.

IV

Sur la mode Parisienne
Le Nord pose ses manteaux lourds,
Comme sur une Athénienne
Un Scythe étendrait sa peau d'ours.

Where scant-clad Venus stands beside
Athenian Phocion,[73] there, on
Her base, Winter has glorified
The shivering nymph of Clodion.[74]

III

Ladies beneath the trees walk past—
Ermined *dames*, sabled *demoiselles*;
Goddesses chill, in marble cast,
Sporting frost's winter dress as well.

Venus Anadyomenes
In hooded cape, is there no less.[75]
Flora, teased, tousled by the breeze,
Conceals her hands in muff's recess.[76]

And shepherdessses, for the season—
Coustou's and Coysevox's too—[77]
Necks cold in flimsy scarves—have reason
To wrap in boas' curlicue.

IV

The North spreads its thick mantles with
Parisian style, just as a fair
Athenian *dame*, clothed by some Scyth,
Might be decked out in skin of bear.

Partout se mélange aux parures
Dont Palmyre habille l'Hiver,
Le faste russe des fourrures
Que parfume le vétyver.

Et le Plaisir rit dans l'alcôve
Quand, au milieu des Amours nus,
Des poils roux d'une bête fauve
Sort le torse blanc de Vénus.

V

Sous le voile qui vous protège,
Défiant les regards jaloux,
Si vous sortez par cette neige,
Redoutez vos pieds andalous;

La neige saisit comme un moule
L'empreinte de ce pied mignon
Qui, sur le tapis blanc qu'il foule,
Signe, à chaque pas, votre nom.

Ainsi guidé, l'époux morose
Peut parvenir au nid caché
Où, de froid la joue encor rose,
A l'Amour s'enlace Psyché.

Lush Russian furs, by khuskhus-root
Perfumed,[78] blend with the modes that she—
Palmyre, *modiste* of rich repute—[79]
Creates for Winter's finery.

And Pleasure laughs behind the stairs
In naked alcove-loves, by night,
When, from wild beasts' red, tawny hairs,
Venus's breast heaves, rises, white.

V

Beneath the veil you hide behind
From jealous glances indiscreet,
Should you tread on this snow, pray mind
Your dainty Andalusian feet:[80]

With every step they take thereon,
Snow seizes, like a mold, each trace
On the white carpet, whereupon
They sign your name with every pace.

Guided there, your dour husband will
Easily find the secret nest
Where, cheek still pink with winter chill,
Lie Love and Psyche, breast to breast.[81]

LA SOURCE

Tout près du lac filtre une source,
Entre deux pierres, dans un coin;
Allégrement l'eau prend sa course
Comme pour s'en aller bien loin.

Elle murmure : Oh! quelle joie!
Sous la terre il faisait si noir!
Maintenant ma rive verdoie,
Le ciel se mire à mon miroir.

Les myosotis aux fleurs bleues
Me disent : Ne m'oubliez pas!
Les libellules de leurs queues
M'égratignent dans leurs ébats;

A ma coupe l'oiseau s'abreuve;
Qui sait?—Après quelques détours
Peut-être deviendrai-je un fleuve
Baignant vallons, rochers et tours.

Je broderai de mon écume
Ponts de pierre, quais de granit,
Emportant le steamer qui fume
A l'Océan où tout finit.

THE SPRING

By the lake, in a corner, seeps,
Bubbling betwixt two rocks, a spring;[82]
Flowing, in happy little leaps,
As if bent on long voyaging.

She babbles: "Ah, what joy! For I
Lay pent beneath ground's dark expanse!
Now my bank sprouts its green; and sky
Mirrors in me its heavenly glance.

"The myosotis—flowers of blue—
Tell me: 'Forget me not!' Look! See
How dragonflies dart fro and to,
Tails a-flit, skimming, scratching me.

"Birds come sip from my billows, and,
In my meanderings, after all,
I might grow to a river grand
And bathe vales, cliffs, and towers tall.

"My foam will tat its lace upon
Stone bridges, granite quais. And it
Will draw smoke-puffing steamers on
Into the Ocean's infinite..."

Ainsi la jeune source jase,
Formant cent projets d'avenir;
Comme l'eau qui bout dans un vase,
Son flot ne peut se contenir;

Mais le berceau touche à la tombe;
Le géant futur meurt petit;
Née à peine, la source tombe
Dans le grand lac qui l'engloutit!

And so the young spring gaily goes
Prattling on fate that might have been,
As water, boiling, overflows
The pot that cannot hold it in.

But tomb was by the cradle lying:
Scarce born, the future giant, doomed,
Followed her course—mere trickle!—dying
In the vast lake, swallowed, consumed...

BUCHERS ET TOMBEAUX

Le squelette était invisible
Au temps heureux de l'Art païen;
L'homme, sous la forme sensible,
Content du beau, ne cherchait rien.

Pas de cadavre sous la tombe,
Spectre hideux de l'être cher,
Comme d'un vêtement qui tombe
Se déshabillant de sa chair,

Et quand la pierre se lézarde,
Parmi les épouvantements,
Montrant à l'œil qui s'y hasarde
Une armature d'ossements;

Mais au feu du bûcher ravie
Une pincée entre les doigts,
Résidu léger de la vie,
Qu'enserrait l'urne aux flancs étroits;

Ce que le papillon de l'âme
Laisse de poussière après lui,
Et ce qui reste de la flamme
Sur le trépied, quand elle a lui!

PYRES AND TOMBS

In pagan Art's contented time
One never viewed the skeleton
Beneath the flesh; beauty sublime
Was quite enough for everyone;

No hideous spectral corpse—a dear
Departed's phantom form—within
The tomb, and shedding like a drear
Garment its covering of skin;

Nor, when the horrors of the grave
Begin to crack and split the stone,
Showing the eye that dares to brave
The scene, a panoply of bone;

But, wrested from the funeral pyre,
A pinch of flesh not wont to burn,
Merest vestige of life that fire
Leaves spared, enclosed within the urn;

Trace of the soul—that butterfly
A-wing: ash left to linger here:
After the fires go flaming high,
A bit of dust upon the bier!

Entre les fleurs et les acanthes,
Dans le marbre joyeusement,
Amours, ægipans et bacchantes
Dansaient autour du monument;

Tout au plus un petit génie
Du pied éteignait un flambeau;
Et l'art versait son harmonie
Sur la tristesse du tombeau.

Les tombes étaient attrayantes :
Comme on fait d'un enfant qui dort,
D'images douces et riantes
La vie enveloppait la mort;

La mort dissimulait sa face
Aux trous profonds, au nez camard,
Dont la hideur railleuse efface
Les chimères du cauchemar.

Le monstre, sous la chair splendide
Cachait son fantôme inconnu,
Et l'œil de la vierge candide
Allait au bel éphèbe nu.

Seulement, pour pousser à boire,
Au banquet de Trimalcion,
Une larve, joujou d'ivoire,
Faisait son apparition;

In joyous, sculptured carousel,
Mid flowering blooms, acanthus-vined,
Goat-gods, maenads—Cupids as well
Would, round the marble, dance entwined.[83]

At most, a wee small sprite, whose toe
Damped down a torch's flame... No gloom,
But only art's stately tableaux
To cheer the sadness of the tomb.

Graves shone with a beauty beguiling:
Life gently cradled death, embraced,
Like a child, sleeping, swathed in smiling
Images fair, all sweetness-graced.

Death hid its face, deep-holed between
Bare bones; noseless, the gaping head
Whose hideous, mocking sneer sweeps clean
Chimera-creatures nightmare-bred.

The monster, wondrous-fleshed, would hide
His spectre, lurking unrevealed,
Whilst the pale virgin, lustful-eyed,
Craved the ephebe, nude, unconcealed.

But, that his guests might quaff contented,
Trimalchio, at his banquet, had
An ivory skeleton presented,
Bauble brought by a servant-lad;[84]

Des dieux que l'art toujours révère
Trônaient au ciel marmoréen;
Mais l'Olympe cède au Calvaire,
Jupiter au Nazaréen;

Une voix dit : Pan est mort! — L'ombre
S'étend. — Comme sur un drap noir,
Sur la tristesse immense et sombre
Le blanc squelette se fait voir;

Il signe les pierres funèbres
De son paraphe de fémurs,
Pend son chapelet de vertèbres
Dans les charniers, le long des murs,

Des cercueils lève le couvercle
Avec ses bras aux os pointus;
Dessine ses côtes en cercle
Et rit de son large rictus;

Il pousse à la danse macabre
L'empereur, le pape et le roi,
Et de son cheval qui se cabre
Jette bas le preux plein d'effroi;

Il entre chez la courtisane
Et fait des mines au miroir,
Du malade il boit la tisane,
De l'avare ouvre le tiroir;

And, though gods' art-long pedigree—
Revered!—ruled heavens' death-marbled scene,
Olympus yields to Calvary;
Jupiter, to the Nazarene;

A voice says: "Pan is dead!" The shade[85]
Spreads like a pall—vast, dark, immense.
Stripped white, the skeleton is laid
Over its stark malevolence.

It autographs the graveyard stones
With femur-flourish; lavishly
Strews catacomb walls with the bones
Of its vertebral rosary;

And, with its sharp-boned arms, lifts wide
The coffin-lids, with ghastly leer
At fleshly relics laid inside,
Rib-cage curved in a semi-sphere;[86]

It summons to fate's deathly dance
The emperor, the pope, the king,
And tumbles from his steed—a-prance,
Dancing—the gallant, cowering;

It pays the courtesan a call,
Grimaces in her looking glass;
It drinks the sick man's teas; steals all
The miser's hidden hoard, alas;

Piquant l'attelage qui rue
Avec un os pour aiguillon,
Du laboureur à la charrue
Termine en fosse le sillon;

Et, parmi la foule priée,
Hôte inattendu, sous le banc,
Vole à la pâle mariée
Sa jarretière de ruban.

A chaque pas grossit la bande;
Le jeune au vieux donne la main;
L'irrésistible sarabande
Met en branle le genre humain.

Le spectre en tête se déhanche,
Dansant et jouant du rebec,
Et sur fond noir, en couleur blanche,
Holbein l'esquisse d'un trait sec.

Quand le siècle devient frivole
Il suit la mode; en tonnelet
Retrousse son linceul et vole
Comme un Cupidon de ballet

Au tombeau-sofa des marquises
Qui reposent, lasses d'amour,
En des attitudes exquises,
Dans les chapelles Pompadour.

With a bone, spurs the oxen-hitch
As tiller plows the furrows; and
Tills them a-tangle in the ditch
Rather than plowing straight the land;

And, wedding-guest unbidden, it
Crawls by the pale bride's bench, and there
Filches her garter in a fit
Of deathly pique, to her despair...

Resistless is the saraband,
Growing—before, beside, behind:
The young take elders by the hand,
And death's round stirs all humankind.

A lithe-hipped spectre leads the pack—
Dancing, plucking his rebec-strings—
Whom Holbein, with his white on black,
Sketches in quick, sharp renderings.[87]

And when the age grows frivolous,
It does so too: petticoat-wise,
It lifts its shroud-skirt high, and thus,
Like ballet-Cupid, straightway flies

To sofa-graves of *belles marquises,*
Who, surfeited on their amour,
In sumptuous poses take their ease
In chapels à la Pompadour.[88]

Mais voile-toi, masque sans joues,
Comédien que le ver mord,
Dupuis assez longtemps tu joues
Le mélodrame de la Mort.

Reviens, reviens, bel art antique,
De ton paros étincelant
Couvrir ce squelette gothique;
Dévore-le, bûcher brûlant!

Si nous sommes une statue
Sculptée à l'image de Dieu,
Quand cette image est abattue,
Jetons-en les débris au feu.

Toi, forme immortelle, remonte
Dans la flamme aux sources du beau,
Sans que ton argile ait la honte
Et les misères du tombeau!

Cover your cheekless mask, I pray,
You, actor lifeless now, on whom
Gnaws the worm... Long enough you play
The melodrama of the Tomb!

Return, O ancient art, redone
In Paros marble's sheen august,[89]
To hide that Gothic skeleton;
O pyre, burn it to deadly dust!

If in God's image we are wrought—
Mere statues!—then, when we expire,
Cast down, and when they come to naught,
Let their remains go feed the fire!

But thou, immortal form! Let not
Your clay suffer the tomb's base shame!
Rise high above death's rue and rot
To beauty's source amidst the flame!

LE SOUPER DES ARMURES

Biorn, étrange cénobite
Sur le plateau d'un roc pelé,
Hors du temps et du monde, habite
La tour d'un burg démantelé.

De sa porte l'esprit moderne
En vain soulève le marteau.
Biorn verrouille sa poterne
Et barricade son château.

Quand tous ont les yeux vers l'aurore,
Biorn, sur son donjon perché,
A l'horizon contemple encore
La place du soleil couché.

Ame rétrospective, il loge
Dans son burg et dans le passé;
Le pendule de son horloge
Depuis des siècles est cassé.

Sous ses ogives féodales
Il erre, éveillant les échos,
Et ses pas, sonnant sur les dalles,
Semblent suivis de pas égaux.

THE ARMORS' SUPPER

Far from the here and now, Sir Bjorn,
Strange hermit-monk, lives in his manse— [90]
Decrepit tower, now time-forlorn—
On a cliff's craggy, bare expanse.

Should modern spirit urge his gate
To raise its latch, Sir Bjorn is quite
Unmoved; and, ever obdurate,
Bars, bolts, and locks the manor tight.

When others gaze at dawning morn
To hail the newly-rising sun,
From his dark tower-perch, Sir Bjorn
Fixes the spot where day lies done.

Soul wrought of time's residuum,
The manor's past: his sole domain.
Even his old clock's pendulum
For centuries has lifeless lain.

Beneath the feudal arched vaults, he
Wanders, as echoes past awaken,
Striking the flagstones evenly
In rhythmic pace with each step taken.

Il ne voit ni laïcs, ni prêtres,
Ni gentilshommes, ni bourgeois,
Mais les portraits de ses ancêtres
Causent avec lui quelquefois.

Et certains soirs, pour se distraire,
Trouvant manger seul ennuyeux,
Biorn, caprice funéraire,
Invite à souper ses aïeux.

Les fantômes, quand minuit sonne,
Viennent armés de pied en cap;
Biorn, qui malgré lui frissonne,
Salue en haussant son hanap.

Pour s'asseoir, chaque panoplie
Fait un angle avec son genou,
Dont l'articulation plie
En grinçant comme un vieux verrou;

Et tout d'une pièce, l'armure,
D'un corps absent gauche cercueil,
Rendant un creux et sourd murmure,
Tombe entre les bras du fauteuil.

Landgraves, rhingraves, burgraves,
Venus du ciel ou de l'enfer,
Ils sont tous là, muets et graves,
Les roides convives de fer!

He sees no priests, no laymen, no
Commoners, no fine gentlemen;
But portraits of his forebears—lo!—
Stop to chat with him now and then.

On certain evenings, lonely grown,
Indulging in a morbid whim—
Finding it dull to dine alone—
Bjorn prays his kin come dine with him.

Armor-clad tip to toe, when toll
The midnight bells, the ghosts draw nigh;
And Bjorn, quaking beyond control,
Greets one and all, tankard held high.

Each suit of armor, as it sits,
Bent to an angle at the knee,
Creeks with a screech that more befits
A gate-latch grating eerily;

Each awkward metal coffin drawls
A hollow moan, as each—a space
Empty of body, groaning—sprawls
Into a waiting chair's embrace.

Landgraves, rhinegraves, burgraves. Each guest—[91]
From heaven or hell bemetaled come—
Stiff in each silent, somber *geste*,
Attends the weird convivium.

Dans l'ombre, un rayon fauve indique
Un monstre, guivre, aigle à deux cous,
Pris au bestiaire héraldique
Sur les cimiers faussés de coups.

Du mufle des bêtes difformes
Dressant leurs ongles arrogants,
Partent des panaches énormes,
Des lambrequins extravagants;

Mais les casques ouverts sont vides
Comme les timbres du blason;
Seulement deux flammes livides
Y luisent d'étrange façon.

Toute la ferraille est assise
Dans la salle du vieux manoir,
Et, sur le mur, l'ombre indécise
Donne à chaque hôte un page noir.

Les liqueurs aux feux des bougies
Ont des pourpres d'un ton suspect;
Les mets dans leurs sauces rougies
Prennent un singulier aspect.

Parfois un corselet miroite,
Un morion brille un moment;
Une pièce qui se déboîte
Choit sur la nappe lourdement.

A tawny light pierces the very
Shades round each crest, battered, abject;
Helmets' heraldic bestiary
Spawns eagle-snake, fierce, double-necked.[92]

From shapeless monsters' spectral snout—
Menacing monsters, surly-clawed—
Enormous plumes appear to sprout,
And lambrequin-cloths, passing odd.

Opened, the helmets, headless looming,
Faceless symbols of heraldry!
In their place, two flames, flashing, fuming,
Glow ghastly pale, uncannily.

Metal sits, fills the old manse-hall,
And each invited guest therein,
From the dimmed shadows on the wall,
Welcomes a varlet black of skin.

The liquors lit by candle-glare
Gleam in crimson mysteriousness;
And each dish of the phantom fare—
Gravy tinged red—flares weird no less.

Betimes, a corselet shimmers... One
Moment a helmet shines... Some thing[93]
Metallic comes unhinged, undone,
Falls, strikes the table, echoing...

L'on entend les battements d'ailes
D'invisibles chauves-souris,
Et les drapeaux des infidèles
Palpitent le long du lambris.

Avec des mouvements fantasques
Courbant leurs phalanges d'airain,
Les gantelets versent aux casques
Des rasades de vin du Rhin,

Ou découpent au fil des dagues
Des sangliers sur des plats d'or...
Cependant passent des bruits vagues
Par les orgues du corridor.

La débauche devient farouche,
On n'entendrait pas tonner Dieu;
Car, lorsqu'un fantôme découche,
C'est le moins qu'il s'amuse un peu.

Et la fantastique assemblée
Se tracassant dans son harnois,
L'orgie a sa rumeur doublée
Du tintamarre des tournois.

Gobelets, hanaps, vidrecomes,
Vidés toujours, remplis en vain,
Entre les mâchoires des heaumes
Forment des cascades de vin.

One hears the sound of bats, detested,
Unseen, but fluttering their wings;
And flags from godless foemen wrested
Shudder about the wainscotings.

Bending their brass joints in the air,
The gauntlets flailing, trunk to chin,
Grasping the helmets gaping bare,
Pour drafts of Rhenish wine therein;

Or cut with dagger-blades, on plates
Of gold, thick slices of wild boar,
As organ music ululates—
Vaguely—throughout the corridor.

Louder the revel than God's thunder,
This wild carouse of wine, of victual!...
—When spectre quits his bed, no wonder:
Best he amuse himself a little!

Fantastic, this knight-errantry
Is clad in clanging armor, whence,
To the orgy's cacophony,
It joins the din of tournaments.

Betwixt the helmets' yawning jaws,
Loving-cup, brimming tankard, stein,
Pour their cascades with never a pause:
Emptied, filled, emptied... Wine... More wine...

Les hauberts en bombent leurs ventres,
Et le flot monte aux gorgerins;
— Ils sont tous gris comme des chantres,
Les vaillants comtes suzerains!

L'un allonge dans la salade
Nonchalamment ses pédieux,
L'autre à son compagnon malade
Fait un sermon fastidieux.

Et des armures peu bégueules
Rappellent, dardant leur boisson,
Les lions lampassés de gueules
Blasonnés sur leur écusson.

D'une voix encore enrouée
Par l'humidité du caveau,
Max fredonne, ivresse enjouée,
Un lied, en treize cents, nouveau.

Albrecht, ayant le vin féroce,
Se querelle avec ses voisins,
Qu'il martèle, bossue et rosse,
Comme il faisait des Sarrasins.

Echauffé, Fritz ôte son casque,
Jadis par un crâne habité,
Ne pensant pas que sans son masque
Il semble un tronc décapité.

Beneath their mail their bellies swell;
Up to their chin-guards floods rise free;
All drunk as deacons, truth to tell:[94]
This fruit of fiefdom's suzerainty!

One—legs outstretched in casual wise—
Plants his feet in the salad, while
His priggish friend will sermonize
On end, and his debauch revile.

Some—not prudes in the slightest!—guzzle,
Glut on their drink; and they recall
Lions, tongues hanging from their muzzle,[95]
That their escutcheons sport withal.

Voice hoarsened by the humid air,
Max, in a drunk fortissimo,
Drones with the brashest devil-may-care
A *lied* from centuries ago.

Albrecht—wild wine-imbiber he—
Pounds on his neighbors... Strikes again...
Again... Pummels them murderously,
As once he thrashed the Saracen.

Fritz, hot with rash exuberance,
Will his once skull-filled helmet doff,
Not thinking that, in faceless stance,
Mere trunk he seems, with head cut off.

Bientôt ils roulent pêle-mêle
Sous la table, parmi les brocs,
Tête en bas, montrant la semelle
De leurs souliers courbés en crocs.

C'est un hideux champ de bataille
Où les pots heurtent les armets
Où chaque mort par quelque entaille,
Au lieu de sang vomit des mets.

Et Biorn, le poing sur la cuisse,
Les contemple, morne et hagard,
Tandis que, par le vitrail suisse,
L'aube jette son bleu regard.

La troupe, qu'un rayon traverse,
Pâlit comme au jour un flambeau,
Et le plus ivrogne se verse
Le coup d'étrier du tombeau.

Le coq chante, les spectres fuient
Et, reprenant un air hautain,
Sur l'oreiller de marbre appuient
Leurs têtes lourdes du festin!

Soon, rousting to a fare-thee-well—
Under the tables, champing, churning,
Rolling among the mugs, pell-mell—
They crouch, heads low and feet upturning.

Ghastly battlefield this, with its
Clashing of cups and helmets, where
Each corpse pukes through his armor's slits
Not blood but what was supper-fare!

And Bjorn, somber and woebegone,
Looks on, fist on his thigh, as through
Tracery stained-glass skylight, dawn
A-borning casts its glance of blue.

Light darts a ray: the ancestors
Pale, torch-like in morn's lightening gloom;
And the most drunk amongst them pours
The stirrup-cup to reach the tomb.

Cockcrow... That haughty phantom frown
Theirs once again, the spectres flee,
On marble pillows laying down
Their heads, heavy with revelry!

LA MONTRE

Deux fois je regarde ma montre,
Et deux fois à mes yeux distraits
L'aiguille au même endroit se montre;
Il est une heure... une heure après.

La figure de la pendule
En rit dans le salon voisin,
Et le timbre d'argent module
Deux coups vibrant comme un tocsin.

Le cadran solaire me raille
En m'indiquant, de son long doigt,
Le chemin que sur la muraille
A fait son ombre qui s'accroît.

Le clocher avec ironie
Dit le vrai chiffre et le beffroi,
Reprenant la note finie,
A l'air de se moquer de moi.

Tiens! la petite bête est morte.
Je n'ai pas mis hier encor,
Tant ma rêverie était forte,
Au trou de rubis la clef d'or!

THE POCKET WATCH

I open twice my pocket watch.
What? Have my poor eyes wrongly reckoned?
The hand moved not one blessèd notch:
One o'clock both times, first and second...

The great clock leering in the hall
Laughs as he sees me thus confounded,
And, like a jeering signal-call,
Peels twice his bell-voice, silver-sounded.

The sundial mocks and twits with his
Long finger, pointing at me, showing
The wall, and how well-trod it is,
Tracked by its shadow, ever growing.

The steeple-clock, ironic, sneers
The time exact; and the bell-tower,
Repeating the same note he hears,
Smirks at me as he tolls the hour.

Alas, the little beast lies dead.
The golden key? Yes, I forgot
Again last night—where was my head?—
To wind it in his rubied slot!

Et je ne vois plus, dans sa boîte,
Le fin ressort du balancier
Aller, venir, à gauche, à droite,
Ainsi qu'un papillon d'acier.

C'est bien de moi! Quand je chevauche
L'Hippogriffe, au pays du Bleu,
Mon corps sans âme se débauche,
Et s'en va comme il plaît à Dieu!

L'éternité poursuit son cercle
Autour de ce cadran muet,
Et le temps, l'oreille au couvercle,
Cherche ce cœur qui remuait;

Ce cœur que l'enfant croit en vie,
Et dont chaque pulsation
Dans notre poitrine est suivie
D'une égale vibration,

Il ne bat plus, mais son grand frère
Toujours palpite à mon côté.
—Celui que rien ne peut distraire,
Quand je dormais, l'a remonté!

Now, in his case, no more I spy
The wee spring of his balance-wheel,
A-flit—left, right—before my eye,
Like fluttering butterfly of steel.

Just like me, as I mount upon
The Hippogryph, in Blue domain—[96]
Soulless, and reveling on and on—
Off to wherever God might deign!

Eternity, mute, runs apace
About his dial; and time, once more
Pressing an ear against his case,
Seeks out that heart that beat before;

Heart that the child thinks must still be
Alive, ticking time's ebb and flow,
Whose beats echoed unerringly
Within my pulsing breast. But no...

Silence! Yet his big brother, who
Lies by me, pulses, beats away:
—He who does all He chooses to,
Rewound him as I, sleeping, lay.

LES NEREIDES

J'ai dans ma chambre une aquarelle
Bizarre, et d'un peintre avec qui
Mètre et rime sont en querelle,
—Théophile Kniatowski.

Sur l'écume blanche qui frange
Le manteau glauque de la mer
Se groupent en bouquet étrange
Trois nymphes, fleurs du gouffre amer.

Comme des lis noyés, la houle
Fait dans sa volute d'argent
Danser leurs beaux corps qu'elle roule,
Les élevant, les submergeant.

Sur leurs têtes blondes, coiffées
De pétoncles et de roseaux,
Elles mêlent, coquettes fées,
L'écrin et la flore des eaux.

Vidant sa nacre, l'huître à perle
Constelle de son blanc trésor
Leur gorge, où le flot qui déferle
Suspend d'autres perles encor.

THE NEREIDS

An aquarellist's work have I —
Artist of most uncommon style,
Whose names meter and rhyme defy:
One Kniatowski, Théophile.

Water-nymphs three — bizarre bouquet,
Grouped on the white froth fringing this
Sea-mantle, sallow, glaucous — they
Rise flower-like from the abyss.

Like lilies drowned, their lovely, fair
Shapes, as the silvered foam unfurls,
Now rise, now fall — grace debonair —
Wrapped in the rolling water-swirls.

With fairy-like coquettishness,
Their blond heads coifed in disarray —
All reeds and cockleshells, no less! —
Gems mingle with seaweed display.

Opening wide her treasure-chest,
The oyster, from her lucent shell,
Sprinkles white stars upon each breast,
Dappled with other pearls as well.

Et, jusqu'aux hanches soulevées
Par le bras des Tritons nerveux,
Elles luisent, d'azur lavées,
Sous l'or vert de leurs longs cheveux.

Plus bas, leur blancheur sous l'eau bleue
Se glace d'un visqueux frisson,
Et le torse finit en queue,
Moitié femme, moitié poisson.

Mais qui regarde la nageoire
Et les reins aux squameux replis,
En voyant les bustes d'ivoire
Par le baiser des mers polis?

A l'horizon,—piquant mélange
De fable et de réalité,—
Paraît un vaisseau qui dérange
Le chœur marin épouvanté.

Son pavillon est tricolore;
Son tuyau vomit la vapeur;
Ses aubes fouettent l'eau sonore,
Et les nymphes plongent de peur.

Sans crainte elles suivaient par troupes
Les trirèmes de l'Archipel,
Et les dauphins, arquant leurs croupes,
D'Arion attendaient l'appel.

Unto their very hips they glow,
Held aloft—in pure azure bathed—
By Triton's sinewed arms, and, lo![97]
Stand forth in gold-green tresses swathed,

Below, beneath the waters blue,
Their torsos white turn viscous, grayed,
And there grow tails, joined thereunto:
Creatures combined—part fish, part maid.

Yet who will gaze on tail or fin,
On squamous back, on scales' design,
When shines their busts' fair ivory skin
By water's kisses polished fine?

But look! Beyond... A boat, appearing—
Real? Or a dream?—plying its way
On the horizon, ever nearing...
Our sea-choir shudders in dismay.

Its flag waves colors three; it spews
Steam from its pipes; its paddles, shaking,
Whip up the humming waters, whose
Nymphs, numb with fright, dive, plunging, quaking...[98]

Fearless, their troupes once plied the sea,
Stalked by the Greek Isles' triremes all,
As dolphins arched their backs to be
Ready to heed Arion's call.[99]

Mais le steam-boat avec ses roues,
Comme Vulcain battant Vénus,
Souffletterait leurs belles joues
Et meurtrirait leurs membres nus.

Adieu, fraîche mythologie!
Le paquebot passe et, de loin,
Croit voir sur la vague élargie
Une culbute de marsouin.

Alas! The bladed wheel well might—
Should Vulcan thrash Venus's charms—[100]
Slap their soft cheeks, and, with its bite,
Bruise black and blue their naked arms!...[101]

Enough, fresh-sprung mythologies!
The boat slips past—nor slows, nor halts—
And, from afar, it thinks it sees
Porpoises turning somersaults...

LES ACCROCHE-CŒURS

Ravivant les langueurs nacrées
De tes yeux battus et vainqueurs,
En mèches de parfum lustrées
Se courbent deux accroche-cœurs.

A voir s'arrondir sur tes joues
Leurs orbes tournés par tes doigts,
On dirait les petites roues
Du char de Mab fait d'une noix;

Ou l'arc de l'Amour dont les pointes,
Pour une flèche à décocher,
En cercle d'or se sont rejointes
A la tempe du jeune archer.

Pourtant un scrupule me trouble,
Je n'ai qu'un cœur, alors pourquoi,
Coquette, un accroche-cœur double?
Qui donc y pends-tu près de moi?

THE LOVE LOCKS

Bringing to life your dark-ringed eyes'
Triumphant languor opaline,
A pair of love-locks fragrant lies,
Lustrous hair swirled against your skin.

To see them on your cheeks a-curl,
Twirled by your fingers with a dab,
One might think them the wheels that whirl
The walnut-shell coach of Queen Mab;[102]

Or Cupid's bow, whose tips—when he
Pulls tight to loose his dart—are now
Joined in a circle, goldenly,
Against the archer's boyish brow.

A qualm, however... Please explain:
One heart have I; why must there be
Two lovely kiss-curls, love-locks twain?
Whom do you hang here next to me?

LA ROSE-THE

La plus délicate des roses
Est, à coup sûr, la rose-thé.
Son bouton aux feuilles mi-closes
De carmin à peine est teinté.

On dirait une rose blanche
Qu'aurait fait rougir de pudeur,
En la lutinant sur la branche,
Un papillon trop plein d'ardeur.

Son tissu rose et diaphane
De la chair a le velouté;
Auprès, tout incarnat se fane
Ou prend de la vulgarité.

Comme un teint aristocratique
Noircit les fronts bruns de soleil,
De ses sœurs elle rend rustique
Le coloris chaud et vermeil.

Mais, si votre main qui s'en joue,
A quelque bal, pour son parfum,
La rapproche de votre joue,
Son frais éclat devient commun.

THE TEA-ROSE

Of all the roses, surely must
The tea-rose be the daintiest:
Her leaves half-closed, her bud is just
A slightly crimsoned hue at best.

One might indeed even suppose
She were a white rose—blushing, shy—
Tweaked on the twig by one of those:
An all-too-amorous butterfly!

Her fabric pink, diaphanous—
Bloom of flesh-tinted velvet, she.
All other reds beside her, thus,
Fade or turn vulgar frippery.

Her hue, aristocratic, pure...
Such that her sisters' sun-bronzed skin
Seems almost dark as rustic boor,
Though warm its rich incarnadine.

Yet, at some ball, if your hand goes
To breathe her scent, and gently brings
Her to your cheek, this lustrous rose
Becomes the most banal of things.

Il n'est pas de rose assez tendre
Sur la palette du printemps,
Madame, pour oser prétendre
Lutter contre vos dix-sept ans.

La peau vaut mieux que le pétale,
Et le sang pur d'un noble cœur
Qui sur la jeunesse s'étale,
De tous les roses est vainqueur!

No rose is there—my love, my sweet—
Born of spring's tender palette green,
That would dare venture to compete
Against your seasons seventeen.[103]

Ah! Better flesh than petals, surely!
And blood of noble heart well-bred
Spread over youthful beauty purely,
Bests every other pink and red!

CARMEN

Carmen est maigre, — un trait de bistre
Cerne son œil de gitana.
Ses cheveux sont d'un noir sinistre,
Sa peau, le diable la tanna.

Les femmes disent qu'elle est laide,
Mais tous les hommes en sont fous :
Et l'archevêque de Tolède
Chante la messe à ses genoux;

Car sur sa nuque d'ambre fauve
Se tord un énorme chignon
Qui, dénoué, fait dans l'alcôve
Une mante à son corps mignon.

Et, parmi sa pâleur, éclate
Une bouche aux rires vainqueurs;
Piment rouge, fleur écarlate,
Qui prend sa pourpre au sang des cœurs.

Ainsi faite, la moricaude
Bat les plus altières beautés,
Et de ses yeux la lueur chaude
Rend la flamme aux satiétés.

CARMEN

Carmen is gaunt; bronzed shadow lies
Ringing her gypsy eyes within.
Her black hair shines in evil wise:
The devil himself wrought tan her skin.

Women disdain her look, but all
Men love her madly and adore her.
Toledo's bishop, too, would fall
On his knees and sing mass before her!

For an enormous chignon-bun
Twists on her tawny-amber nape;
Which, in the alcove, come undone,
Mantles her body's graceful shape.

Grown pale betimes, her lips explode
Into triumphant laughter, red
As pepper, scarlet bloom-bestowed,
Crimson as blood from men's hearts bled.

Thus does this swarthy creature beat
Those beauties of the haughtiest,
And from her eyes her passion's heat
Enflames even the calmest breast.

Elle a dans sa laideur piquante
Un grain de sel de cette mer
D'où jaillit nue et provocante,
L'âcre Vénus du gouffre amer.

Hers, in her piquant ugliness,
A grain of salt found in that sea—
That bitter deep, vast, fathomless—
Whence surged nude Venus, tauntingly.[104]

CE QUE DISENT LES HIRONDELLES

Chanson d'automne

Déjà plus d'une feuille sèche
Parsème les gazons jaunis;
Soir et matin, la brise est fraîche,
Hélas! les beaux jours sont finis!

On voit s'ouvrir les fleurs que garde
Le jardin, pour dernier trésor :
Le dahlia met sa cocarde
Et le souci sa toque d'or.

La pluie au bassin fait des bulles;
Les hirondelles sur le toit
Tiennent des conciliabules :
Voici l'hiver, voici le froid!

Elles s'assemblent par centaines,
Se concertant pour le départ.
L'une dit : « Oh! que dans Athènes
Il fait bon sur le vieux rempart!

« Tous les ans j'y vais et je niche
Aux métopes du Parthénon.
Mon nid bouche dans la corniche
Le trou d'un boulet de canon. »

WHAT THE SWALLOWS SAY

An Autumn Song

Over the dry and yellowed grass,
Many a withered leaf lies spread.
Days, nights, the breeze blows cool. Alas!
Too soon the year's fair days are dead!

One sees late garden-treasures yet
Appear—saved for the last; unfold
Their petals: dahlia's proud rosette,
Cocked headdress of the marigold.

Raindrops raise bubbles on the pond;
In council, on the roof, the swallows
Meet to decide what lies beyond:
Winter is here, soon the freeze follows!

By hundreds they assemble there
To make the plans for their migration.
Says one: "To Athens, I declare!
Fair her ramparts' accommodation!

"Each year I find the very best
Frieze in the Parthenon... The wall
Has a hole where I build my nest,
Pierced by an errant cannonball."

L'autre : « J'ai ma petite chambre
A Smyrne, au plafond d'un café.
Les Hadjis comptent leurs grains d'ambre
Sur le seuil d'un rayon chauffé.

« J'entre et je sors, accoutumée
Aux blondes vapeurs des chibouchs,
Et parmi les flots de fumée,
Je rase turbans et tarbouchs. »

Celle-ci : « J'habite un triglyphe
Au fronton d'un temple, à Balbeck.
Je m'y suspends avec ma griffe
Sur mes petits au large bec. »

Celle-là : « Voici mon adresse :
Rhodes, palais des chevaliers;
Chaque hiver, ma tente s'y dresse
Au chapiteau des noirs piliers. »

La cinquième : « Je ferai halte,
Car l'âge m'alourdit un peu,
Aux blanches terrasses de Malte,
Entre l'eau bleue et le ciel bleu. »

La sixième : « Qu'on est à l'aise
Au Caire, en haut des minarets!
J'empâte un ornement de glaise,
Et mes quartiers d'hiver sont prêts. »

"I roost in Smyrna, if you please,
On café ceiling," chirps this one,
"While Hajjis tell their rosaries[105]
On counter-ledge warmed by the sun.

"I go and come as suits my whim,
Amid blond chibouk-clouds," he says.[106]
"And, flitting midst the smoke, I skim
Many a turban, many a fez."

Another pipes: "At Balbec, I[107]
Visit a temple, perched outside,
Hanging from a triglyph on high,[108]
Above my brood, beaks gaping wide."

Another: "My winter address?
Rhodes, Palace of the *Chevaliers*...
Pillared tent's lofty, dark recess:
Thither I fly, and there I stay."

The fifth: "Age weighs me down. Perchance
Shall I stop for a day or two
On Malta's white-terraced expanse
Between the sky's and water's blue."

The sixth: "High Cairo minaret!
I coat with lime and line with twigs
A fancy niche, all snug, and set
About to make my winter digs."

« A la seconde cataracte,
Fait la dernière, j'ai mon nid;
J'en ai noté la place exacte,
Dans le pschent d'un roi de granit. »

Toutes : « Demain combien de lieues
Auront filé sous notre essaim,
Plaines brunes, pics blancs, mers bleues
Brodant d'écume leur bassin! »

Avec cris et battements d'ailes,
Sur la moulure aux bords étroits,
Ainsi jasent les hirondelles,
Voyant venir la rouille aux bois.

Je comprends tout ce qu'elles disent,
Car le poète est un oiseau;
Mais, captif, ses élans se brisent
Contre un invisible réseau!

Des ailes! des ailes! des ailes!
Comme dans le chant de Ruckert,
Pour voler, là-bas avec elles
Au soleil d'or, au printemps vert!

"Hard by the second cataract,"
Twitters the last, "I settle down,
Always in one same spot, in fact:
A granite pharaoh's twofold crown."[109]

Then all: "How many leagues will be
Spun out beneath our flock? All these
Brown plains, white mountain peaks, blue sea,
Shores edged with foam-embroideries!"

With peeps and fluttering of wings,
Over the molding narrow-ledged,
Our swallows chirp their jabberings,
Watching the woods turn russet-hedged...

I understand this chatter, for
The poet is a bird serene;
But, captive, when he seeks to soar,
He crashes on a web unseen!

Ah! Wings! Wings! Wings!... As Rückert wrote![110]
Oh, to be able to take wing
And with the swallows, fly, afloat,
To goldening sun and greening spring!

NOEL

Le ciel est noir, la terre est blanche;
—Cloches, carillonnez gaîment!—
Jésus est né;—la Vierge penche
Sur lui son visage charmant.

Pas de courtines festonnées
Pour préserver l'enfant du froid;
Rien que les toiles d'araignées
Qui pendent des poutres du toit.

Il tremble sur la paille fraîche,
Ce cher petit enfant Jésus,
Et pour l'échauffer dans sa crèche
L'âne et le bœuf soufflent dessus.

La neige au chaume coud ses franges,
Mais sur le toit s'ouvre le ciel
Et, tout en blanc, le chœur des anges
Chante aux bergers : « *Noël! Noël!* »

NOEL

The earth is white, dark is the sky
—Bells, peal your joy!—for Jesus, he
Is born; the Virgin, kneeling by,
Nods her fair face adoringly.

No drapes festooned, no flounce, no frill
Is there: nothing at all, it seems,
To keep the child safe from the chill
But cobwebs hanging from the beams.

As Jesus, tender babe, lies there
In straw—cold, trembling limb to limb—
The ass and bull blow warm the air
With gentle breath to blanket him.

Snow sews the thatch, unraveling;
Roof bathes in heaven's light nonpareil;[111]
And to the shepherd, angels sing—
Clad all in white—*"Noel! Noel!"*

LES JOUJOUX DE LA MORTE

La petite Marie est morte,
Et son cercueil est si peu long
Qu'il tient sous le bras qui l'emporte
Comme un étui de violon.

Sur le tapis et sur la table
Traîne l'héritage enfantin.
Les bras ballants, l'air lamentable,
Tout affaissé, gît le pantin.

Et si la poupée est plus ferme,
C'est la faute de son bâton;
Dans son œil une larme germe,
Un soupir gonfle son carton.

Une dînette abandonnée
Mêle ses plats de bois verni
A la troupe désarçonnée
Des écuyers de Franconi.

La boîte à musique est muette;
Mais, quand on pousse le ressort
Où se posait sa main fluette,
Un murmure plaintif en sort.

THE LITTLE DEAD GIRL'S TOYS

Little Marie is dead. So small[112]
The coffin that they lay her in,
It can be carried, corpse and all,
Like the case of a violin.

On carpet and on table, there
Lies childhood wealth to others left:
Poor puppet, with his doleful air,
Arms dangling, sprawling, strength bereft.

More firm of form, the doll, for she
Sports a stick; and a tear wells fresh
Upon her eye, as mournfully
A sigh swells from her cardboard flesh.

Dolls' dining-set, abandoned too,
Of polished wood, dawdles among
Franconi's squires, cavaliers who[113]
Lie strewn, unsaddled and unstrung.

The music box is mute; but when
Your hand chances to flick the spring,
Touched by her tiny fingers, then
A plaintive sob comes murmuring.

L'émotion chevrote et tremble
Dans : *Ah! vous dirai-je maman!*
Le *Quadrille des Lanciers* semble
Triste comme un enterrement,

Et des pleurs vous mouillent la joue
Quand *la Donna è mobile*,
Sur le rouleau qui tourne et joue,
Expire avec un son filé.

Le cœur se navre à ce mélange
Puérilement douloureux,
Joujoux d'enfant laissés par l'ange,
Berceau que la tombe a fait creux!

"Ah! vous dirai-je, maman!" bleats shrill[114]
Its quivering notes, sad as can be,
And even "The Lancers' Quadrille"[115]
Plinks a lugubrious harmony.

Tears wet your cheeks at thoughts of her;
The air "La Donna è mobile,"[116]
From the revolving cylinder,
Tinkles to life then dies away...

Such this-and-that sorely bereaves
The heart, with scenes of childhood doom:
Youngster's toys that the angel leaves,
Cradle left empty by the tomb!

APRES LE FEUILLETON

Mes colonnes sont alignées
Au portique du feuilleton;
Elles supportent résignées
Du journal le pesant fronton.

Jusqu'à lundi je suis mon maître.
Au diable chefs-d'œuvre mort-nés!
Pour huit jours je puis me permettre
De vous fermer la porte au nez.

Les ficelles des mélodrames
N'ont plus le droit de se glisser
Parmi les fils soyeux des trames
Que mon caprice aime à tisser.

Voix de l'âme et de la nature,
J'écouterai vos purs sanglots,
Sans que les couplets de facture
M'étourdissent de leurs grelots.

Et portant, dans mon verre à côtes,
La santé du temps disparu,
Avec mes vieux rêves pour hôtes
Je boirai le vin de mon cru :

AFTER THE ARTICLE

My article is done; aligned,
My columns—which they relegate
To page's bottom!—stand resigned
To bear the ponderous masthead's weight.

Till Monday, now, all my toil ceases;
I can cry, as the door is slammed
On you, abortive masterpieces:
"For a week may you all be damned!"

The melodramas' tangling strings
Have no right now to slip within
The silken-thread meanderings
That my caprices choose to spin.

I shall heed your pure sobs sublime,
O voice of nature, voice of soul,
Nor let dull, hackneyed money-rhyme
Bore me with jangling rigmarole.

And, feting my past dreams, shall I—
In my old ribbed-glass goblet fine,
Toasting the health of time gone by—
Drink deep of my own vintage wine;

Le vin de ma propre pensée,
Vierge de toute autre liqueur,
Et que, par la vie écrasée,
Répand la grappe de mon cœur!

The wine of no thoughts but my own,
Virgin—all other drafts apart—
Pressed by the crush of life, and sown
By grapes of none but my own heart!

LE CHATEAU DU SOUVENIR

La main au front, le pied dans l'âtre,
Je songe et cherche à revenir,
Par delà le passé grisâtre,
Au vieux château du Souvenir.

Une gaze de brume estompe
Arbres, maisons, plaines, coteaux,
Et l'œil au carrefour qui trompe
En vain consulte les poteaux.

J'avance parmi les décombres
De tout un monde enseveli,
Dans le mystère des pénombres,
A travers des limbes d'oubli.

Mais voici, blanche et diaphane,
La Mémoire, au bord du chemin,
Qui me remet, comme Ariane,
Son peloton de fil en main.

Désormais la route est certaine;
Le soleil voilé reparaît,
Et du château la tour lointaine
Pointe au-dessus de la forêt.

THE CASTLE OF MEMORY

Foot by the hearth, hand on my brow,
I muse, and yearn once more to see—
Bridging the ashen past—here, now,
The old Castle of Memory.

Gossamer mist befogs the plain,
Hills, houses, trees, dimmed through the gray;
And the unsure eye seeks in vain
For signposts pointing out the way.

I tread the shambles; panoply
Of a life lying buried... Rotten
Debris eclipsed in mystery:
The limbo of a world forgotten.

Ah! But as I trudge on ahead,
Diaphanous, there Memory stands,
Tall; and, like Ariadne's thread,
A ball of twine thrusts in my hands.[117]

Now is the route made clear, and I
Perceive the sun unveiled, and see
The distant castle's tower rise high
Above the forest canopy.

Sous l'arcade où le jour s'émousse,
De feuilles en feuilles tombant,
Le sentier ancien dans la mousse
Trace encor son étroit ruban.

Mais la ronce en travers s'enlace;
La liane tend son filet,
Et la branche que je déplace
Revient et me donne un soufflet.

Enfin au bout de la clairière,
Je découvre du vieux manoir
Les tourelles en poivrière
Et les hauts toits en éteignoir

Sur le comble aucune fumée
Rayant le ciel d'un bleu sillon;
Pas une fenêtre allumée
D'une figure ou d'un rayon.

Les chaînes du pont sont brisées;
Aux fossés la lentille d'eau
De ses taches vert-de-grisées
Etale le glauque rideau.

Des tortuosités de lierre
Pénètrent dans chaque refend,
Payant la tour hospitalière
Qui les soutient... en l'étouffant.

Beneath the vaults where light turns shade,
Falling in leaf-swept interlacing,
The old path, on the moss-strewn glade,
Ribbons once more its narrow tracing.

Brambles lurk though they fain would hide;
Vines set their traps swaying through space;
And the branch that I turn aside
Snaps a sharp slap across my face.

Then, there! A sudden clearing, where
Turrets, like pepper-shakers, rise,
And candle-snuffers pierce the air:
An ancient manse against the skies.

Atop, no stripe of smoke, no gray,
Furrowing wake splitting the blue;
No empty window with a ray
Of light; no face to welcome you.

The drawbridge chains hang uselessly,
Broken; with droplets, glaucous green,
The ditches spread their verdigris
Like a drape hung betwixt, between...

Ivy vines clambering tortuously
Into each cranny, every slit,
Repay the hospitality
The tower extends... by stifling it!

Le porche à la lune se ronge,
Le temps le sculpte à sa façon,
Et la pluie a passé l'éponge
Sur les couleurs de mon blason.

Tout ému, je pousse la porte
Qui cède et geint sur ses pivots;
Un air froid en sort et m'apporte
Le fade parfum des caveaux.

L'ortie aux morsures aiguës,
La bardane aux larges contours,
Sous les ombelles des ciguës,
Prospèrent dans l'angle des cours.

Sur les deux chimères de marbre,
Gardiennes du perron verdi,
Se découpe l'ombre d'un arbre
Pendant mon absence grandi.

Levant leurs pattes de lionne
Elles se mettent en arrêt.
Leur regard blanc me questionne,
Mais je leur dis le mot secret.

Et je passe. — Dressant sa tête,
Le vieux chien retombe assoupi,
Et mon pas sonore inquiète
L'écho dans son coin accroupi.

The porch, by moonlight, stands defaced:
Time gnaws, sculpts as it will, contorted;
And rains have washed clean and erased
The colors once my blazon sported.

Breathless, I push the door... I hear
The hinges whine and creak, pell-mell;
A dank draft hits me with the drear
Waft of the cellars' brackish smell.

Thorned nettles that bite sharp and prick
The flesh; the burdock, broad of line,
Grow in the courtyard corners, thick,
Beneath the sprawling hemlock vine.

Chimera-beasts, still standing there
Astride the steps of age-greened stone;
And a tree shades the marble pair,
Since last I saw it, taller grown.

Lance-paws held high, like lioness's,
They are as they have always been:
Their blank gaze stares, silently guesses...
I say the password and go in.

The old dog lifts his head and then
Resumes his pose, a-dozing, slouching;
My hollow footsteps rouse again
The echo in its corner crouching.

Un jour louche et douteux se glisse
Aux vitres jaunes du salon
Où figurent, en haute lisse,
Les aventures d'Apollon.

Daphné, les hanches dans l'écorce,
Etend toujours ses doigts touffus;
Mais aux bras du dieu qui la force
Elle s'éteint, spectre confus.

Apollon, chez Admète, garde
Un troupeau, des mites atteint;
Les neuf Muses, troupe hagarde,
Pleurent sur un Pinde déteint;

Et la Solitude en chemise
Trace au doigt le mot : « Abandon »
Dans la poudre qu'elle tamise
Sur le marbre du guéridon.

Je retrouve au long des tentures,
Comme des hôtes endormis,
Pastels blafards, sombres peintures,
Jeunes beautés et vieux amis.

Ma main tremblante enlève un crêpe
Et je vois mon défunt amour,
Jupons bouffants, taille de guêpe,
La Cidalise en Pompadour!

Through yellowed panes, the portico
Casts a dull light, whose sullen shades
Cover walled tapestries that show
Apollo at his escapades.

Daphne, her hips in tree-bark trapped,[118]
Spreads leaf-grown fingers; vainly tries
To flee, in his rude arms enwrapped;
But—phantom form—dims, fades, and dies...

Apollo, by Admetus' side,[119]
Tends to his herd—scene all worm-eaten;
The Muses Nine, troop fearsome-eyed,
Weep on the Pindus, weather-beaten;[120]

And Solitude, in bare blouse, stands
Tracing the single word "Alone"
In the dust sifting from her hands
Over the tabouret of stone...

As down the somber halls I go,
On the walls sleeping guests I see:
Brash pastel portraits, grave tableaux,
Young beauties, old friends dear to me.

With trembling hand I lift a pall...
Lo! My dead love, still sporting these:
Wasp-waist, skirts flared, a-flounce and all—
Pompadour-decked, our Cydalise![121]

Un bouton de rose s'entr'ouvre
A son corset enrubanné,
Dont la dentelle à demi couvre
Un sein neigeux d'azur veiné.

Ses yeux ont de moites paillettes;
Comme aux feuilles que le froid mord,
La pourpre monte à ses pommettes,
Eclat trompeur, fard de la mort!

Elle tressaille à mon approche,
Et son regard, triste et charmant,
Sur le mien d'un air de reproche,
Se fixe douloureusement.

Bien que la vie au loin m'emporte,
Ton nom dans mon cœur est marqué,
Fleur de pastel, gentille morte,
Ombre en habit de bal masqué!

La nature de l'art jalouse,
Voulant dépasser Murillo,
A Paris créa l'Andalouse
Qui rit dans le second tableau.

Par un caprice poétique,
Notre climat brumeaux para
D'une grâce au charme exotique
Cette autre Petra Camara.

A rosebud, scarcely opened, on
The ribboned bodice round her pressed,
Barely ruffles its lace upon
An azure-veined and snow-white breast.[122]

Moist sequins circle round her eyes;
Like leaves in the cold's biting breath,
Crimson hues to her cheekbones rise:
Deceitful flush—the rouge of death!

As I approach to touch her, she
Quivers, then strikes a doleful air—
Charming withal—reproachfully,
Fixing on me a sad-eyed stare...

Yes, time has drawn us far apart—
Pastel flower, lifeless grace, sweet shade—
Yet is your name carved on my heart,
Dear corpse dressed for the masquerade!...

In the next portrait Nature bade
One best Murillo's art, and brought
The laughing Andalusian maid
To life in Paris, artful-wrought.[123]

Our fog-bound clime, through some quixotic
Whimsy, had graced with the éclat
Of a mien winsome and exotic
This second Petra Cámara.[124]

De chaudes teintes orangées
Dorent sa joue au fard vermeil;
Ses paupières de jais frangées
Filtrent des rayons de soleil.

Entre ses lèvres d'écarlate
Scintille un éclair argenté,
Et sa beauté splendide éclate
Comme une grenade en été.

Au son des guitares d'Espagne
Ma voix longtemps la célébra.
Elle vint, un jour, sans compagne,
Et ma chambre fut l'Alhambra.

Plus loin une beauté robuste,
Aux bras forts cerclés d'anneaux lourds,
Sertit le marbre de son buste
Dans les perles et le velours.

D'un air de reine qui s'ennuie
Au sein de sa cour à genoux,
Superbe et distraite, elle appuie
La main sur un coffre à bijoux.

Sa bouche humide et sensuelle
Semble rouge du sang des cœurs,
Et, pleins de volupté cruelle,
Ses yeux ont des défis vainqueurs.

On rouged cheek gold-tinged glints bestow
The warm blush of a crimsoned hue,
And jet-fringed eyelids let the glow
Of sunshine, beaming, filter through.

A flash of brilliance argentine
Flares betwixt lips of scarlet red,
And beauty bursts upon the scene
Like pomegranate, summer-bred!

Long would I sing praise to her name,
And Spain's guitars would pluck and strum!
Once, when—duenna-less!—she came,
All mine, Alhambra's glorydom!

Next, a fine beauty, firm of flesh,[125]
Stout arms with many a bracelet-ring;
Her marbled bosom, gleaming fresh,
Set in pearled velvet, glistening.

Queenly her air... Supremely bored
As subjects kneel before Her Grace,
She stands, scornng the groveling horde,
Hand resting on her jewel-case.

Moist, her lips' sensuous cruelty,
Red with the blood of hearts' distress;
Her eyes' defiant victory,
Ruthless in their voluptuousness.

Ici, plus de grâce touchante,
Mais un attrait vertigineux.
On dirait la Vénus méchante
Qui préside aux amours haineux.

Cette Vénus, mauvaise mère,
Souvent a battu Cupidon.
O toi, qui fus ma joie amère,
Adieu pour toujours... et pardon!

Dans son cadre, que l'ombre moire,
Au lieu de réfléchir mes traits,
La glace ébauche de mémoire
Le plus ancien de mes portraits.

Spectre rétrospectif qui double
Un type à jamais effacé,
Il sort du fond du miroir trouble
Et des ténèbres du passé.

Dans son pourpoint de satin rose,
Qu'un goût hardi coloria,
Il semble chercher une pose
Pour Boulanger ou Devéria.

Terreur de bourgeois glabre et chauve,
Une chevelure à tous crins
De roi franc ou de lion fauve
Roule en torrent jusqu'à ses reins.

Here, gracious coquetry adieu!
Love lures in a most dizzying fashion;
And she, ill-tempered Venus, who
Flaunts naught but a most hateful passion;

This Venus—mother harsh—would beat
Cupid in hostile tête-à-têtes;
O bitter joy... Nay, bittersweet!...
Farewell forever... My regrets!

Glass, framed in shimmering shade, has dimmed
My own true features, it appears,
And has from memory, rather, limned
The portrait of my earliest years.[126]

Specter in retrospect—a stark
Double, fleshless, but holding fast—
It stalks forth from the mirror's dark
And murky shadows of the past.

In satin vest, *couleur de rose,*
Brash-colored and unseemly gay,
He seems to be striking a pose
For Devéria or Boulanger.[127]

Torrents of curls roll, eddying,
Down his back: sheer anathema—
Like lush-maned lion or Frankish king—
To bald and beardless *bon bourgeois.*

Tel, romantique opiniâtre,
Soldat de l'art qui lutte encor,
Il se ruait vers le théâtre
Quand d'Hernani sonnait le cor.

...La nuit tombe et met avec l'ombre
Ses terreurs aux recoins dormants.
L'inconnu, machiniste sombre,
Monte ses épouvantements.

Des explosions de bougies
Crèvent soudain sur les flambeaux!
Leurs auréoles élargies
Semblent des lampes de tombeaux.

Une main d'ombre ouvre la porte
Sans en faire grincer la clé.
D'hôtes pâles qu'un souffle apporte
Le salon se trouve peuplé.

Les portraits quittent la muraille,
Frottant de leurs mouchoirs jaunis
Sur leur visage qui s'éraille
La crasse fauve du vernis.

D'un reflet rouge illuminée,
La bande se chauffe les doigts
Et fait cercle à la cheminée
Où tout à coup flambe le bois.

Romantic soldier-denizen
Of an art-world still warring, he,
Willful, besieged the theater when
Hernani's horn blared "Victory!"

...Night falls; fills sleeping in-betweens,
Crannies all round—here, there, high, low—
With horror. The Unknown's machines
Prepare a frightening terror-show.

Candles, exploding, burst askance
About the torches! In the gloom's
Expanse, their halo-radiance
Seems fit to light the walls of tombs.

A shadow-hand opens the door
In keyless silence, whereupon,
Swept in one gusting breath—no more—
Pale guests invade the grand salon.

The portraits quit the wall, and dab—
With handkerchiefs jaundiced with age—
Their faces, varnish-cracked and drab
With tawny smudge, time's withering wage.

The ghosts, lit by a sudden red
Reflection, circle round the fire,
Warming their hands, fingers outspread,
As rise the logs' flames, higher, higher...

L'image au sépulcre ravie
Perd son aspect roide et glacé;
La chaude pourpre de la vie
Remonte aux veines du passé.

Les masques blafards se colorent
Comme au temps où je les connus.
O vous que mes regrets déplorent,
Amis, merci d'être venus!

Les vaillants de dix-huit cent trente,
Je les revois tels que jadis.
Comme les pirates d'Otrante
Nous étions cent, nous sommes dix.

L'un étale sa barbe rousse
Comme Frédéric dans son roc,
L'autre superbement retrousse
Le bout de sa moustache en croc.

Drapant sa souffrance secrète
Sous les fiertés de son manteau,
Pétrus fume une cigarette
Qu'il baptise papelito,

Celui-ci me conte ses rêves,
Hélas! jamais réalisés,
Icare tombé sur les grèves
Où gisent les essors brisés.

The graveyard pallor of the chill,
Stiff fingers now is giving way;
And life's warm flush of crimson will
Quicken the veins of yesterday.

The sallow masks glow now, reborn
With colors that they first bore when
I met them... O friends, whom I mourn,
Thank you for having come again!

Those eighteen-thirty braves... Ah yes,
I see us as we used to be,
A hundred then, now ten—or less:
Like the Otranto pirates, we.[128]

Like Barbarossa in his cave,
One a red beard proudly unfurls;[129]
Another, with a lordly wave,
The tips of his mustache twists, twirls.

Pétrus, with woes draped in his cloak's
Arrogant folds, puffing away,
A cigarette urbanely smokes—
A *papelito* he would say.[130]

This one recounts his dreams, well planned
But each, alas, a failure, quite:
Icarus fallen on the strand
Where land so many a fruitless flight.

Celui-là me confie un drame
Taillé sur le nouveau patron
Qui fait, mêlant tout dans sa trame,
Causer Molière et Calderon.

Tom, qu'un abandon scandalise,
Récite « Love's labour's lost ».
Et Fritz explique à Cidalise
Le « Walpurgisnachtstraum » de Faust.

Mais le jour luit à la fenêtre,
Et les spectres, moins arrêtés,
Laissent les objets transparaître
Dans leurs diaphanéités.

Les cires fondent consumées,
Sous les cendres s'éteint le feu,
Du parquet montent des fumées;
Château du Souvenir, adieu!

Encore une autre fois décembre
Va retourner le sablier.
Le présent entre dans ma chambre
Et me dit en vain d'oublier.

This one reveals a *drame* of his
Cut to today's style debonair:
Plot mixed with this and that, it is
Calderón chatting with Molière.[131]

Stunned by love's infidelities,
Tom will *Love's Labour's Lost* recite;[132]
And Fritz explains to Cydalise
Faust's "Dream of Saint Walpurgis' Night."[133]

Daylight brightens the panes anew;
The figures dim, fade spectrally,
And let the hall shine, solid, through
Their gossamer transparency.

The candles melt... The smoke-clouds rise
From the parquet, a-swirl, a-swell.
The fire beneath the embers dies...
Castle of Memory... Ah, farewell!

December, once again, will loom,
Turning the hourglass sands; and yet
Again, the present in my room
Tells me—in vain—I must forget.

CAMELIA ET PAQUERETTE

On admire les fleurs de serre
Qui loin de leur soleil natal,
Comme des joyaux mis sous verre,
Brillent sous un ciel de cristal.

Sans que les brises les effleurent
De leurs baisers mystérieux,
Elles naissent, vivent et meurent
Devant le regard curieux.

A l'abri de murs diaphanes,
De leur sein ouvrant le trésor,
Comme de belles courtisanes,
Elles se vendent à prix d'or.

La porcelaine de la Chine
Les reçoit par groupes coquets,
Ou quelque main gantée et fine
Au bal les balance en bouquets.

Mais souvent parmi l'herbe verte,
Fuyant les yeux, fuyant les doigts,
De silence et d'ombre couverte,
Une fleur vit au fond des bois.

CAMELLIA AND DAISY

Those hothouse flowers, far from the sun
That gave them birth, delight our eye;
Like jewels, gems under glass, each one
Shines bright beneath a crystal sky.

No breeze-lips graze their buds with kiss
Mysterious; they spend their days
A-borning, living, dying. This,
Their lot, before our curious gaze.

Shielded by walls diaphanous—
Like courtesans, who, fancy-free,
Reveal their bosom's treasures, thus—
They sell themselves outrageously.

Standing in China porcelain vase,
They form coquette nosegay arrays,
Or, at the ball, some fine hand's grace—
Begloved—gently wafts their bouquets.

But often, midst the grasses green,
A simple flower its vigil keeps—
Lest it be plucked, lest it be seen—
In the dark, silent woodland deeps.

Un papillon blanc qui voltige,
Un coup d'œil au hasard jeté,
Vous fait surprendre sur sa tige
La fleur dans sa simplicité.

Belle de sa parure agreste
S'épanouissant au ciel bleu,
Et versant son parfum modeste
Pour la solitude et pour Dieu.

Sans toucher à son pur calice
Qu'agite un frisson de pudeur,
Vous respirez avec délice
Son âme dans sa fraîche odeur.

Et tulipes au port superbe,
Camélias si chers payés,
Pour la petite fleur sous l'herbe,
En un instant, sont oubliés!

A fluttering white butterfly,
A careless glance... And, suddenly,
There, on its stem, catching your eye,
The flower, in its simplicity.

Beautiful in its rustic blooming,
Spread beneath heavens azure-hued,
Casting its fragrance unassuming,
For God alone, in solitude.

Even without the merest touch
On calyx, quivering chaste, still might
You sense its perfume-soul so much
That you inhale it with delight.

And tulips tall, of haughty stance,
Camellias of immodest price...
This grass-flower's simple elegance
Makes us forget them in a trice!

LA FELLAH

Sur une aquarelle de la princesse M...

Caprice d'un pinceau fantasque
Et d'un impérial loisir,
Votre fellah, sphinx qui se masque,
Propose une énigme au désir.

C'est une mode bien austère
Que ce masque et cet habit long,
Elle intrigue par son mystère
Tous les Œdipes du salon.

L'antique Isis légua son voile
Aux modernes filles du Nil;
Mais, sous le bandeau, deux étoiles
Brillent d'un feu pur et subtil.

Ces yeux qui sont tout un poème
De langueur et de volupté
Disent, résolvant le problème,
« Sois l'amour, je suis la beauté. »

THE FELLAH

On a Watercolor by Princess Mathilde[134]

Whimsical paintbrush phantasy—
Leisure pose, languid, regal-wise—
Your fellah, masked sphinx, silently
Dares desire solve her riddle-guise.

Her long robe and that mask present
A dark style, stark, mysterious,
Whose enigmatic puzzlement
Intrigues each salon Oedipus.

Isis bequeathed her veil of old
To modern daughters of the Nile.
Beneath the headband, lo! two bold,
Bright-burning stars, pure, free of guile;

Eyes of lascivious bliss, those eyes
That are, themselves, a poem, whereof
To strike a languorous compromise:
"Let me be beauty, you be love..."

LA MANSARDE

Sur les tuiles où se hasarde
Le chat guettant l'oiseau qui boit,
De mon balcon une mansarde
Entre deux tuyaux s'aperçoit.

Pour la parer d'un faux bien-être,
Si je mentais comme un auteur,
Je pourrais faire à sa fenêtre
Un cadre de pois de senteur,

Et vous y montrer Rigolette
Riant à son petit miroir,
Dont le tain rayé ne reflète
Que la moitié de son œil noir;

Ou, la robe encor sans agrafe,
Gorge et cheveux au vent, Margot
Arrosant avec sa carafe
Son jardin planté dans un pot;

Ou bien quelque jeune poète
Qui scande ses vers sibyllins,
En contemplant la silhouette
De Montmartre et de ses moulins.

THE LOFT

Looking out from my balcony—
Where cat risks the tile parapet
To stalk the sipping bird—we see
A loft betwixt two chimneys set.

Were I to lie as authors could,
I might pretend to grace my room's
Window by placing round the wood
A frame of fragrant sweet-pea blooms;

By sporting Rigolette, the dear,[135]
Laughing before her mirror's glass,
Whose silver—scuffed—reflects a mere
Half of her fair black eye, alas;

Or Margot—hair wind-blown, breast bare,
Her dress unpinned, but caring not
A jot!—as she stands sprinkling there
Her garden in a flowerpot;

Or some fine poet prodigy
Mouthing his arcane verse, who frets
And struts, scanning prophetically
Montmartre's windmill silhouettes.

Par malheur, ma mansarde est vraie;
Il n'y grimpe aucun liseron,
Et la vitre y fait voir sa taie,
Sous l'ais verdi d'un vieux chevron.

Pour la grisette et pour l'artiste,
Pour le veuf et pour le garçon,
Une mansarde est toujours triste :
Le grenier n'est beau qu'en chanson.

Jadis, sous le comble dont l'angle
Penchait les fronts pour le baiser,
L'amour, content d'un lit de sangle,
Avec Suzon venait causer.

Mais pour ouater notre joie,
Il faut des murs capitonnés,
Des flots de dentelle et de soie,
Des lits par Monbro festonnés.

Un soir, n'étant pas revenue,
Margot s'attarde au mont Breda,
Et Rigolette entretenue
N'arrose plus son réséda.

Voilà longtemps que le poète,
Las de prendre la rime au vol,
S'est fait *reporter* de gazette,
Quittant le ciel pour l'entresol.

But my loft wears no lying guise:
No vine climbs high to mask the scene.
The window's blemish strikes your eyes
Under the planks turned moldy green.

For bachelor, widower, and tart—
For artist too—a garret's walls
Are ever oh so sad: its art
Shines only in the music-halls.

Time was, so slant the roof above
My cot, that we would bow thereat
To kiss each other, or when love
Summoned Suzon to have a chat.

But now, to comfort us, we need
Lush-padded walls and richly plaited
Laces and silks, and beds—indeed!—
By the great Monbro decorated.[136]

One evening Margot fails to come—
On Breda Street her trade must ply.[137]
Rigolette, deep in mistressdom,
Leaves her reseda high and dry.

Long since, the poet, seeing how
Tired he grows of rhyme's fleeting call,
Has turned gazette reporter now
And moved from loft to entresol.

Et l'on ne voit contre la vitre
Qu'une vieille au maigre profil,
Devant Minet, qu'elle chapitre,
Tirant sans cesse un bout de fil.

And now, before the windowpane,
Only a scrawny crone stands scolding
Old Puss, who, time and time again,
Paws, pulls a bit of thread she's holding...

LA NUE

A l'horizon monte une nue,
Sculptant sa forme dans l'azur :
On dirait une vierge nue
Emergeant d'un lac au flot pur.

Debout dans sa conque nacrée,
Elle vogue sur le bleu clair,
Comme une Aphrodite éthérée,
Faite de l'écume de l'air.

On voit onder en molles poses
Son torse au contour incertain,
Et l'aurore répand des roses
Sur son épaule de satin.

Ses blancheurs de marbre et de neige
Se fondent amoureusement
Comme, au clair-obscur du Corrège,
Le corps d'Antiope dormant.

Elle plane dans la lumière
Plus haut que l'Alpe ou l'Apennin;
Reflet de la beauté première,
Sœur de « l'éternel féminin ».

THE CLOUD

Yonder, a climbing cloud, arrayed
Against the azure, seems to take
A sculpted form, like naked maid
Rising from a pure-rippling lake.

Standing in her shell opal-hued,
She floats over the clear blue air,
Figure of foam and froth, a nude,
Translucent Aphrodite fair.

One sees her vaguely contoured shape
Contort in softly shifting poses,
As on her satin back and nape
The dawning daybreak strews its roses.

Her snow-and-marble whites—like those
Correggio chiaroscuros, showing
Antiope lying a-doze—[138]
Blend, lovingly together flowing...

She glides on light, higher above
Than any Alp or Appenine,
Primal reflection, sister of
Beauty's "eternal feminine."

A son corps, en vain retenue,
Sur l'aile de la passion,
Mon âme vole à cette nue
Et l'embrasse comme Ixion.

La raison dit : « Vague fumée,
Où l'on croit voir ce qu'on rêva,
Ombre au gré du vent déformée,
Bulle qui crève et qui s'en va! »

Le sentiment répond : « Qu'importe!
Qu'est-ce après tout que la beauté,
Spectre charmant qu'un souffle emporte
Et qui n'est rien, ayant été!

« A l'Idéal ouvre ton âme;
Mets dans ton cœur beaucoup de ciel,
Aime une nue, aime une femme,
Mais aime! — C'est l'essentiel! »

My soul, on passion's wings, goes flying
To that cloud-body, bent upon
Love's joy; and, brooking no denying,
Clutches her close, like Ixion.[139]

Reason says: "Only smoke one sees
In shapes born of such dream-display,
Shadow buffeted by the breeze,
Bubble that bursts, then slips away..."

Sentiment answers: "Oh? Dear me!
After all, what is beauty? For
Only a charming specter, she,
Blown on the wind, and then no more!

"Let the ideal infuse your soul;
Love a cloud, love a woman, but,
With heaven-filled heart, love be your goal:
Love what you will!... No matter what!"

LE MERLE

Un oiseau siffle dans les branches
Et sautille gai, plein d'espoir,
Sur les herbes, de givre blanches,
En bottes jaunes, en frac noir.

C'est un merle, chanteur crédule,
Ignorant du calendrier,
Qui rêve soleil, et module
L'hymne d'avril en février.

Pourtant il vente, il pleut à verse;
L'Arve jaunit le Rhône bleu,
Et le salon, tendu de perse,
Tient tous ses hôtes près du feu.

Les monts sur l'épaule ont l'hermine,
Comme des magistrats siégeant.
Leur blanc tribunal examine
Un cas d'hiver se prolongeant.

Lustrant son aile qu'il essuie,
L'oiseau persiste en sa chanson,
Malgré neige, brouillard et pluie,
Il croit à la jeune saison.

THE BLACKBIRD

Bird whistling in the branches, free,
And full of hope... Now forth, now back,
Over the frost-white grasses, he
Wears yellow boots and frock coat black.

Yes, blackbird, this: singer naïve
Calendar-wise, untutored very!
He dreams of sun, wants to believe,
Sings April's hymn in February!

But still, winds howl, rains drench the air:
The Arve yellows the blue Rhone; dire[140]
Cold grips the thick-draped parlors, where
One and all huddle round the fire.

Ermine-cloaked hills: judges who face
The court's defendant, and contend
In frost-tribunal... Theirs, the case
Of winter lasting past its end.

Licking his lustrous wings aglow,
Warbling his song beyond all reason,
Despite the fog, and rain, and snow,
Yet he has faith in the young season.

Il gronde l'aube paresseuse
De rester au lit si longtemps
Et, gourmandant la fleur frileuse,
Met en demeure le printemps.

Il voit le jour derrière l'ombre,
Tel un croyant, dans le saint lieu,
L'autel désert, sous la nef sombre,
Avec sa foi voit toujours Dieu.

A la nature il se confie,
Car son instinct pressent la loi.
Qui rit de ta philosophie,
Beau merle, est moins sage que toi!

He scolds the lazy dawn for staying
Too long abed, well past her hour;
Tells spring the dues she ought be paying,
Taking to task the shivering flower...

Daylight he spies behind the dark,
Like a believer at his prayer:
Nave somber, altar bare and stark...
But in his faith he sees God there.

Nature he trusts implicitly,
Instinct, not law... Ah! all those who
Make sport of your philosophy,
Blackbird, are far less wise than you!

LA FLEUR QUI FAIT LE PRINTEMPS

Les marronniers de la terrasse
Vont bientôt fleurir, à Saint-Jean,
La villa d'où la vue embrasse
Tant de monts bleus coiffés d'argent.

La feuille, hier encor pliée
Dans son étroit corset d'hiver,
Met sur la branche déliée
Les premières touches de vert.

Mais en vain le soleil excite
La sève des rameaux trop lents;
La fleur retardataire hésite
A faire voir ses thyrses blancs.

Pourtant le pêcher est tout rose,
Comme un désir de la pudeur,
Et le pommier, que l'aube arrose,
S'épanouit dans sa candeur.

La véronique s'aventure
Près des boutons d'or dans les prés,
Les caresses de la nature
Hâtent les germes rassurés.

THE FLOWER THAT MAKES THE SPRING

Come Saint John's Day the chestnut trees
Will bloom about the terrace, round
The cottage, whence one, gazing, sees
So many a blue peak, silver-crowned.

The leaf that yesterday had been
In winter corset, soon shall be
Dabbing the first few spots of green
Over the boughs, now swaying free.

And yet, in vain the sun will still
The tardy branches' sap incite:
The laggard flower holds back, and will
Her bashful buds not bring to light.

But pink now does the peach tree stand,
Coy in her modest eloquence;
So too the apple, branches spanned
White, in her dawn-dewed innocence.

The speedwell—eager herb—goes pressing
His pace midst meadow buds of gold,
And nature, in one vast caressing,
Urges her seed be yet more bold.

Il me faut retourner encore
Au cercle d'enfer où je vis;
Marronniers, pressez-vous d'éclore
Et d'éblouir mes yeux ravis.

Vous pouvez sortir pour la fête
Vos girandoles sans péril,
Un ciel bleu luit sur votre faîte
Et déjà mai talonne avril.

Par pitié, donnez cette joie
Au poète dans ses douleurs,
Qu'avant de s'en aller, il voie
Vos feux d'artifice de fleurs.

Grands marronniers de la terrasse,
Si fiers de vos splendeurs d'été,
Montrez-vous à moi dans la grâce
Qui précède votre beauté.

Je connais vos riches livrées,
Quand octobre, ouvrant son essor,
Vous met des tuniques pourprées,
Vous pose des couronnes d'or.

Je vous ai vus, blanches ramées,
Pareils aux dessins que le froid
Aux vitres d'argent étamées
Trace, la nuit, avec son doigt.

Return I must, now, to my room,
That grim hell-circle dwelling-place.
Chestnut trees, hurry pray: let bloom
Your buds before my blissful face.

Now may you waft without ado
Your pinwheels for our roundelay:
Your crest shines in a sky of blue,
April is spurred along by May.

I beg you, let the poet know
This joy, to soothe his woe-filled hours;
Let him, before he turns to go,
Gaze on your firework-blaze of flowers.

Tall terraced chestnut trees, so proud
Of coming splendor! Pray bestir
Yourselves to stand forth, graceful-boughed,
As summer beauty's harbinger.

I know lofty October's fine
Costumes you wear; and I know how
You sport her gown incarnadine,
And her gold crown upon your brow.

You have I seen, limbs decked with lace's
Filigree-forms, like shapes of white
That the cold, with its finger, traces
On silver-frosted panes by night.

Je sais tous vos aspects superbes,
Arbres géants, vieux marronniers,
Mais j'ignore vos fraîches gerbes
Et vos arômes printaniers.

Adieu, je pars lassé d'attendre;
Gardez vos bouquets éclatants!
Une autre fleur suave et tendre,
Seule à mes yeux fait le printemps.

Que mai remporte sa corbeille!
Il me suffit de cette fleur;
Toujours pour l'âme et pour l'abeille
Elle a du miel pur dans le cœur.

Par le ciel d'azur ou de brume
Par la chaude ou froide saison,
Elle sourit, charme et parfume,
Violette de la maison!

I know all your haughty arrays—
Old chestnuts, tall trees towering—
But I know not your fresh bouquets'
Fragrant aromas, born of spring.

Farewell! I have no patience, none!
Little your garish blooms I prize:
One tender flower, and only one,
Betokens springtime in my eyes.

Off with your nosegay basket, May!
This flower alone I crave to see.
Her heart: pure honey's hideaway—
Wealth for the soul, food for the bee.

Mid skies of mist or azure blue
That seasons hot or cold beget,
Her smile, her fragrance charm me through:
The gentle, simple violet![141]

DERNIER VŒU

Voilà longtemps que je je vous aime :
—L'aveu remonte à dix-huit ans!—
Vous êtes rose, je suis blême;
J'ai les hivers, vous les printemps.

Des lilas blancs de cimetière
Près de mes tempes ont fleuri;
J'aurai bientôt la touffe entière
Pour ombrager mon front flétri.

Mon soleil pâli qui décline
Va disparaître à l'horizon,
Et sur la funèbre colline
Je vois ma dernière maison.

Oh! que de votre lèvre il tombe
Sur ma lèvre un tardif baiser,
Pour que je puisse dans ma tombe,
Le cœur tranquille, reposer!

LAST WISH

A long time have I known you... Why,
Full eighteen years, I must confess![142]
All pink are you; pale, blear am I.
Winters, mine; yours, spring's comeliness!

White cemetery lilacs sprout
Over my temples; but soon, now,
The grove entire will bloom about
My head, to shade my withered brow.

Pallid, my sun sinks low, and will
Soon fade on the horizon's face;
And on the mournful, doleful hill
I see my final dwelling-place.

Oh! May you from your lips let fall
A kiss, too long delayed, upon
My own, so that beneath my pall
I may rest, heart at peace, anon...

PLAINTIVE TOURTERELLE

Plaintive tourterelle,
Qui roucoules toujours,
Veux-tu prêter ton aile
Pour servir mes amours!

Comme toi, pauvre amante,
Bien loin de mon ramier
Je pleure et me lamente
Sans pouvoir l'oublier.

Vole, et que ton pied rose
Sur l'arbre ou sur la tour
Jamais ne se repose,
Car je languis d'amour;

Evite, ô ma colombe,
La halte des palmiers
Et tous les toits où tombe
La neige des ramiers.

Va droit sur sa fenêtre,
Près du palais du roi,
Donne-lui cette lettre
Et deux baisers pour moi.

PLAINTIVE TURTLEDOVE

Cooing your song, poor thing—
Dear, plaintive turtledove—
Might you lend me your wing
To serve me in my love!

Like you, poor lover, I
Lament my love, and yet,
Far flown, though sad I sing,
Never can I forget.

Go! Hurry off! Nor rest
Your foot on tower or tree;
For love harries my breast
And I long languorously.

Tarry not, dove, nor light
On palms along the way,
Or roofs, dove-snowflaked white.
Rather, eschew them, pray.

Fly to her window, where
The royal palace stands.
Kiss her twice, give her there
This letter from my hands.

Puis sur mon sein en flamme,
Qui ne peut s'apaiser,
Reviens, avec son âme,
Reviens te reposer.

Then, on my bosom burning,
That cannot solaced be,
Bring me her soul, returning:
Take your rest here with me.

LA BONNE SOIREE

Quel temps de chien!—il pleut, il neige;
Les cochers, transis sur leur siège,
      Ont le nez bleu.
Par ce vilain soir de décembre,
Qu'il ferait bon garder la chambre,
      Devant son feu!

A l'angle de la cheminée
La chauffeuse capitonnée
      Vous tend les bras
Et semble avec une caresse
Vous dire comme une maîtresse,
      « Tu resteras! »

Un papier rose à découpures,
Comme un sein blanc sous des guipures,
      Voile à demi
Le globe laiteux de la lampe
Dont le reflet au plafond rampe,
      Tout endormi.

On n'entend rien dans le silence
Que le pendule qui balance
      Son disque d'or,
Et que le vent qui pleure et rôde,
Parcourant, pour entrer en fraude,
      Le corridor.

THE PLEASANT EVENING

Snow, rain... Foul night! The coachmen sit
Chilled through and through with cold, as it
      Turns blue the nose.
This vile December night! More fitting
Were by the fireside to be sitting,
      Safe from the snows!

The corner hearth-chair, with its air
Of padded elegance, stands there
      Seems to say "No!"
As, with a mistress-like caress,
Reaching across the emptiness,
      It begs: "Don't go!"

Pink paper shade, design-impressed,
Like lace trim edging fair white breast,
      Veils, half-revealing,
The lamp's milky glass globe, as on
And on reflections dance upon
      The dozing ceiling.

Silence. No sound save of the clock's
Golden disk, with its ticks and tocks...
      Each rise and fall.
And of the wind, furtively peeking
About, as it tries to come sneaking
      In through the hall.

C'est bal à l'ambassade anglaise;
Mon habit noir est sur la chaise,
        Les bras ballants;
Mon gilet bâille et ma chemise
Semble dresser, pour être mise,
        Ses poignets blancs.

Les brodequins à pointe étroite
Montrent leur vernis qui miroite,
        Au feu placés;
A côté des minces cravates
S'allongent comme des mains plates
        Les gants glacés.

Il faut sortir!—quelle corvée!
Prendre la file à l'arrivée
        Et suivre au pas
Les coupés des beautés altières
Portant blasons sur leurs portières
        Et leurs appas.

Rester debout contre une porte
A voir se ruer la cohorte
        Des invités;
Les vieux museaux, les frais visages,
Les fracs en cœur et les corsages
        Décolletés;

Ball at the English embassy!...
My frock, arms dangling hopefully;
     My vest, a-yawn;
My white shirt-cuffs, expecting too—
On the chair—as the others do,
     To be put on...

My point-toed, polished boots sit by
The fire, and, as the flames reach high,
     They shimmer, shine:
And, next to many a slim cravat,
Set in a row, like hands laid flat,
     Cold gloves of mine...

But I must leave!... Ah! What a chore!
To join the coaches at the door,
     Following there
Behind the lovelies proud... Approach
In turn, after each crested coach
     And lady fair,

Then stand aside and watch, as pass,
In flurried haste, the hurrying mass
     Of honored guests;
Old snouts, and faces young and fresh,
Deep-plunging necklines, daring flesh
     Of heaving breasts;

Les dos où fleurit la pustule,
Couvrant leur peau rouge d'un tulle
        Aérien;
Les dandys et les diplomates,
Sur leurs faces à teintes mates,
        Ne montrant rien.

Et ne pouvoir franchir la haie
Des douairières aux yeux d'orfraie
        Ou de vautour,
Pour aller dire à son oreille
Petite, nacrée et vermeille,
        Un mot d'amour!

Je n'irai pas!—et ferai mettre
Dans son bouquet un bout de lettre
        A l'Opéra.
Par les violettes de Parme,
La mauvaise humeur se désarme :
        Elle viendra!

J'ai là l'*Intermezzo* de Heine,
Le *Thomas Grain-d'Orge* de Taine,
        Les deux Goncourt;
Le temps, jusqu'à l'heure où s'achève
Sur l'oreiller l'idée en rêve,
        Me sera court.

Backs blooming pimples, pustules, scruff...
Reddened skin masked by muslin fluff
     Flimsy as naught;
The diplomats, the dandies... Those
Whose faces' dull complexion shows
     Never a thought...

And there, the dowagers! Hawk-eyed,
Menacing vultures, side by side,
     Perched in a line;
And I, unable to draw near,
To whisper in her shell-pink ear
     Love's tender words!

No! I'll not go! I'll find a way
Into her Opera-loge bouquet
     To slip a *mot.*
With Parma violets we can cure
The sullen mood's discomfiture:
     She'll come! I know!

Here, Heine's *Intermezzo* and[143]
Taine's *Thomas Grain-d'Orge* in my hand —[144]
     The Goncourts too...[145]
My pillow-thoughts will ageless seem
And, in a moment, turn to dream,
     As oft they do...

L'ART

Oui, l'œuvre sort plus belle
D'une forme au travail
     Rebelle,
Vers, marbre, onyx, émail.

Point de contraintes fausses!
Mais que pour marcher droit
     Tu chausses,
Muse, un cothurne étroit.

Fi du rythme commode
Comme un soulier trop grand,
     Du mode
Que tout pied quitte et prend!

Statuaire, repousse
L'argile que pétrit
     Le pouce,
Quand flotte ailleurs l'esprit;

Lutte avec le carrare,
Avec le paros dur
     Et rare,
Gardiens du contour pur;

ART

Yes, fair-wrought verse shuns pliant
Form; beauty craves the touch
     Defiant:
Marble, onyx, and such.

All false constraints begone!
But, Muse, to walk aright,
     Best don
A cothurn firm and tight.[146]

Like shoe that each foot fits,
Despite too lax a measure!
     For it's
On and off, at its pleasure.

When you sculpt uninspired,
Let your thumb-kneaded clay,
     Unfired,
Be spurned and swept away.

Battle your adversary—
Carrara, Paros pure—[147]
     The very
Keepers of form's contour.

Emprunte à Syracuse
Son bronze où fermement
   S'accuse
Le trait fier et charmant;

D'une main délicate
Poursuis dans un filon
   D'agate
Le profil d'Apollon.

Peintre, fuis l'aquarelle,
Et fixe la couleur
   Trop frêle
Au four de l'émailleur.

Fais les sirènes bleues,
Tordant de cent façons
   Leurs queues,
Les monstres des blasons;

Dans son nimbe trilobe
La Vierge et son Jésus,
   Le globe
Avec la croix dessus.

Tout passe. — L'art robuste
Seul a l'éternité.
   Le buste
Survit à la cité.

Borrow from Syracuse
Her bronze bust-treasures, these,
    And whose
Proud features charm and please.

In agate vein's design
Let your hand gently follow
    The fine,
Firm profile of Apollo.

Painters, shun frail pastel:
Let colors weak and lame
    Bake well
In the enameler's flame.

Paint blue your sirens, and
Monsters blazoned of old,
    Tails spanned
In twistings hundredfold;

Mary and Jesus, furled
In three-foil halo-cloud;
    The world,
Cross erect, standing proud.

Nothing will last... All must
Pass on, save art, strength-rife:
    The bust
Survives this earthly life,

Et la médaille austère
Que trouve un laboureur
　　　Sous terre
Révèle un empereur.

Les dieux eux-mêmes meurent,
Mais les vers souverains
　　　Demeurent
Plus forts que les airains.

Sculpte, lime, cisèle;
Que ton rêve flottant
　　　Se scelle
Dans le bloc résistant!

And when stark coin is found
In plowman's furrowed field,
        A-ground,
An emperor stands revealed.

The gods themselves die; still,
Princely, poems shall reign
        And will
Stronger than brass remain.

Sculpt, chisel, file, and let[148]
Your flotsam dream, wind-blown,
        Be set,
In the resisting stone!

FROM *ESPANA*

1845

DEPART

Avant d'abandonner à tout jamais ce globe,
Pour aller voir là-haut ce que Dieu nous dérobe,
Et de faire à mon tour au pays inconnu
Ce voyage dont nul n'est encor revenu,
J'ai voulu visiter les cités et les hommes
Et connaître l'aspect de ce monde où nous sommes.
Depuis mes jeunes ans d'un grand désir épris,
J'étouffais à l'étroit dans ce vaste Paris;
Une voix me parlait et me disait : — « C'est l'heure;
« Va, déracine-toi du seuil de ta demeure;
« L'arbre pris par le pied, le minéral pesant,
« Sont jaloux de l'oiseau, sont jaloux du passant;
« Et puisque Dieu t'a fait de nature mobile,
« Qu'il t'a donné la vie, et le sang et la bile,
« Pourquoi donc végéter et te cristalliser
« A regarder les jours sous ton arche glisser?
« Il est au monde, il est des spectacles sublimes,
« Des royaumes qu'on voit en gravissant les cimes,
« De noirs Escurials, mystérieux granits,
« Et de bleus océans, visibles infinis.
« Donc, sans t'en rapporter à son image ronde,
« Par toi-même connais la figure du monde. »
Tout bas à mon oreille ainsi la voix chantait,
Et le désir ému dans mon cœur palpitait.
Comme au jour du départ on voit parmi les nues
Tournoyer et crier une troupe de grues,

LEAVE-TAKING

Before quitting this sphere for good, to rise
Unto God's heights and peer—here, there—with eyes
Of wonder at what he conceals from us;
Before leaving for that mysterious
Domain, whence none returns, I thought I should
Travel about this earthly neighborhood
Of ours, to know the lands, cities, and men
Who people them... When young, time and again,
I found that this vast Paris stifled me
And hemmed me in. A voice said: "Go! Be free!
It is time to uproot yourself and quit
Your lodging! Be not like the tree, unfit—
Heavy of foot!—to rise aloft and fly;
Or like earth's ores, jealous of passersby
And of the birds who flit whither they will.
God made of you a creature volatile,
Imbued with life, and blood, and passion! What?
Must you sit meekly vegetating, shut
Tight in a crystal mass, watching the days
Pass, slipping through the arching of your gaze?
The earth has spectacles sublime to view
From high atop great mountains, oceans blue,
Infinite; dark Escurials strange-hewn[1]
Of granite blocks... Indeed, visions in tune
With wonders of your being, for you to know."
My heart throbbed with desire as, soft and low,

Mes rêves palpitants, prêts à prendre leur vol,
Tournoyaient dans les airs et dédaignaient le sol;
Au colombier, le soir, ils rentraient à grand'peine,
Et des hôtes pensifs qui hantent l'âme humaine,
Il ne s'asseyait plus à mon triste foyer
Que l'ennui, ce fâcheux qu'on ne peut renvoyer!

L'amour aux longs tourments, aux plaisirs éphémères,
L'art et la fantaisie aux fertiles chimères,
L'entretien des amis et les chers compagnons
Intimes dont souvent on ignore les noms,
La famille sincère où l'âme se repose,
Ne pouvaient plus suffire à mon esprit morose;
Et sur l'âpre rocher où descend le vautour
Je me rongeais le foie en attendant le jour.
Je sentais le désir d'être absent de moi-même;
Loin de ceux que je hais et loin de ceux que j'aime,
Sur une terre vierge et sous un ciel nouveau,
Je voulais écouter mon cœur et mon cerveau,
Et savoir, fatigué de stériles études,
Quel baume contenait l'urne des solitudes,
Quel mot balbutiait avec ses bruits confus,
Dans la rumeur des flots et des arbres touffus,
La nature, ce livre où la plume divine
Ecrit le grand secret que nul œil ne devine!

Sang the voice... And, like flocks of cranes, twist-turning,
On high among the clouds, a-shriek, my yearning,
Pulsing dreams, eager to take flight, whirled round
About the air, flouting the lowly ground.
At night, how difficult for them to come
Back to the roost, back to the dull humdrum
Of lodging and of soul, where ever held
Sway that ennui that will not be dispelled!

Loves long-tormenting, fleeting pleasure-fraught;
Phantasy, art of rich chimeras wrought;
Chats with boon friends, bosom companions whose
Very names, in a moment, I might lose;
My family, sincere seat of my soul...
No, naught restored my spirit, hale and whole;
And I awaited dawn as, on the rock,
I fed my liver to the swooping hawk,
Nor desired aught more than the chance to be
Free: from myself, from those I hated, free
Even from those I loved! On virgin ground,
Beneath new skies, I sought the virgin sound
Of heart and head; and, in the tedious calm
Of sterile studies, hoped to learn what balm
It was that filled the urn of loneliness;
What word it was that nature's deep recess
Muttered, burbled amid the waves, the trees
A-tangle in their lush varieties;
Nature: book wherein quill divine professes
The secret that the mind nor knows nor guesses!

Je suis parti, laissant sur le seuil inquiet,
Comme un manteau trop vieux que l'on quitte à regret,
Cette lente moitié de la nature humaine,
L'habitude au pied sûr qui toujours y ramène,
Les pâles visions, compagnes de mes nuits,
Mes travaux, mes amours et tous mes chers ennuis.
La poitrine oppressée et les yeux tout humides,
Avant d'être emporté par les chevaux rapides,
J'ai retourné la tête à l'angle du chemin,
Et j'ai vu, me faisant des signes de la main,
Comme un groupe plaintif d'amantes délaissées,
Sur la porte debout ma vie et mes pensées.
Hélas! que vais-je faire et que vais-je chercher?
L'horizon charme l'œil : à quoi bon le toucher?
Pourquoi d'un pied réel fouler les blondes grèves
Et les rivages d'or de l'univers des rêves?
Poète, tu sais bien que la réalité
A besoin, pour couvrir sa propre nudité,
Du manteau que lui file à son rouet d'ivoire
L'imagination, menteuse qu'il faut croire;
Que tout homme en son cœur porte son Chanaan,
Et son Eldorado par-delà l'Océan.
N'as-tu pas dans tes mains assez crevé de bulles,
De rêves gonflés d'air et d'espoirs ridicules?
Plongeur, n'as-tu pas vu sous l'eau du lac d'azur
Les reptiles grouiller dans le limon impur?
L'objet le plus hideux, que le lointain estompe,
Prend une belle forme où le regard se trompe.

I left; and, leaving at the threshold there,
Sadly, like an old cloak too worn to wear,
My human nature's stolid half—the sure,
Steadying pace of habit's safe, secure,
Pale visions, night-companions, I cast free
My loves, drear studies, and my dear ennui.
Eyes moist with tears, bosom oppressed, before
The stallion, fleet of hoof, straightaway bore
Me off, I turned my head, angled against the road,
Saw at the open door of my abode,
Standing abandoned, like a company
Of belles once loved, waving farewell to me,
My very life, my thoughts... Alas! What now
To do? What now to seek? And why? And how?
The far horizon charms the eye; what good
To reach out and to touch it? And what would
It profit me to tread with fleshly feet
The universe of dream unreal, replete
With sand-blond strands? Poet, you know the world
Must clothe its nakedness, in dream-lies furled,
Spun from its ivory spinning-wheel; and that
Man's heart yearns for its Canaan habitat,
Its El Dorado far beyond the seas.[2]
Must your hands burst more bubble-phantasies'
Frivolous hopes! Diver, has azure's swell
Not retched up loathsome reptiles from the fell,
Foul mire and muck? Yet, when seen from afar,
Though hideous as such fulsome creatures are,

Le mont chauve et pelé doit à l'éloignement
Les changeantes couleurs de son beau vêtement;
Approchez, ce n'est plus que rocs noirs et difformes,
Escarpements abrupts, entassements énormes,
Sapins échevelés, broussailles aux poils roux,
Gouffre vertigineux et torrents en courroux :
Je le sais, je le sais. Déception amère!
Hélas! J'ai trop souvent pris au vol ma chimère!
Je connais quels replis terminent ces beaux corps,
Et la sirène peut m'étaler ses trésors :
A travers sa beauté je vois, sous les eaux noires,
Frétiller vaguement sa queue et ses nageoires.
Aussi ne vais-je pas, de vains mots ébloui,
Chercher sous d'autres cieux mon rêve épanoui;
Je ne crois pas trouver devant moi, toutes faites,
Au coin des carrefours les strophes des poètes,
Ni pouvoir en passant cueillir à pleines mains
Les fleurs de l'idéal aux chardons des chemins.
Mais je suis curieux d'essayer de l'absence,
Et de voir ce que peut cette sourde puissance;
Je veux savoir quel temps, sans être enseveli,
Je flotterai sur l'eau qui ne garde aucun pli,

The distance quite softens the sight, and some
Think the repulsive now most fair become.
Even the mountain tops, piercing the air,
Owe the shimmering hues that cloak their bare,
Bald pates, merely to distance. Look! Draw near...
You will see rocks, jagged black peaks, and sheer
Cliffs plunging into the abyss; root-tangled
Fir tree and pine; tawny dark briars in mangled
Masses of nettle; torrents fierce, un-pent,
Gushing... But oh, the disillusionment!
I know, I know! Naught is what it would seem!
Alas! Too often have I seized my dream —
Wingèd chimera! — and only too well
Would see the beauty of my siren belle
End in the flutterings of her undine tail
And fin; her treasures turned to mermaid's scale
Within the brackish waves! No more shall I,
Dazzled by empty words, go looking high
And low, beneath a foreign sky, to find
The phantasy dear to my heart and mind;
Nor poet's stanzas, ready-wrought, spread thick
Over the crossroads; nor shall I go pick
Handfuls of the Ideal's fair flowers, born
Among the pathways brambled deep with thorn...
Ah! But I would defy the powers that spring
From emptiness's absent wandering,
To see how long I float at liberty,
Without a billow's swell enfolding me;

Et dans combien de jours, comme un peu de fumée,
Des cœurs éteints s'envole une mémoire aimée.

Le voyage est un maître aux préceptes amers;
Il vous montre l'oubli dans les cœurs les plus chers,
Et vous prouve, — ô misère et tristesse suprême! —
Qu'ingrat à votre tour, vous oubliez vous-même!
Pauvre atome perdu, point dans l'immensité,
Vous apprenez ainsi votre inutilité.
Votre départ n'a rien dérangé dans le monde;
Déjà votre sillon s'est refermé sur l'onde.
Oublié par les uns, aux autres inconnu,
Dans des lieux où jamais votre nom n'est venu,
Parmi des yeux distraits et des visages mornes,
Vous allez sur la terre et sur la mer sans bornes.
Par l'absence à la mort vous vous accoutumez.
Cependant l'araignée à vos volets fermés
Suspend sa toile ronde, et la maison déserte
Semble n'avoir plus d'âme et pleurer votre perte,
Et le chien qui s'ennuie et voudrait vous revoir
Au détour du chemin va hurler chaque soir.

Before love's smoke-wisp memory, free to waft
Above, quits the heart's embers, soars aloft...

Travel teaches us many a precept dour.
It proves to us that in the hearts most sure,
Most dear, forgetfulness holds sway; it shows—
O sadness next to none! O bitter throes
Of misery supreme!—that one day you
Will be the victim of oblivion too!
Poor atom! Mere minuscule nothing, cast
Aside and lost, lonely speck in the vast
Expanse; you learn your uselessness: you leave,
And nothing changes in the world. Waves heave
About a bit, close up your wake... By some
Forgot, by others never known, you come,
Unheralded, over the endless seas,
Met with blank looks and eyes' mute inquiries,
As your long absence draws you ever on,
Accustoming your life to death anon...
Meanwhile, the spider hangs her web about
The shuttered windows, and the house, without
A trace of life, a trace of soul, stands weeping
Your loss... And there, the lonely hound, still keeping
A faithful, futile watch, bays his distress,
Each night, at the path's utter emptiness.

LE PIN DES LANDES

On ne voit en passant par les Landes désertes,
Vrai Sahara français, poudré de sable blanc,
Surgir de l'herbe sèche et des flaques d'eaux vertes
D'autre arbre que le pin avec sa plaie au flanc,

Car, pour lui dérober ses larmes de résine,
L'homme, avare bourreau de la création,
Qui ne vit qu'aux dépens de ce qu'il assassine,
Dans son tronc douloureux ouvre un large sillon!

Sans regretter son sang qui coule goutte à goutte,
Le pin verse son baume et sa sève qui bout,
Et se tient toujours droit sur le bord de la route,
Comme un soldat blessé qui veut mourir debout.

Le poète est ainsi dans les Landes du monde;
Lorsqu'il est sans blessure, il garde son trésor.
Il faut qu'il ait au cœur une entaille profonde
Pour épancher ses vers, divines larmes d'or!

THE PINE OF THE LANDES COUNTRY

In passing through the barren Landes, one sees —[3]
Over the French Sahara's sand dust-white
Poking among the brackish pools, no trees
In the parched grass, save pine, with slashes right

And left, ripping their bark... For man, creation's
Villain, who lives on what he kills, will steal
Their resin-tears, furrow his depradations
Along their flanks. And yet, the pine will feel

No loss of sap-blood, trickling drop by drop;
Yielding his bubbling balm, with head held high,
By the road, upright, proudly, toe to top,
Like wounded soldier who stands tall to die.

Landes-like, the poet with his poetry,
Unwounded, holds his treasure well controlled.
But he must bear a deep heart-gash if he
Would spread his verses' heavenly tears of gold!

SAINTE CASILDA

A Burgos, dans un coin de l'église déserte,
Un tableau me surprit par son effet puissant :
Un ange, pâle et fier, d'un ciel fauve descend,
A sainte Casilda portant la palme verte.

Pour l'œuvre des bourreaux la vierge découverte
Montre sur sa poitrine, albâtre éblouissant,
A la place des seins, deux ronds couleur de sang,
Distillant un rubis par chaque veine ouverte.

Et les seins déjà morts, beaux lis coupés en fleurs,
Blancs comme les morceaux d'une Vénus de marbre,
Dans un bassin d'argent gisent au pied d'un arbre.

Mais la sainte en extase, oubliant sa douleur,
Comme aux bras d'un amant de volupté se pâme,
Car aux lèvres du Christ elle suspend son âme !

Burgos

SAINT CASILDA

Burgos... Deserted church... And stunned, my stare
Falls on a canvas: Saint Casilda in
Travail. An angel—haughty, pale therein—
Offers her a green palm for her despair.[4]

The virgin, nude, goading her hangman's glare,
Sports bosom's splendrous alabaster skin;
Two globes replace her breasts, incarnadine,
Blood-rubies beading from veined tips laid bare.

Dead breasts—fair lilies hacked in bloom—remain
White as fragments of marble Venus, found
Tree-side, in silver pool, sparkling the ground.

But she swoons, blissful, putting by her pain,
As when love's soft caress embraces, grips...
And her soul, clinging to the Christ's own lips!

Burgos

EN ALLANT A LA CHARTREUSE DE MIRAFLORES

Oui, c'est une montée âpre, longue et poudreuse,
Un revers décharné, vrai site de Chartreuse.
Les pierres du chemin, qui croulent sous les pieds,
Trompent à chaque instant les pas mal appuyés.
Pas un brin d'herbe vert, pas une teinte fraîche;
On ne voit que des murs bâtis en pierre sèche,
Des groupes contrefaits d'oliviers rabougris,
Au feuillage malsain couleur de vert-de-gris,
Des pentes au soleil que nulle fleur n'égaie,
Des roches de granit et des ravins de craie,
Et l'on se sent le cœur de tristesse serré...
Mais, quand on est en haut, coup d'œil inespéré!
L'on aperçoit là-bas, dans le bleu de la plaine,
L'église où dort le Cid près de doña Chimène!

Cartuja de Miraflorès

ON THE WAY TO THE MIRAFLORES CHARTERHOUSE

Long, dusty rise... Behind, the landscape—bare,
Fleshless—stripped to the bone; and perching there,
The Charterhouse... Arduous climb, on crumbling
Pebbles, with every step, faltering, stumbling...
No wisp of grass, no cool shades fresh and green;
Walls of parched stone, nothing more to be seen
But clumps of sickly, stunted olive-tree
Leaves, woebegone, color of verdigris;
Slopes in the sun, flowerless, cheerless; rock,
Granite cliff, deep ravines carved in the chalk;[5]
A wrenching sadness grips your heart, dejected...
But, at the top, at last, an unexpected
Sight! In the plain's blue, one spies there and then
The church where sleep the Cid with his Chimène![6]

Charterhouse of Miraflores

LA FONTAINE DU CIMETIERE

A la morne Chartreuse, entre des murs de pierre,
En place de jardin l'on voit un cimetière,
Un cimetière nu comme un sillon fauché,
Sans croix, sans monument, sans tertre qui se hausse :
L'oubli couvre le nom, l'herbe couvre la fosse;
La mère ignorerait où son fils est couché.
Les végétations maladives du cloître
Seules sur ce terrain peuvent germer et croître,
Dans l'humidité froide à l'ombre des longs murs :
Des morts abandonnés douces consolatrices,
Les fleurs n'oseraient pas incliner leurs calices
Sur le vague tombeau de ces dormeurs obscurs.
Au milieu, deux cyprès à la noire verdure
Profilent tristement leur silhouette dure,
Longs soupirs de feuillage élancés vers les cieux!
Pendant que du bassin d'une avare fontaine
Tombe en frange effilée une nappe incertaine,
Comme des pleurs furtifs qui débordent des yeux.
Par les saints ossements des vieux moines filtrée,
L'eau coule à flots si clairs dans la vasque éplorée,
Que pour en boire un peu je m'approchai du bord...
Dans le cristal glacé quand je trempai ma lèvre,

THE CEMETERY FOUNTAIN

Charterhouse gloom's stone walls... No garden spread
Between, only a graveyard there instead,
Barren; no crosses, tombs, no gentle mound,
Only a cemetery's naked ground,
Like furrow scythed to naught... Oblivion
Casts its pall round, covering everyone,
Everything, every name—just as the grass
Covers the pit. Each mother's son, alas,
Is doomed to lie unfound, unknown. No life
Save in the cloister's vines, its long wall rife
With dank and sickly-sprouting vegetation,
Chill in the shade, whilst, as a consolation
To the forsaken dead, the flowers would dare
Not nod their head to those who, sleeping there
In utter desolation lie... In dark,
Dim green, two cypresses rise, sad and stark,
Laying their silhouettes, with long-drawn sighs,
Against the air, plunge upward to the skies!
Fringing a meager fountain's pool, come seeping
Droplets, in vague rhythm unsure, like weeping
Eyes casting furtive tears... The waters flow
Through relic bones of long-gone monks, and then
Join in the basin's dirge, a-drip... Again,
Again... Thirsting, I wet my lip, when, lo!
I am seized by a shudder's fevered breath,
Kneeling there by the edge... Though crystal-cool

Je me sentis saisi par un frisson de fièvre :
Cette eau de diamant avait un goût de mort!

Cartuja de Miraflorès

And saintly pure, the waters of the pool,
In diamantine splendor, taste of death![7]

   Charterhouse of Miraflores

LES YEUX BLEUS DE LA MONTAGNE

On trouve dans les monts des lacs de quelques toises,
Purs comme des cristaux, bleus comme des turquoises,
Joyaux tombés du doigt de l'ange Ithuriel,
Où le chamois craintif, lorsqu'il vient pour y boire,
S'imagine, trompé par l'optique illusoire,
        Laper l'azur du ciel.

Ces limpides bassins, quand le jour s'y reflète,
Ont comme la prunelle une humide paillette;
Et ce sont les yeux bleus, au regard calme et doux,
Par lesquels la montagne en extase contemple,
Forgeant quelque soleil dans le fond de son temple,
        Dieu, l'ouvrier jaloux!

Guadarrama

THE BLUE EYES OF THE MOUNTAIN

Lakes—here, there—only arms-lengths wide,
Dot in a turquoise blue the mountainside...
Crystal gems that Ithuriel, on high,[8]
Dropped from his hands; where timid chamois sips,
Imagining his eyes deceive his lips,
   And laps the azure sky.

These limpid pools, when they reflect the day,
Are like a glinting pupil, moist; and they
Are the blue eyes, with glance calm and sedate,
Through which, in bliss, the mountain looks upon
God, in his shrine, sun-forging paragon,
   Artisan obdurate!

Guadarrama[9]

A MADRID

Dans le boudoir ambré d'une jeune marquise,
Grande d'Espagne, belle, et d'une grâce exquise,
Au milieu de la table, à la place de fleurs,
Frais groupe mariant et parfums et couleurs,
Grimaçait sur un plat une tête coupée,
Sculptée en bois et peinte, et dans le sang trempée,
Le front humide encor des suprêmes sueurs,
L'œil vitreux et blanchi de ces pâles lueurs
Dont la lampe de l'âme en s'éteignant scintille;
Chef-d'œuvre affreux, signé Montañès de Séville,
D'une vérité telle et d'un si fin travail,
Qu'un bourreau n'aurait su reprendre un seul détail.

La marquise disait : —Voyez donc quel artiste!
Nul sculpteur n'a jamais fait les saint Jean-Baptiste
Et rendu les effets du damas sur un col
Comme ce Sévillan, Michel-Ange espagnol!
Quelle imitation dans ces veines tranchées,
Où le sang perle encore en gouttes mal séchées!
Et comme dans la bouche on sent le dernier cri
Sous le fer jaillissant de ce gosier tari! —
En me disant cela d'une voix claire et douce,
Sur l'atroce sculpture elle passait son pouce,
Coquette, souriant d'un sourire charmant,
L'œil humide et lustré comme pour un amant.

Madrid

IN MADRID

In amber-scented boudoir of a fair,
Young marquise of that grandiose Spanish air
And wondrous grace, lay, tabled there, instead
Of fragrant, bright bouquet, a severed head,
Leering—of painted sculpted wood—and set
In pool of blood, brow moist with noble sweat,
Eye pallid, empty-stared, with glassy white
Of the soul's dying lamp's last flickering light...
Horrendous masterwork of Montañés[10]
De Sevilla, wrought true, with such finesse
That executioner, to no avail,
Might criticize the merest, least detail.

Said the marquise: "What art! No sculptor—no,
None!—bests this Spanish Michelangelo!
Never such skill was lavished on Saint John
The Baptist's head, the damask pressed upon
His neck!... This great Sevillian! See each bead
Of blood, scarce dry, pearl from slit veins! Indeed,
One seems to hear those dying lips emit
The throat's last cry as the blade severs it!..."
So saying, clear had her gentle voice become,
As over the vile bust she passed her thumb,
Smiling a smile of charm's coquettishness,
Moist-eyed, like lover's lustrous, coy caress.

Madrid

SUR LE PROMETHEE DU MUSEE DE MADRID

Sonnet

Hélas! il est cloué sur les croix du Caucase,
Le Titan qui, pour nous, dévalisa les cieux!
Du haut de son calvaire il insulte les dieux,
Raillant l'Olympien dont la foudre l'écrase.

Mais du moins, vers le soir, s'accoudant à la base
Du rocher où se tord le grand audacieux,
Les nymphes de la mer, des larmes dans les yeux,
Echangent avec lui quelque plaintive phrase.

Toi, cruel Ribeira, plus dur que Jupiter,
Tu fais de ses flancs creux, par d'affreuses entailles,
Couler à flots de sang des cascades d'entrailles!

Et tu chasses le chœur des filles de la mer;
Et tu laisses hurler, seul dans l'ombre profonde,
Le sublime voleur de la flamme féconde!

Madrid

ON THE PROMETHEUS IN THE MADRID MUSEUM

Sonnet

Alas! From the heights of his calvary,
Nailed to the crosses of the Caucasus,
The Titan who dared rob the heavens for us
Sneers at Olympus' gods, especially

The one whose lightning crushes him... But he,
Brash overreacher, come day's end, as thus,
At the base of the rock where, tortuous,
He writhes, he and the sea-nymphs, weeping free,

Exchange laments... O you, Ribeira, yet[11]
More fierce than Jove, pour a cascading flood—
From deep-gashed, gaping flanks—of guts and blood!

You cast the sea-nymph chorus off, and let
Him, in his deepening shadows, wail and moan—
Sublime thief of the fecund flame—alone!

Madrid

L'ESCURIAL

Posé comme un défi tout près d'une montagne,
L'on aperçoit de loin dans la morne campagne
Le sombre Escurial, à trois cents pieds du sol,
Soulevant sur le coin de son épaule énorme,
Eléphant monstrueux, la coupole difforme,
Débauche de granit du Tibère espagnol.

Jamais vieux Pharaon, au flanc d'un mont d'Egypte,
Ne fit pour sa momie une plus noire crypte;
Jamais sphinx au désert n'a gardé plus d'ennui;
La cigogne s'endort au bout des cheminées;
Partout l'herbe verdit les cours abandonnées;
Moines, prêtres, soldats, courtisans, tout a fui!

Et tout semblerait mort, si du bord des corniches,
Des mains des rois sculptés, des frontons et des niches,
Avec leurs cris charmants et leur folle gaîté,
Il ne s'envolait pas des essaims d'hirondelles,
Qui, pour le réveiller, agacent à coups d'ailes
Le géant assoupi qui rêve éternité!...

Escurial

THE ESCURIAL

Afar, hard by a mountain, set in pose
Defiant, stands—in landscape dull, morose—
The dour Escurial, three-hundred-foot
Above the ground; and, on its shoulder vast—
Elephantine—shapeless dome, granite-cast,[12]
By Spain's Tiberius! Never Pharaoh put[13]

On Egypt's hillock-flanks a crypt more dark
To house his mummy. Never a sphinx more stark
In desert boredom stood... The stork stands tall,
In empty chimneys now, staunchly, asleep.
Grass greens abandoned courtyards; weeds grow deep,
Thick... Gone the soldiers, monks, priests, courtiers all!

Everything would seem dead but for the flights
Of swallows, from their niches' cornice-heights—
Kings' statue-hands—swarming on pediments,
With fluttering wings, chirping their ecstasy
To wake him from dreams of eternity:
This giant, slumbering now, and ages hence...

Escurial

LE ROI SOLITAIRE

Je vis cloîtré dans mon âme profonde,
Sans rien d'humain, sans amour, sans amis,
Seul comme un dieu, n'ayant d'égaux au monde
Que mes aïeux sous la tombe endormis!
Hélas! grandeur veut dire solitude.
Comme une idole au geste surhumain,
Je reste là, gardant mon attitude,
La pourpre au dos, le monde dans la main.

Comme Jésus, j'ai le cercle d'épines;
Les rayons d'or du nimbe sidéral
Percent ma peau comme des javelines,
Et sur mon front perle mon sang royal.
Le bec pointu du vautour héraldique
Fouille mon flanc en proie aux noirs soucis :
Sur son rocher, le Prométhée antique
N'était qu'un roi sur son fauteuil assis.

De mon olympe entouré de mystère,
Je n'entends rien que la voix des flatteurs;
C'est le seul bruit qui des bruits de la terre
Puisse arriver à de telles hauteurs;
Et si parfois mon peuple, qu'on outrage,
En gémissant entre-choque ses fers :
—Sire! dormez, me dit-on, c'est l'orage;
Les cieux bientôt vont devenir plus clairs.

THE SOLITARY KING

Like cloistered god, deep in my soul, and with
No friends, no love, I live; no one with whom
To share my days; with neither kin, nor kith,
Nor kind, save forebears sleeping in the tomb!
Grandeur, alas, is ever solitary.
Like idol, more than human, here I stand,
On my back, purple; in my hand, the very
World itself, reaching vast from land to land.

Like Jesus', mine a crown of thorns. And in
Gold glory, star-shine's halo, round me spread,
Shoots forth its javelin rays, piercing my skin,
And my brow beads with droplets royal-red.
Heraldic vulture, sharp-beaked, unremitting,
Plucks my flank's dark chagrin. Prometheus, he
Of old, is like a king in comfort sitting
Bound to his rock, compared to such as me.

On my mystery-cloaked olympus round,
I hear naught but the voice of sybarites,
Flatterers; theirs the only earthly sound
Able to well up to my august heights.
And if, betimes, my people's mournful cries
Of woe, their rattling chains, rise to my ear,
One tells me: "Sire, 'tis but the angry skies...
But wait... In but a trice the storm will clear."

Je puis tout faire, et je n'ai plus d'envie.
Ah! si j'avais seulement un désir!
Si je sentais la chaleur de la vie!
Si je pouvais partager un plaisir!
Mais le soleil va toujours sans cortège;
Les plus hauts monts sont aussi les plus froids;
Et nul été ne peut fondre la neige
Sur les sierras et dans le cœur des rois!

Escurial

All power is mine, yet have I no desire.
No, none!... Ah, might I have but one! Were there
Once more in me the heat of passion-fire!
Might I have but one pleasure yet to share!
But no! The grandiose sun no courtiers knows,
And highest peaks feel, fierce, the cold that clings:
There is no summer that can melt the snows
On mountain tops and in the hearts of kings.

  Escurial

IN DESERTO

Les pitons des sierras, les dunes du désert,
Où ne pousse jamais un seul brin d'herbe vert;
Les monts aux flancs zébrés de tuf, d'ocre et de marne,
Et que l'éboulement de jour en jour décharne;
Le grès plein de micas papillotant aux yeux,
Le sable sans profit buvant les pleurs des cieux,
Le rocher renfrogné dans sa barbe de ronce,
L'ardente solfatare avec la pierre-ponce,
Sont moins secs et moins morts aux végétations
Que le roc de mon cœur ne l'est aux passions.
Le soleil de midi, sur le sommet aride,
Répand à flots plombés sa lumière livide,
Et rien n'est plus lugubre et désolant à voir
Que ce grand jour frappant sur ce grand désespoir.
Le lézard pâmé bâille, et parmi l'herbe cuite
On entend résonner les vipères en fuite.
Là, point de marguerite au cœur étoilé d'or,
Point de muguet prodigue égrenant son trésor;
Là, point de violette ignorée et charmante,
Dans l'ombre se cachant comme une pâle amante :
Mais la broussaille rousse et le tronc d'arbre mort,
Que le genou du vent comme un arc plie et tord;
Là, pas d'oiseau chanteur, ni d'abeille en voyage,
Pas de ramier plaintif déplorant son veuvage :
Mais bien quelque vautour, quelque aigle montagnard,
Sur le disque enflammé fixant son œil hagard,

IN DESERTO

The desert dunes, the sierra's mountain tops,
Where grows no blade of grass, no tuft of copse;
Mounts zebra-flanked in layered stripes of marl,
Ochre, and chalky tuff, that the days gnarl
Away to pebble-dust; the slate-dry slabs
Flicking their glints with little flashing dabs
Of mica, blinking on the eyes; the sand
Drinking to no avail the sky's tears; and
The cliff, sullen, bearded in thorn and sedge;
Hot sulfur springs, pumice ringing their edge...
None is more sickly-dry—dead, I confess!—
Than is my rock soul, barren, passionless.
The midday sun, flooding the arid height,
Spreads roundabout its pallid, leaden light,
And nothing is more sad, more ghastly bare
Than noon's rays lashing at this pale despair.
The lizard gapes a-swoon; one hears the snakes'
Slithering flight through grass the hot air bakes
To brown. There, no gold-breasted daisy, no
Lush lily of the valley, quick to show
Her petal-treasure; no violet unseen
But charming still, bashful and pale gamine
Hiding her love in shade... Here, naught but brush,
The tangled thicket with its ruddy blush;
The tree trunk, dead, that the wind's knee bends, twists;
No chirping birds, no bees in honeyed trysts,

Et qui, du haut du pic où son pied prend racine,
Dans l'or fauve du soir durement se dessine.
Tel était le rocher que Moïse, au désert,
Toucha de sa baguette, et dont le flanc ouvert,
Tressaillant tout à coup, fit jaillir en arcade
Sur les lèvres du peuple une fraîche cascade.
Ah! s'il venait à moi, dans mon aridité,
Quelque reine des cœurs, quelque divinité,
Une magicienne, un Moïse femelle,
Traînant dans les déserts les peuples après elle,
Qui frappât le rocher dans mon cœur endurci,
Comme de l'autre roche, on en verrait aussi
Sortir en jets d'argent des eaux étincelantes,
Où viendraient s'abreuver les racines des plantes;
Où les pâtres errants conduiraient leurs troupeaux,
Pour se coucher à l'ombre et prendre le repos;
Où, comme en un vivier, les cigognes fidèles
Plongeraient leurs grands becs et laveraient leurs ailes.

La Guardia

No ring dove moaning of his solitary
Widowerhood; but there, in mountain aerie,
Vulture or eagle stands, with sunset stare
Fixed on the flaming orb, in wild-eyed glare,
Clawing the peak, seeming to root, outstretched
Against the evening's savage gold, stark-etched.
Such was the rock that, on the desert sand,
Time past, was struck by Moses, wand in hand;
The rock whose quivering flank suddenly burst
In cool cascades, slaking the people's thirst...
Ah! If some queen of hearts—a sorceress,
A goddess—some Moses in woman's dress
Might come, leading her people, desert-borne,
To strike the rock of my hard heart forlorn,
Then would one see, as with that other, streaming
Silver jets, water glistening and gleaming,
Where thirsting plants would delve their roots to find
Sustenance, and where shepherd, flocks behind,
Would, shaded, rest; where storks, in crystal springs,
Would plunge their giant beaks and wash their wings!

La Guardia[14]

STANCES

Maintenant,—dans la plaine ou bien dans la montagne,
Chêne ou sapin, un arbre est en train de pousser,
En France, en Amérique, en Turquie, en Espagne,
Un arbre sous lequel un jour je puis passer.

Maintenant,—sur le seuil d'une pauvre chaumière,
Une femme, du pied agitant un berceau,
Sans se douter qu'elle est la parque filandière,
Allonge entre ses doigts l'étoupe d'un fuseau.

Maintenant,—loin du ciel à la splendeur divine,
Comme une taupe aveugle en son étroit couloir,
Pour arracher le fer au ventre de la mine,
Sous le sol des vivants plonge un travailleur noir.

Maintenant,—dans un coin du monde que j'ignore,
Il existe une place où le gazon fleurit,
Où le soleil joyeux boit les pleurs de l'aurore,
Où l'abeille bourdonne, où l'oiseau chante et rit.

Cet arbre qui soutient tant de nids sur ses branches,
Cet arbre épais et vert, frais et riant à l'œil,
Dans son tronc renversé l'on taillera des planches,
Les planches dont un jour on fera mon cercueil!

STANZAS

Now... On the mountainside or on the plain,
A tree—an oak or fir—grows on its way
In France, America, Turkey, or Spain;
A tree beneath which I may pass one day.

Now... By a poor thatched hut a woman spreads
A spindled skein betwixt her fingers; and
Her foot gentles a cradle as the threads,
Unbeknownst, take shape in her Fate-wrought hand.

Now... Far off from the heaven-splendored air,
Like a blind mole in narrow confines bound,
A miner, black, digs in earth's belly, where[15]
A vein of iron ore runs underground.

Now... In a corner of our globe, unknown,
There is a spot where grass grows, flourishing;
Where sun's beams quaff the dawn's tears, joyful-sown;
Where buzz the bees and where birds chaff and sing.

And there, a tree, whose boughs bear many a nest—
A tree, thick, green, cool-shaded, laughing free—
From whose trunk, lying downcast, one will wrest
The planks that one day will envelop me!...

Cette étoupe qu'on file, et qui, tissée en toile,
Donne une aile au vaisseau dans le port engourdi,
A l'orgie une nappe, à la pudeur un voile,
Linceul, revêtira mon cadavre verdi!

Ce fer que le mineur cherche au fond de la terre
Aux brumeuses clartés de son pâle fanal,
Hélas! le forgeron quelque jour en doit faire
Le clou qui fermera le couvercle fatal!

A cette même place où mille fois peut-être
J'allai m'asseoir, le cœur plein de rêves charmants,
S'entr'ouvrira le gouffre où je dois disparaître,
Pour descendre au séjour des épouvantements!

Manche

That skein one spins: sail hanging from mast's head
To give a wing to boat becalmed in port;
Or table linen for the orgy spread;
Or veil—modesty's first and best resort;

Or shroud to wrap my dead and greening skin!
The iron that the miner digs, dim lit,
Will nail my fatal coffin lid, each pin
Hammered hot by the smithy forging it!

And, in that place where I would sit, with heart
Full of dreams, at my ease, soon must I go
Toward the abyss as earth splits, pulls apart,
And descend to the horror-realm below.

La Mancha[16]

EN PASSANT PRES D'UN CIMETIERE

Qu'est-ce que le tombeau? — Le vestiaire où l'âme,
Au sortir du théâtre et son rôle joué,
Dépose ses habits d'enfant, d'homme ou de femme,
Comme un masque qui rend un costume loué!

Manche

PASSING BY A CEMETERY

What is the tomb?... Soul's costume studios
Where, as they leave the theater, roles now done,
Actors—men, women, children, every one!—
Stop to return their rented acting-clothes!

La Mancha

J'ETAIS MONTE PLUS HAUT...

J'étais monté plus haut que l'aigle et le nuage;
Sous mes pieds s'étendait un vaste paysage,
Cerclé d'un double azur par le ciel et la mer;
Et les crânes pelés des montagnes géantes
En foule jaillissaient des profondeurs béantes,
Comme de blancs écueils sortant du gouffre amer.

C'était un vaste amas d'éboulements énormes,
Des rochers grimaçant dans des poses difformes,
Des pics dont l'œil à peine embrasse la hauteur,
Et, la neige faisant une écume à leur crête,
On eût dit une mer prise un jour de tempête,
Un chaos attendant le mot du Créateur.

Là dorment les débris des races disparues,
Le vieux monde noyé sous les ondes accrues,
Le Béhémot biblique et le Léviathan.
Chaque mont de la chaîne, immense cimetière,
Cache un corps monstrueux dans son ventre de pierre,
Et ses blocs de granit sont des os de Titan!

Sierra-Nevada

HIGHER I CLIMBED...

Higher I climbed than cloud and eagle; there,
Sea and sky, spread below, in azure pair,
Circled as one the landscape broad and steep:[17]
Bald-pated giant mountain summits, come
Surging high, like a great white squall, up from
The valley's jaws, quitting the bitter deep.

Huge, formless mass, grimacing rock-falls pose
In wild array, scattered all round. And those
Summits, too high for eye to grasp, each peak,
Snow-frothed... As if a violent, storm-wracked sea,
A-sweep, lies fixed for all eternity:
A chaos waiting for the Lord to speak...

Ruins of vanished races sleep. The ground,
Swept by great waves—biblical world long drowned,
Behemoth and Leviathan of stones—[18]
Reveals a graveyard vast, tomb upon tomb,
Monster concealed deep in its rockbound womb,
Whose blocks of granite are the Titans' bones!

Sierra Nevada

CONSOLATION

Ne sois pas étonné si la foule, ô poète,

Dédaigne de gravir ton œuvre jusqu'au faîte;

La foule est comme l'eau qui fuit les hauts sommets,

Où le niveau n'est pas, elle ne vient jamais.

Donc, sans prendre à lui plaire une peine perdue,

Ne fais pas d'escalier à ta pensée ardue :

Une rampe aux boiteux ne rend pas le pied sûr.

Que le pic solitaire escalade l'azur,

L'aigle saura l'atteindre avec un seul coup d'aile,

Et posera son pied sur la neige éternelle,

La neige immaculée, au pur reflet d'argent,

Pour que Dieu, dans son œuvre allant et voyageant,

Comprenne que toujours on fréquente les cimes

Et qu'on monte au sommet des poèmes sublimes.

Sierra-Nevada

CONSOLATION

Wonder not, Poet, that the public might
Refuse to climb your work's loftymost height.
The throng, like water, spurns the summits... Where
No level ground lies spread, it will not dare
To tread. Try not to please: you waste your time.
Build them no staircase for the arduous climb
Thereto: a ramp makes not the lame more sure
Of foot. Leave the lone peak in peace secure
In its azure ascent. The eagle, he,
Will reach it in one wing-thrust, easily,
Lighting on the eternal, silver snows,
So that God, toiling as he comes and goes,
Sees that there are, indeed, those who would deign
Ascend to poetry's sublime domain.

  Sierra Nevada

DANS LA SIERRA

J'aime d'un fol amour les monts fiers et sublimes!
Les plantes n'osent pas poser leurs pieds frileux
Sur le linceul d'argent qui recouvre leurs cimes;
Le soc s'émousserait à leurs pics anguleux.

Ni vigne aux bras lascifs, ni blés dorés, ni seigles;
Rien qui rappelle l'homme et le travail maudit.
Dans leur air libre et pur nagent des essaims d'aigles,
Et l'écho du rocher siffle l'air du bandit.

Ils ne rapportent rien et ne sont pas utiles;
Ils n'ont que leur beauté, je le sais, c'est bien peu;
Mais, moi, je les préfère aux champs gras et fertiles,
Qui sont si loin du ciel qu'on n'y voit jamais Dieu!

Sierra-Nevada

IN THE SIERRA

How madly do I love the mountains proud,[19]
Sublime! Plants dare not place their shivering toes
Upon their lofty summits' silvered shroud;
Their craggy peaks would dull the plow; no rows

Of golden grain, languid-limbed vines... There, flocks
Of eagles, swimming through the air, pure, free,
And bandits' tunes whistling from rocks to rocks...
Nothing to sing man's work, his industry

Accursed; no profit's use to labor for.
But I prefer them to our fields' lush sod—
Though they have only beauty, nothing more—
So heaven-removed that never one sees God!

Sierra Nevada

LE POETE ET LA FOULE

Le plaine un jour disait à la montagne oisive :
—Rien ne vient sur ton front des vents toujours battu!
Au poète, courbé sur sa lyre pensive,
La foule aussi disait :—Rêveur, à quoi sers-tu?

La montagne en courroux répondit à la plaine :
—C'est moi qui fais germer les moissons sur ton sol;
Du midi dévorant je tempère l'haleine;
J'arrête dans les cieux les nuages au vol!

Je pétris de mes doigts la neige en avalanches;
Dans mon creuset je fonds les cristaux des glaciers,
Et je verse, du bout de mes mamelles blanches,
En longs filets d'argent, les fleuves nourriciers.

Le poète, à son tour, répondit à la foule :
—Laissez mon pâle front s'appuyer sur ma main.
N'ai-je pas, de mon flanc dont mon âme s'écoule,
Fait jaillir une source où boit le genre humain?

Sierra-Nevada

THE POET AND THE MASSES

The plain addressed the idle mountain thus:
"Your barren brow, wind-battered, all day through,
Produces nothing valuable to us!"
And the masses addressed the poet too,[20]

Bent on his pensive lyre: "Dreamer, what good
Are you?" Angry, the mountain told the plain:
"Without those storms that lash me, nothing would
You sprout for harvesting! Here I remain,

Calming the noon's devouring breath... I stop
Clouds in their flight! My fingers knead the snow:
Crystal cascades plunge, melting, from atop
My crucible... From my white teats, there flow

Silver, life-giving streams..." The poet, he,
Told the throng: "Let me dream, my pallid face
Held in my hands... Does not my soul burst free,
A-flood, to slake the thirsting human race?"[21]

Sierra Nevada

LE CHASSEUR

Je suis enfant de la montagne;
Comme l'isard, comme l'aiglon,
Je ne descends dans la campagne
Que pour ma poudre et pour mon plomb;
Puis je reviens, et de mon aire
Je vois en bas l'homme ramper,
Si haut placé que le tonnerre
Remonterait pour me frapper.

Je n'ai pour boire, après ma chasse,
Que l'eau du ciel dans mes deux mains;
Mais le sentier par où je passe
Est vierge encor de pas humains.
Dans mes poumons nul souffle immonde!
En liberté je bois l'air bleu,
Et nul vivant en ce bas monde
Autant que moi n'approche Dieu.

Pour mon berceau j'eus un nid d'aigle
Comme un héros ou comme un roi,
Et j'ai vécu sans frein ni règle,
Plus haut que l'homme et que la loi.
Après ma mort une avalanche
De son linceul me couvrira,

THE HUNTER

Child of the mountain top am I;
Like chamois of the Pyrenees,[22]
Or eaglet, ever perched on high,
Never descending, save for these:
Powder and lead! And then, withal,
Back to my heights, from where I see
Lowly man, far beneath, a-crawl;
And I, so high that, verily,
Lightning would have to scale the air
To strike me! And, if I would slake
My thirst after my hunting, there
Is naught whereof I might partake
Save heavenly waters: cupped my hands
To quaff them... And the path I tread,
Virgin of humans on the land's
Expanse... My lungs, unfrequented
By sullied breath! I drink the blue,
Pure air, free as I please; and no
Creature approaches God as do
I alone, in the here-below.
My cradle was an eagle's nest—
Like king or hero—and I dwelt
Untrammeled, high above the rest,
And never yielded, never knelt
Before man or his law! And when
I die, an avalanche will be

Et sur mon corps la neige blanche,
Tombeau d'argent, s'élèvera.

Sierra-Nevada

My snow-white shroud; and, rising then,
A silver grave will cover me.

Sierra Nevada

SERENADE

Sur le balcon où tu te penches
Je veux monter... efforts perdus!
Il est trop haut, et tes mains blanches
N'atteignent pas mes bras tendus.

Pour déjouer ta duègne avare,
Jette un collier, un ruban d'or;
Ou des cordes de ta guitare
Tresse une échelle; ou bien encor...

Ote tes fleurs, défais ton peigne,
Penche sur moi tes cheveux longs,
Torrent de jais dont le flot baigne
Ta jambe ronde et tes talons.

Aidé par cette échelle étrange,
Légèrement je gravirai,
Et jusqu'au ciel, sans être un ange,
Dans les parfums je monterai!

SERENADE

You lean over your balcony.
I would climb up, would that I might...
And though your arms reach out to me —
In vain! Too high, those hands of white!
To dupe your prude duenna, pray
Throw down to me your necklace, or
Your golden ribbon... Find the way
To braid a ladder-rope from your
Guitar-strings; or put by your flowers,
Undo your comb, let fall your hair
In jet cascades, whose torrent showers
Your full-fleshed leg and heel... And there,
On that strange ladder climbing, though
No angel I, yet shall I rise,
Weightless, as higher, higher I go
Among the perfumes of the skies!

J'AI DANS MON CŒUR...

J'ai dans mon cœur, dont tout voile s'écarte,
Deux bancs d'ivoire, une table en cristal,
Où sont assis, tenant chacun leur carte,
Ton faux amour et mon amour loyal.

J'ai dans mon cœur, dans mon cœur diaphane,
Ton nom chéri qu'enferme un coffret d'or;
Prends-en la clef, car nulle main profane
Ne doit l'ouvrir ni ne l'ouvrit encor.

Fouille mon cœur, ce cœur que tu dédaignes
Et qui pourtant n'est peuplé que de toi,
Et tu verras, mon amour, que tu règnes
Sur un pays dont nul homme n'est roi!

Grenade

IN THE DEPTHS OF MY HEART...

In the depths of my heart, unveiled, there stand
Two ivory seats before a crystal-glass
Table, where sit, with playing-cards in hand,[23]
Two loves: mine faithful, and yours false, alas!

In the depths of my heart, diaphanous,
Lies a gold chest, with your dear name inset.
Here, take the key: no vain hand impious
Must open it, nor has one done so yet.[24]

Plumb deep my heart that proudly you disdain,
This heart with none but you inhabiting;
Then shall you see, my love, that there you reign
Over a realm where no one else is king![25]

Grenada

LE LAURIER DU GENERALIFE

Dans le Généralife, il est un laurier-rose,
Gai comme la victoire, heureux comme l'amour.
Un jet d'eau, son voisin, l'enrichit et l'arrose;
Une perle reluit dans chaque fleur éclose,
Et le frais émail vert se rit des feux du jour.

Il rougit dans l'azur comme une jeune fille;
Ses fleurs, qui semblent vivre, ont des teintes de chair.
On dirait, à le voir sous l'onde qui scintille,
Une odalisque nue attendant qu'on l'habille,
Cheveux en pleurs, au bord du bassin au flot clair.

Ce laurier, je l'aimais d'une amour sans pareille;
Chaque soir, près de lui, j'allais me reposer;
A l'une de ses fleurs, bouche humide et vermeille,
Je suspendais ma lèvre, et parfois, ô merveille!
J'ai cru sentir la fleur me rendre mon baiser...

Généralife

THE OLEANDER OF THE GENERALIFE

In the Generalife, joyous, stands
An oleander, fancy-free as love
Victorious, watered by neighboring hands—
A jet, nourishing round the garden-land's
Expanse; and pearls shine in the blooms thereof.

Its cool-enameled green scorns daylight's fire;
Like blushing maid, its flower-pink flesh would seem
An odalisque, awaiting her attire—
Azure-clad nude, with weeping hair... And higher,
Above the limpid pool, sparks glitter, gleam...

My laurel love, that shrub. Each night I would
Take my ease by it, reveling in my bliss,
Kissing a moist, red flower-mouth!—Oh, could[26]
It be?... I pressed my eager lips, and stood
Awed, as I felt the flower return my kiss!...

Generalife

LA LUNE

Le soleil dit à la lune :
—Que fais-tu sur l'horizon ?
Il est bien tard, à la brune,
Pour sortir de sa maison.

L'honnête femme, à cette heure,
Défile son chapelet,
Couche son enfant qui pleure,
Et met la barre au volet.

Le follet court sur la dune ;
Gitanas, chauves-souris,
Rôdent en cherchant fortune ;
Noirs ou blancs, tous chats sont gris.

Des planètes équivoques
Et des astres libertins,
Croyant que tu les provoques,
Suivront tes pas clandestins.

La nuit, dehors on s'enrhume.
Vas-tu prendre encor ce soir
Le brouillard pour lit de plume
Et l'eau du lac pour miroir ?

THE MOON

Sun addresses Moon: "I say,
Why come you a-rising here?
Dark it is at close of day,
You had best stay home, my dear!

"Woman honest and well-bred
Sits and tells her beads, come night;
Puts her squealing babe to bed;
Closes, bars the shutter tight.

"Silly are those ne'er-do-wells
Flitting round the dunes, or those
Bats and gypsy damosels,
Bent on pleasure, heaven knows!

"Black or white, all cats are gray![27]
Stars and planets, wary-wise—
Dubious libertines, astray—
Follow you in furtive guise.

"Nighttime air can make you ill.
Rather than a featherbed,
Will you choose to sleep your fill
Outstretched on the fog instead?

Réponds-moi. — J'ai cent retraites
Sur la terre et dans les cieux,
Monsieur mon frère : et vous êtes
Un astre bien curieux!

Généralife

"For your mirror, will you look
On the lake?... I pray, reply!"
"Many a cranny, many a nook,
Have I over earth and sky,

"Wherein I may bide... and do!"
Whereupon she asks the other:
"Questions! Questions!... Why must you
Be so curious, star, my brother!"

  Generalife

J'ALLAIS PARTIR...

J'allais partir; doña Balbine
Se lève et prend à sa bobine
  Un long fil d'or;
A mon bouton elle le noue,
Et puis me dit, baisant ma joue :
  —Restez encor!

Par l'un des bouts ce fil, trop frêle
Pour retenir un infidèle,
  Tient à mon cœur...
Si vous partez, mon cœur s'arrache :
Un nœud si fort à vous m'attache,
  O mon vainqueur!

—Pourquoi donc prendre à ta bobine
Pour me fixer, doña Balbine,
  Un fil doré?
A ton lit qu'un cheveu m'enchaîne,
Se brisât-il, sois-en certaine,
  Je resterai!

 Grenade

AS I NO LONGER WOULD REMAIN...

As I no longer would remain,
Doña Balbine plucked from her skein
    A long gold thread.
She took my button in her hand,
Twisted it round, kissing me, and
    "Pray stay," she said.

"My heart hangs by this thread, but none
So fine can keep a faithless one
    From fell design.
Quit me, and my heart quits me too;
Such the knot that binds me to you,
    O conqueror mine!"

"Since you would fain have me remain,
Doña Balbine, why from your skein
    Pluck that thread, pray?
One hair, to your bed so binds me,
That, should it break, yet shall I be
    Bound, here to stay!"

Grenada

J'AI LAISSE DE MON SEIN DE NEIGE...

J'ai laissé de mon sein de neige
Tomber un œillet rouge à l'eau.
Hélas! comment le reprendrai-je
Mouillé par l'onde du ruisseau?
Voilà le courant qui l'entraîne!
Bel œillet aux vives couleurs,
Pourquoi tomber dans la fontaine?
Pour t'arroser j'avais mes pleurs!

Grenade

A RED CARNATION... MY SNOW BREAST...

A red carnation... My snow breast
Let it fall in the brook. I leave it.
Alas! Soaked through it is! So best
I take no trouble to retrieve it!
Swiftly the current bears it off!...
Carnation fair, of brilliant hue,
Why fall into the stream? Enough
Tears my eyes shed to moisten you!

Grenada

LE SOUPIR DU MORE

Ce cavalier qui court vers la montagne,
 Inquiet, pâle au moindre bruit,
C'est Boabdil, roi des Mores d'Espagne,
 Qui pouvait mourir, et qui fuit !

Aux Espagnols, Grenade s'est rendue ;
 La croix remplace le croissant,
Et Boabdil pour sa ville perdue
 N'a que des pleurs et pas de sang...

Sur un rocher nommé Soupir-du-More,
 Avant d'entrer dans la Sierra,
Le fugitif s'assit, pour voir encore
 De loin Grenade et l'Alhambra :

 « Hier, dit-il, j'étais calife ;
 Comme un dieu vivant adoré,
 Je passais du Généralife
 A l'Alhambra peint et doré !
 J'avais, loin des regards profanes,
 Des bassins aux flots diaphanes
 Où se baignaient trois cents sultanes ;
 Mon nom partout jetait l'effroi !
 Hélas ! ma puissance est détruite ;
 Ma vaillante armée est en fuite,
 Et je m'en vais sans autre suite
 Que mon ombre derrière moi !

THE MOOR'S LAST SIGH

That horseman plunging breathless, who would fain
    Fly to a mountain refuge... He,
Great Boabdil, king of the Moors of Spain,
    Pale, faced with death, was forced to flee.

The Spaniards held Grenada now; the cross
    Relives; the Crescent—lo!—has left,
And Boabdil laments his city's loss,
    With many a tear but blood-bereft...

He stops to rest by the Sierra's edge—
    A spot known as "The Moor's Last Sigh"[28]
Today—and sits upon a rocky ledge,
    Looks back and casts a doleful eye:

    Grenada, Alhambra left behind!
    "Alas! A caliph proud, adored
    Was I but yesterday, enshrined
    In the Generalife, lord
    Of fine Alhambra, golden-walled.
    Three hundred fair sultanas lolled
    In limpid pools; my name appalled
    And held at bay the enemy!
    But now, cast down am I, distraught.
    My army lies outdone, outfought,
    Destroyed! And no one, nothing, naught
    But my dark shadow follows me!

« Fondez, mes yeux, fondez en larmes!
Soupirs profonds venus du cœur,
Soulevez l'acier de mes armes :
Le Dieu des chrétiens est vainqueur!
Je pars, adieu, beau ciel d'Espagne,
Darro, Jénil, verte campagne,
Neige rose de la montagne;
Adieu, Grenade, mes amours!
Riant Alhambra, tours vermeilles,
Frais jardins remplis de merveilles,
Dans mes rêves et dans mes veilles,
Absent, je vous verrai toujours! »

Sierra d'Elvire

"Weep, weep my eyes! Pray let my sighs,
Deep in my heart, come welling! Oh,
That my steel arms once more might rise!
The Christian god has laid me low!
Bright skies of Spain, I may not bide...
Darro, Jenil, green countryside,[29]
Pink mountain snows, off must I ride!
Farewell, Grenada-loves galore!
Laughing Alhambra's crimson towers...
Cool gardens fraught with wondrous flowers,
Still, in my dreams, my waking hours,
Long will I see you, evermore!"

Sierra d'Elvire[30]

PERSPECTIVE

Sur le Guadalquivir, en sortant de Séville,
Quand l'œil à l'horizon se tourne avec regret,
Les dômes, les clochers font comme une forêt :
A chaque tour de roue il surgit une aiguille.

D'abord la Giralda, dont l'ange d'or scintille,
Rose dans le ciel bleu darde son minaret;
La cathédrale énorme à son tour apparaît
Par-dessus les maisons, qui vont à sa cheville.

De près, l'on n'aperçoit que des fragments d'arceaux :
Un pignon biscornu, l'angle d'un mur maussade
Cache la flèche ouvrée et la riche façade.

Grands hommes, obstrués et masqués par les sots,
Comme les hautes tours sur les toits de la ville,
De loin vos fronts grandis montent dans l'air tranquille!

   Sur le Guadalquivir

VIEW

Leaving behind Seville's fair company,
One gazes back over the Guadalquivir[31]
In wistful wise, and he sees looming there
Belfries' and domes' forest-like panoply.

With each wheel's turning, new peaks rise. First, he
Spies the Giralda's angel, sparkling, clear,[32]
In gold; pink minaret, dart in the sheer
Blue of the sky: cathedral in a sea

Of houses, scarcely ankle-deep; nearby.
Arch-fragments, crooked gable, sullen wall
Masking the finely crafted spire, and all

That lush façade... Great men, you, standing high,
Hidden by fools, tall towers rising there:
Your noble brows soar in the tranquil air.

On the Guadalquivir

AU BORD DE LA MER

La lune de ses mains distraites
A laissé choir, du haut de l'air,
Son grand éventail à paillettes
Sur le bleu tapis de la mer.

Pour le ravoir elle se penche
Et tend son beau bras argenté;
Mais l'éventail fuit sa main blanche,
Par le flot qui passe emporté.

Au gouffre amer pour te le rendre,
Lune, j'irais bien me jeter,
Si tu voulais du ciel descendre,
Au ciel si je pouvais monter!

Malaga

BY THE SEASHORE

The moon, with absentminded hand,
From heavens' height, unthinkingly,
Let fall her sequined fan, outspanned,
On the blue carpet of the sea.

To take it back she leans a bit,
Holds out her silvered arm... Denied,
Her white hand grasps it not; for it
Goes fleeing off, borne on the tide.

Ah! To return it, Moon, I should
Dive to the deeps if, from the sky,
You might descend; or even would
Plunge skyward, could I climb so high![33]

Málaga[34]

SAINT CHRISTOPHE D'ECIJA

J'ai vu dans Ecija, vieille ville moresque,
Aux clochers de faïence, aux palais peints à fresque,
Sous les rayons de plomb du soleil étouffant,
Un colosse doré qui portait un enfant.
Un pilier de granit, d'ordre salomonique,
Servait de piédestal au vieillard athlétique.
Sa colossale main sur un tronc de palmier
S'appuyait largement et le faisait plier;
Et tous ses nerfs roidis par un effort étrange,
Comme ceux de Jacob dans sa lutte avec l'ange,
Semblaient suffire à peine à soutenir le poids
De ce petit enfant qui tenait une croix!
—Quoi! géant aux bras forts, à la poitrine large,
Tu te courbes, vaincu par cette faible charge,
Et ta dorure, où tremble une fauve lueur,
Semble fondre et couler sur ton corps en sueur!

—Ne sois pas étonné si mes genoux chancellent,
Si mes nerfs sont roidis, si mes tempes ruissellent,
Certes, je suis de bronze et taillé de façon
A passer les vigueurs d'Hercule et de Samson!
Mon poignet vaut celui du vieux Crotoniate;
Il n'est pas de taureau que d'un coup je n'abatte,
Et je fends les lions avec mes doigts nerveux;
Car nulle Dalila n'a touché mes cheveux.
Je pourrais, comme Atlas, poser sur mes épaules

SAINT CHRISTOPHER OF ECIJA

In Ecija, old Moorish town, where stand
Bright-frescoed palaces, and where the land
Sports steeples earthen-tiled, I laid my eyes—
Under a sun, stifling in lead-hot skies—
Upon a huge colossus wrought of gold,
Holding a babe; a pillar, twined in bold
Wreaths Solomonic, held up the defiant,[35]
Mighty, old athlete's back-bowed stance. His giant
Hand, laid upon a palm's trunk, bent it low,
With curious force, all sinews taut; and, though
As powerful as Jacob when he fought
The angel, yet it seemed that he could not
Bear the weight of that babe, who, raising high
His hand, held up a cross before my eye!
"What, powerful colossus, massive-breasted,
Can it be that you let your strength be bested
By one so small and weak, and that you let
Your tawny gilt blend, trembling, with your sweat!"

"Be not surprised if my knees fail me, or
If wet my brow and taut my sinews; for
True, I am made of bronze, with qualities
That neither Samson nor great Hercules
Could match! Nor would Croton's old champion[36]
Surpass my might. I smite a bull with one
Blow of my fist—but one! And I can split

La corniche du ciel et les essieux des pôles;
Mais je ne puis porter cet enfant de six mois
Avec son globe bleu surmonté d'une croix;
Car c'est le fruit divin de la Vierge féconde,
L'enfant prédestiné, le rédempteur du monde;
C'est l'esprit triomphant, le Verbe souverain :
Un tel poids fait plier même un géant d'airain!

Ecija

Fierce lions' flesh asunder, rending it
Under my quivering fingers! For, my hair
Never lay trapped in some Delilah's snare.
Like Atlas, I could bear from pole to pole
The very earth, and could support the whole
Heavenly realm... Yet am I powerless
To clasp this infant in his weightlessness;
To hold, unbowed, this babe of half a year,
Whose hands grasp round a cross-surmounted sphere;
For fruit divine of Virgin's womb is he,
This world-redeemer, child of destiny;
Spirit triumphant, sovereign Word! See how,
Beneath such weight, a giant's brass must bow!"

   Ecija

PENDANT LA TEMPETE

La barque est petite et la mer immense;
La vague nous jette au ciel en courroux,
Le ciel nous renvoie au flot en démence :
Près du mât rompu prions à genoux!

De nous à la tombe il n'est qu'une planche.
Peut-être ce soir, dans un lit amer,
Sous un froid linceul fait d'écume blanche,
Irons-nous dormir, veillés par l'éclair!

Fleur du paradis, sainte Notre-Dame,
Si bonne aux marins en péril de mort,
Apaise le vent, fais taire la lame,
Et pousse du doigt notre esquif au port.

Nous te donnerons, si tu nous délivres,
Une belle robe en papier d'argent,
Un cierge à festons pesant quatre livres,
Et, pour ton Jésus, un petit saint Jean.

Cadix

DURING THE STORM

The barque is small and endless is the sea;
The waves hurl us up to the frenzied sky,
The sky casts us back down to watery
Chaos of maddened, raging tide... Hard by

The broken masts, we kneel to pray! A plank
Is all that separates us from the tomb.
Perhaps tonight, in white foam's bitter, dank
Shroud will we lie, mid lightning's blare and boom!

You, hope of sailors in the throes of death,
Flower of paradise... Our Lady, if
You calm the waves, muffle the tempest's breath,
And push safely to port our battered skiff...

If we are saved, your statue will be gowned
In gleaming silver foil, O heavenly Queen!
For you, a candle, four full pounds, wreathed round,
And for your Son, a Saint-Jean figurine... [37]

Cadiz[38]

ADIEUX A LA POESIE

Allons, ange déchu, ferme ton aile rose;
Ote ta robe blanche et tes beaux rayons d'or;
Il faut, du haut des cieux où tendait ton essor,
Filer comme une étoile, et tomber dans la prose.

Il faut que sur le sol ton pied d'oiseau se pose.
Marche au lieu de voler : il n'est pas temps encor;
Renferme dans ton cœur l'harmonieux trésor;
Que ta harpe un moment se détende et repose.

O pauvre enfant du ciel, tu chanterais en vain
Ils ne comprendraient pas ton langage divin;
A tes plus doux accords leur oreille est fermée!

Mais, avant de partir, mon bel ange à l'œil bleu,
Va trouver de ma part ma pâle bien-aimée,
Et pose sur son front un long baiser d'adieu!

FAREWELL TO POETRY

Come, fallen angel, and your pink wings close;
Doff your white robe, your rays that gild the skies;
You must—from heaven, where once you used to rise—
Streak, like a shooting star, fall into prose.

Your bird's feet now must strike an earthly pose.
It is no time to fly: walk! Lock your prize—
Your harp's fair harmonies—in resting wise,
Within your heart: vain, worthless treasures those!

Poor child of heaven, but vainly would you sing:
To them your tongue divine means not a thing!
Their ear is closed to your sweet chords! But this

I beg: O blue-eyed angel, first, before
You leave, find my pale love, whom I adore,
And give her brow one long, last farewell kiss.

FROM "PIECES DIVERSES" IN

POESIES NOUVELLES

1845

VOUS VOULEZ DE MES VERS...

Vous voulez de mes vers, reine aux yeux fiers et doux!
Hêlas! vous savez bien qu'avec les chiens jaloux,
Les critiques hargneux, aux babines froncées,
Qui traînent par lambeaux les strophes dépecées,
Toute la pâle race au front jauni de fiel
Dont le bonheur d'autrui fait le deuil éternel,
J'aboie à pleine gueule, et plus fort que les autres.
O poètes divins, je ne suis plus des vôtres :
On m'a fait une niche où je veille tapi,
Dans le bas du journal comme un dogue accroupi;
Et j'ai pour bien longtemps, sur l'autel de mon âme,
Renversé l'urne d'or où rayonnait la flamme.
Pour moi plus de printemps, plus d'art, plus de sommeil;
Plus de blonde chimère au sourire vermeil,
De colombe privée, au col blanc, au pied rose,
Qui boive dans ma coupe et sur mon doigt se pose.
Ma poésie est morte, et je ne sais plus rien,
Sinon que tout est laid, sinon que rien n'est bien.
Je trouve, par état, le mal dans toute chose,
Les taches du soleil, le ver de chaque rose;
Triste infirmier, je vois l'ossement sous la peau,
La coulisse en dedans et l'envers du rideau.
Ainsi je vis.—Comment la belle Muse antique,
Droite sous les longs plis de sa blanche tunique,
Avec ses cheveux noirs en deux flots déroulés,
Comme le firmament de fleurs d'or étoilés,

YOU CRAVE MY VERSE...

You crave my verse, queen of the soft brown eyes![1]
Alas! You know that I, in wretched wise,
Worse than the rest, howl my disdain, like those
Barking dogs—critic-hounds!—who, in the throes
Of jealousy, jaws sneering, wild fangs baring—
Sallow race, brows jaundiced with gall—stand tearing,
Ripping to shreds my stanzas... They, on whom
Another's joy casts an eternal gloom.
No, divine poets! Brothers no more, we!
I have been thrown unceremoniously
Down to the rank of lowly gazetteer,
To crouch with dogs; I, who, for many a year,
Poured the flame from the golden urn upon
The altar of my soul. My spring is gone,
My art, my slumber... Now, no more the fair,
Mysterious chimera's flaxen hair,
Scarlet-lipped smile; no more my private dove—
White breast, pink claws—who fluttered from above
And, settling by my cup, therein would sip,
Gently perching upon my fingertip...
My poetry is dead; I know no more,
Save that this life is ugly to the core!
No good in anything is there. I find
Evil in everything, lurking behind:
Sunlight turns shade, worms hide in every rose,
Beneath the skin I see the skull's foul pose;

Sans se blesser la plante à ces tessons de verre,
Pourrait-elle descendre auprès de moi sur terre?
Mais les belles toujours sont puissantes sur nous :
Les lions sur leurs pieds posent leurs mufles roux.
Ce que ne ferait pas la Muse aux grandes ailes,
La Vierge aonienne aux grâces éternelles,
Avec son doux baiser et la gloire pour prix,
Vous le faites, ô reine! et dans mon cœur surpris
Je sens germer les vers, et, toute réjouie,
S'ouvrir comme une fleur la rime épanouie!

1841

The curtain's underside, what the wings hold
Backstage... Ah, life! How might the Muse of old,
Wrapped in her long white tunic-fold
With her black tresses flowing free, bedecked
With flowers of gold—star-speckled sky... How might
Her tender soles expect safely to light
Upon our jagged glass-defended walls
To join me here? Alas!... Yet it befalls
That beauties wield great power: enough to cause
The lion fierce to nuzzle his tawny jaws
Quietly at their feet! But what the Muse
Broad of wing cannot do, the Virgin whose
Aonian grace is timeless, with soft kiss[2]
And glory's prize... Yes, you, my queen!... Yes, this
You do! And I, amazed, feel in my heart
Come sprouting back to life my poet's art,
And sense that rhyme's delight, fresh-spirited,
Will, like a flower, once more its petals spread![3]

1841

PRIERE

Comme un ange gardien prenez-moi sous votre aile;
Tendez, en souriant et daignant vous pencher,
A ma petite main votre main maternelle,
Pour soutenir mes pas et me faire marcher!

Car Jésus le doux maître, aux célestes tendresses,
Permettait aux enfants de s'approcher de lui;
Comme un père indulgent il souffrait leurs caresses,
Et jouait avec eux sans témoigner d'ennui.

O vous qui ressemblez à ces tableaux d'église
Où l'on voit, sur fond d'or, l'auguste Charité
Préservant de la faim, préservant de la bise
Un groupe frais et blond dans sa robe abrité;

Comme le nourrisson de la mère divine,
Par pitié, laissez-moi monter sur vos genoux,
Moi pauvre jeune fille, isolée, orpheline,
Qui n'ai d'espoir qu'en Dieu, qui n'ai d'espoir qu'en vous!

PRAYER

Beneath your guardian-angel wing I pray
You keep me safe, with mother's hand extending,
Guiding my steps as I wend on life's way,
And my small hand in yours, as you smile, bending

Over me... For, sweet master Jesus—he
Of fatherhood's most heavenly tendernesses—
Suffered the little ones, indulgently,
Before him; bore their sport and their caresses...

O you, image of those church paintings, where
Charity, most august, on field of gold,
Spreads warm her robe for children fresh and fair,
Protecting them from hunger, wind, and cold;

Pray, like the infant of the holy mother,
Let me come nestle on your lap, me too,
Poor orphan maid, alone, who have no other
Reasons to hope, save God above, and you!

A UNE JEUNE ITALIENNE

Février grelottait blanc de givre et de neige;
La pluie, à flots soudains, fouettait l'angle des toits;
Et déjà tu disais : « O mon Dieu! quand pourrai-je
Aller cueillir enfin la violette au bois? »

Notre ciel est pleureur, et le printemps de France,
Frileux comme l'hiver, s'assied près des tisons;
Paris est dans la boue au beau mois où Florence
Egrène ses trésors sous l'émail des gazons.

Vois! les arbres noircis contournent leurs squelettes;
Ton âme s'est trompée à sa douce chaleur :
Tes yeux bleus sont encor les seules violettes,
Et le printemps ne rit que sur ta joue en fleur!

    1843

FOR AN ITALIAN MISS

White February shook with frost and snow;
Rain's sudden floods whipped at the corners of
The roofs... You asked: "Good God, when shall I go,
At last, pick violets in the woods?" Above,

Our sky weeps, yes; but here in France the spring
Shivers like winter huddled round hot embers...
Paris is muck, whilst Florence tells her string
Of treasure-beads, enameled lawns, remembers,

Recounts them... Look! Black bones of writhing trees...
Your soul's sweet warmth mistakes the season's power.
Your eyes of blue: the only violets these,
And spring laughs only on your cheek in flower!

1843

DANS UN BAISER, L'ONDE AU RIVAGE...

Dans un baiser, l'onde au rivage
    Dit ses douleurs;
Pour consoler la fleur sauvage
    L'aube a des pleurs;
Le vent du soir conte sa plainte
    Au vieux cyprès,
La tourterelle au térébinthe
    Ses longs regrets.

Aux flots dormants, quand tout repose,
    Hors la douleur,
La lune parle, et dit la cause
    De sa pâleur.
Ton dôme blanc, Sainte-Sophie,
    Parle au ciel bleu,
Et, tout rêveur, le ciel confie
    Son rêve à Dieu.

Arbre ou tombeau, colombe ou rose,
    Onde ou rocher,
Tout, ici-bas, a quelque chose
    Pour s'épancher...
Moi, je suis seule, et rien au monde
    Ne me répond,
Rien que ta voix morne et profonde,
    Sombre Hellespont!

1845

KISSING THE SHORE, THE SUFFERING SEA...

Kissing the shore, the suffering sea
    Recounts its pain;
Dawn soothes the wild flowers tenderly
    With weeping rain;
The aged cypress hears the woe
    Of evening breeze;
The turtledove moans long and low
    To resin trees.

When all save pain at rest remains,
    The moon makes free
And to the dozing waves explains
    Why pale is she.
Your dome, Santa Sophia, gleams[4]
    Beneath blue sky;
And sky, in turn, reveals its dreams
    To God on high.

Here below, trees, graves, cliffs and tides,
    Roses and doves...
To something everything confides
    Its woes, its loves.
But naught before my lonely eyes
    Echoes my wants:
Only your deep, drear voice replies—
    The Hellespont's!

1845

SULTAN MAHMOUD

Dans mon harem se groupe,
    Comme un bouquet
Débordant d'une coupe
    Sur un banquet,
Tout ce que cherche ou rêve,
    D'opium usé,
Et son ennui sans trêve,
    Un cœur blasé;

Mais tous ces corps sans âmes
    Plaisent un jour...
Hélas! j'ai six cents femmes,
    Et pas d'amour!

✳

La biche et l'antilope,
    J'ai tout ici,
Asie, Afrique, Europe,
    En raccourci;
Teint vermeil, teint d'orange,
    Œil noir ou bleu,
Le charmant et l'étrange,
    De tout un peu;

SULTAN MAHMOUD

About my harem spread
    Like a bouquet...
Opium-surfeited,
    Man's heart blasé
Finds full to overflowing
    The cup that he
Seeks for his ever-growing
    Endless ennui.

These soulless bodies! Fie!
    One day's joy! One!
Six hundred wives have I...
    But love? Nay, none!

✲

Here, earth's munificence—
    Brown, blackamoor:
Fruit of the continents
    In miniature...
Antelope, doe... Eyes blue,
    Eyes black... The fair,
The odd... The bronze of hue,
    The ruddy, rare.

Mais tous ces corps sans âmes
    Plaisent un jour...
Hélas! j'ai six cents femmes,
    Et pas d'amour!

✳

Ni la vierge de Grèce,
    Marbre vivant;
Ni la fauve négresse,
    Toujours rêvant;
Ni la vive Française,
    A l'air vainqueur;
Ni la plaintive Anglaise,
    N'ont pris mon cœur!

Tous ces beaux corps sans âmes
    Plaisent un jour...
Hélas! j'ai six cents femmes,
    Et pas d'amour!

1845

These soulless bodies! Fie!
    One day's joy! One!
Six hundred wives have I...
    But love? Nay, none!

✱

Nor Grecian virgin, nay—
    Life marble-wrought;
Nor black, alackaday,
    Bowed deep in thought;
Nor haughty French "mam'zelle."
    Proud, set apart;
Nor plaintive English belle...
    None moves my heart!

Fair, soulless flesh! Oh, fie!
    One day's joy! One!
Six hundred wives have I...
    But love? Nay, none!

1845

A TRAVERS LA FORET DE FOLLES ARABESQUES...

A travers la forêt de folles arabesques
Que le doigt du sommeil trace au mur de mes nuits,
Je vis, comme l'on voit les Fortunes des fresques,
Un jeune homme penché sur la bouche d'un puits.

Il jetait, par grands tas, dans cette gueule noire
Perles et diamants, rubis et sequins d'or,
Pour faire arriver l'eau jusqu'à sa lèvre, et boire;
Mais le flot flagellé ne montait pas encor.

Hélas! que d'imprudents s'en vont aux puits sans corde,
Sans urne pour puiser le cristal souterrain,
Enfouir leur trésor afin que l'eau déborde,
Comme fit le corbeau dans le vase d'airain!

Hélas! et qui n'a pas, épris de quelque femme,
Pour faire monter l'eau du divin sentiment,
Jeté l'or de son cœur au puits sans fond d'une âme,
Sur l'abîme muet penché stupidement!

1840

MID THE WILD-GROWING FOREST FILIGREE...

Mid the wild-growing forest filigree
Traced by night's finger on my walls of sleep,
I saw—as one might Fortune's frescoes see—
A young man bending on a well dug deep.

Diamonds, pearls, rubies, golden coins he flails
Into the water, thinks to make it rise
High from that black pit's throat, to drink... He fails:
No drop he sips, however hard he tries.

Many there are—poor fools!—who, bucket-less,
Rope-less, cast wealth in wells hoping to bring
Their crystal to the surface, but who guess
Amiss... Unlike the crow who thought to fling

Pebbles down a brass vase! For who has not,[5]
Loving a lass, flung his heart's wealth, like this,
But raised her soul's divine love not a jot,
Foolishly bent over the mute abyss!

1840

L'ESCLAVE

Captive et peut-être oubliée,
Je songe à mes jeunes amours,
        A mes beaux jours,
Et par la fenêtre grillée
Je regarde l'oiseau joyeux
        Fendant les cieux.

Douce et pâle consolatrice,
Espérance, rayon d'en haut,
        Dans mon cachot
Fais-moi, sous ta clarté propice,
A ton miroir faux et charmant
        Voir mon amant!

Auprès de lui, belle Espérance,
Porte-moi sur tes ailes d'or,
        S'il m'aime encor,
Et, pour endormir ma souffrance,
Suspends mon âme sur son cœur
        Comme une fleur!

1840

THE SLAVE

Captive, perhaps forgotten too,
I muse on my lost loves, and on
    Youth's joys now gone,
As, by the window, gazing through
The bars, the joyous bird I spy
    Cleaving the sky.

Hope—gentle, pale, consoling balm—
Come, cast into this cell of mine
    Your ray divine;
Grant me the vision, clear and calm,
Of lover mine in your fair glass,
    Though false, alas!

I pray, dear Hope, on golden wing,
You bear me to his side, if he
    Yearns yet for me;
And there, to soothe my suffering,
Flower-like, hang my soul, apart,
    Upon his heart!

1840

FROM "POESIES DIVERSES," PUBLISHED

WITH *LA COMEDIE DE LA MORT*

1833 – 1838

TOMBEE DU JOUR

Le jour tombait, une pâle nuée
Du haut du ciel laissait nonchalamment,
Dans l'eau du fleuve à peine remuée,
Tremper les plis de son blanc vêtement.

La nuit parut, la nuit morne et sereine,
Portant le deuil de son frère le jour,
Et chaque étoile à son trône de reine,
En habits d'or s'en vint faire sa cour.

On entendait pleurer les tourterelles,
Et les enfants rêver dans leurs berceaux;
C'était dans l'air comme un frôlement d'ailes,
Comme le bruit d'invisibles oiseaux.

Le ciel parlait à voix basse à la terre;
Comme au vieux temps ils parlaient en hébreu.
Et répétaient un acte du mystère;
Je n'y compris qu'un seul mot : c'était Dieu.

1834

DAY'S END

The day was ending and a pallid cloud
From heaven's height, in leisured languidness,
Barely stirring the stream below, allowed
To dip therein the folds of her white dress.

Night appeared, night serenely somber, sad,
Decked out in mourning for her brother, day;
And each star came to court her, golden-clad,
Glowing before her throne's queenly array.

Turtledoves wept, and one could hear the sound
Of children dreaming in their cradles there:
The hum of rustling wings, spreading all round,
Like birds unseen, but fluttering in the air.

Sky and earth whispered each to each, hushed low—
In Hebrew, as in olden times… I heard
Their ancient mystery repeated, though
Only one word I knew: "God" was that word…

1834

LA DERNIERE FEUILLE

Dans la forêt chauve et rouillée
Il ne reste plus au rameau
Qu'une pauvre feuille oubliée,
Rien qu'une feuille et qu'un oiseau.

Il ne reste plus dans mon âme
Qu'un seul amour pour y chanter,
Mais le vent d'automne qui brame
Ne permet pas de l'écouter;

L'oiseau s'en va, la feuille tombe,
L'amour s'éteint, car c'est l'hiver.
Petit oiseau, viens sur ma tombe
Chanter, quand l'arbre sera vert!

1837

THE LAST LEAF

In the wood, balding, hued with rust,
There clings to branch's nakedness
One poor lone leaf, forgotten... Just
One, and one bird, alone no less.

In my soul clings one love as well—
Only one, with its song to sing;
But autumn's winds and gales—a-swell,
A-howl—allow no listening.

Off flies the bird, the leaf goes falling.
Love's flame fades, dying winterly...
You, little bird, pray heed my calling:
Sing on my grave when green the tree![1]

1837

LE SPECTRE DE LA ROSE

Soulève ta paupière close
Qu'effleure un songe virginal;
Je suis le spectre d'une rose
Que tu portais hier au bal.
Tu me pris encore emperlée
Des pleurs d'argent de l'arrosoir,
Et parmi la fête étoilée
Tu me promenas tout le soir.

O toi qui de ma mort fus cause,
Sans que tu puisses le chasser,
Toutes les nuits mon spectre rose
A ton chevet viendra danser.
Mais ne crains rien, je ne réclame
Ni messe ni *De profundis*;
Ce léger parfum est mon âme,
Et j'arrive du paradis.

Mon destin fut digne d'envie :
Pour avoir un trépas si beau,
Plus d'un aurait donné sa vie,
Car j'ai ta gorge pour tombeau.
Et sur l'albâtre où je repose
Un poète avec un baiser
Ecrivit : Ci-gît une rose
Que tous les rois vont jalouser.

THE SPECTRE OF THE ROSE

Flutter awake your lid, a-doze,
By virgin dream grazed, soft and light.
I am the spectre of the rose
That you wore at the ball last night.
You took me, silver tear-dropped yet
With pearls fresh-sprinkled tenderly;
And all through the star-twinkling fête
I sported you about with me.

You, friend, source of my death, my woes,
Cannot sweep it away; instead,
All the night through, my spectral rose
Will come dance roundabout your head.
Fear not. I seek no mass, no psalm—
No *De profundis.* Here come I,
Wafting my soul, faint-perfumed balm,
From my home, paradise on high.

Greatly my fate was coveted:
To have so fair a deathly doom,
Many would gladly have lain dead,
For your fair bosom is my tomb;
A poet kissed this grave I chose—
This alabaster loveliness—
And then he wrote: "Here lies a rose
That every king would fain possess."

L'HIPPOPOTAME

L'hippopotame au large ventre
Habite aux Jungles de Java,
Où grondent, au fond de chaque antre,
Plus de monstres qu'on n'en rêva.

Le boa se déroule et siffle,
Le tigre fait son hurlement,
Le buffle en colère renifle,
Lui dort ou paît tranquillement.

Il ne craint ni kriss ni zagaies,
Il regarde l'homme sans fuir,
Et rit des balles des cipayes
Qui rebondissent sur son cuir.

Je suis comme l'hippopotame :
De ma conviction couvert,
Forte armure que rien n'entame,
Je vais sans peur par le désert.

THE HIPPOPOTAMUS

Javanese jungle-denizen,
Big-bellied hippopotamus
Snuffles from deep within his den
Mid monsters, some undreamt by us.

While boa coiled uncoils, a-hiss,
And tiger roars, fierce as you please,
And buffalo snorts wildly, this
Creature sleeps, pastures, takes his ease.

He fears nor kris, nor javelin,[2]
Defies man, staunch and scornful-eyed;
The Sepoy's bullets graze his skin,
Glance harmless from his leather hide.

Like hippopotamus am I,
Protected by my moral stand—
Armor whence blows fall all awry;
Fearless, I roam the desert sand.

FROM *PREMIERES POESIES*

1830 – 1845

MEDITATION

> ...Ce monde où les meilleures choses
> Ont le pire destin.
>
> —Malherbe

Virginité du cœur, hélas! si tôt ravie!
Songes riants, projets de bonheur et d'amour,
Fraîches illusions du matin de la vie,
Pourquoi ne pas durer jusqu'à la fin du jour?

Pourquoi?... Ne voit-on pas qu'à midi la rosée
De ses larmes d'argent n'enrichit plus les fleurs,
Que l'anémone frêle, au vent froid exposée,
Avant le soir n'a plus ses brillantes couleurs?

Ne voit-on pas qu'une onde, à sa source limpide,
En passant par la fange y perd sa pureté;
Que d'un ciel d'abord pur un nuage rapide
Bientôt ternit l'éclat et la sérénité?

Le monde est fait ainsi : loi suprême et funeste!
Comme l'ombre d'un songe au bout de peu d'instants,
Ce qui charme s'en va, ce qui fait peine reste :
La rose vit une heure et le cyprès cent ans.

MEDITATION

> ...This world, where the most lovely things
> Suffer the foulest fate.
>
> —Malherbe

Heart's virgin joy, ravished, alas, so soon!
Life's laughing-dawn illusions, swept away;
Purloined, its happiness, love's tender boon...
Why may they last not till the end of day?

Why? Do we not see that, come noon, no more
Are petals richly silvered by the dew's
Bright tears; that frail anemone, before
Night's fall, wind-blown, has lost her brilliant hues?

Do we not see that, limpid though the spring,
The billow, passing through the mire, must be
Befouled; that a pure cloud, swift-wandering,
Soon dulls sky's shine and its tranquility?

Life's morose law supreme! For so it goes.
Dream-shadows fade... Life's charm soon disappears,
Its woes remain: one brief hour lives the rose,
But death's dour cypress lasts a hundred years.

ELEGIE I

> Dame, d'amer déesse,
> Pour votre grâce avoir,
> Vous offre ma jeunesse,
> Mes biens et mon avoir.
> —A. Chartier

Nuit et jour, malgré moi, lorsque je suis loin d'elle,
A ma pensée ardente un souvenir fidèle
La ramène :—il me semble ouïr sa douce voix
Comme le chant lointain d'un oiseau; je la vois
Avec son collier d'or, avec sa robe blanche,
Et sa ceinture bleue, et la fraîche pervenche
De son chapeau de paille, et le sourire fin
Qui découvre ses dents de perle,—telle enfin
Que je la vis un soir dans ce bois de vieux ormes
Qui couvrent le chemin de leurs ombres difformes;
Et je l'aime d'amour profond : car ce n'est pas
Une femme au teint pâle et mesurant ses pas,
Au regard nuagé de langueur, une Anglaise
Morne comme le ciel de Londres, qui se plaise,
La tête sur sa main, à rêver longuement,
A lire Grandisson et Werther; non, vraiment;
Mais une belle enfant inconstante et frivole,
Qui ne rêve jamais; une brune créole
Aux grands sourcils arqués, aux longs yeux de velours
Dont les regards furtifs vous poursuivent toujours;

ELEGY I

> Goddess of love, in truth,
> Be your grace mine alone,
> I offer you my youth
> And everything I own.
> —A. Chartier

Day and night, when I wander far from her,
A faithful memory oft will bestir
My burning brain, despite myself, and bring
Her back... I seem to hear her sweet voice sing
Like distant bird; I see her white robe bound
About with sash of blue, a collar round
Her neck, in glistening gold; and her straw hat,
Topped with a periwinkle bloom... With that,
I see her smile, her teeth, pearls without flaw,
Gleaming between her lips, just as I saw
Her stand one night, back then, in forest realm's
Jagged and shapeless shadow that the elms
Cast on her path... I love her endlessly,
For no prim, mincing English miss is she,
Pallid and wan, like clouded London sky,
Head in her hands, with languor-shrouded eye,
And who will sit, dreaming her dream outspun,
Betwixt her Werther and her Grandison.[1]
No! Mine, a flighty, sweet young thing is, who
Dreams not; a Creole maiden brown, with two

A la taille élancée, à la gorge divine,
Que sous les plis du lin la volupté devine.

Great arching eyebrows, eyes of velvet, whose
Pupils stand bold; whose glance ever pursues
You furtively; waist slender, breasts' outline,
Bliss-guessed beneath her shift: bosom divine!

PAYSAGE

...omnia plenis
Rura natant fossis.
—P. Virgilus Maro

Pas une feuille qui bouge,
Pas un seul oiseau chantant;
Au bord de l'horizon rouge
Un éclair intermittent;

D'un côté, rares broussailles,
Sillons à demi noyés,
Pans grisâtres de murailles,
Saules noueux et ployés;

De l'autre, un champ que termine
Un large fossé plein d'eau,
Une vieille qui chemine
Avec un pesant fardeau,

Et puis la route qui plonge
Dans le flanc des coteaux bleus,
Et comme un ruban s'allonge
En minces plis onduleux.

LANDSCAPE

> Then the ditches overflow
> and all the fields are flooded.
> —P. Virgilus Maro

Leaves in utter stillness spread,
No birds' chirping melody;
Over the horizon red,
Lightning flashing fitfully.[2]

Here, scarce any brush at all;
Furrows stretching drenched, half-drowned;
Dull gray corners of a wall;
Willows gnarled, bent toward the ground;

There, a field; and, bordering,
Water-filled ditch… On the road,
An old woman, carrying,
As she lopes, a heavy load;

Then the road that plunges deep,
And in twisted pleatings lies
On blue hillock flanks, a-creep,
Undulating, ribbon-wise…

SERMENT

> ...L'on ne seust en nule terre
> Nul plus bel cors de fame querre.
> —*Roman de la Rose*

Par tes yeux si beaux sous les voiles
De leurs franges de longs cils noirs,
Soleils jumeaux, doubles étoiles,
D'un cœur ardent ardents miroirs;

Par ton front aux pâleurs d'albâtre,
Que couronnent des cheveux bruns,
Où l'haleine du vent folâtre
Parmi la soie et les parfums;

Par tes lèvres, fraîche églantine,
Grenade en fleur, riant corail
D'où sort une voix argentine
A travers la nacre et l'émail;

Par ton sein rétif qui s'agite
Et bat sa prison de satin,
Par ta main étroite et petite,
Par l'éclat vermeil de ton teint;

Par ton doux accent d'Espagnole,
Par l'aube de tes dix-sept ans,
Je t'aimerai, ma jeune folle,
Un peu plus que toujours,—longtemps!

OATH

> No woman's flesh one finds more fair
> Though one seek here, there, everywhere.
> —*Roman de la Rose*

By your eyes' twin stars, burning pair
Of suns veiled by a lovely lass's
Fringe of fine lashes—long, black, fair—
Glowing heart's glowing looking-glasses;[3]

By your brow, alabaster-pale,
Wreathed in brown hair, soft-tousled, whence
Mischievous wind wafts round its veil,
Blowing its silk and fragrant scents;

By your pearl lips, smooth, coral-smiling—
Dog-rose and pomegranate hue—
And that bright silvered voice beguiling,
Passing between, betwixt the two;

By your breast, pounding restively
Its satin prison, pent within;
By your hand, dainty as can be;
By the rose brilliance of your skin;

By your sweet Spanish accent, this
Morn of your years—plus three: a score...
I pledge my love, my madcap miss,
Long, long... Forever? Yes... And more.

LA JEUNE FILLE

La vierge est un ange d'amour.
—A. Guiraud

Dieu l'a faite une heureuse et belle créature.
—Inédit. M*****

Brune à la taille svelte, aux grands yeux noirs, brillants,
A la lèvre rieuse, aux gestes sémillants,
Blonde aux yeux bleus rêveurs, à la peau rose et blanche,
La jeune fille plaît : ou réservée ou franche,
Mélancolique ou gaie, il n'importe; le don
De charmer est le sien, autant par l'abandon
Que par la retenue; en Occident, Sylphide,
En Orient, Péri, vertueuse, perfide,
Sous l'arcade moresque en face d'un ciel bleu,
Sous l'ogive gothique assise auprès du feu,
Ou qui chante, ou qui file, elle plaît; nos pensées
Et nos heures, pourtant si vite dépensées,
Sont pour elle. Jamais, imprégné de fraîcheur,
Sur nos yeux endormis un rêve de bonheur
Ne passe fugitif, comme l'ombre du cygne
Sur le miroir des lacs, qu'elle n'en soit, d'un signe
Nous appelant vers elle, et murmurant des mots
Magiques, dont un seul enchante tous nos maux.
Eveillés, sa gaîté dissipe nos alarmes,
Et lorsque la douleur nous arrache des larmes,
Son baiser à l'instant les tarit dans nos yeux.

MAIDEN FAIR

> Angel of love is virgin maid.
> —A. Guiraud

> God made of her a happy creature fair.
> —M*****, unpublished

Brunette, svelte-waisted, with great black eyes gleaming,
Laughing lips, twinkling hands; or blonde, with dreaming
Eyes of blue, pink-white skin... All the same... Be
She poised, sedate, or full of levity,
Of melancholic mood or joyful bent,
Maiden fair pleases! Hers, the temperament
That charms, entices, whether she give way
To gay abandon, or pose calm, soigné;
Occident's Sylphe or Oriental Peri:[4]
Soul pure or filled with guile; beneath a dreary,
Old, pointed Gothic vault of stone, before
The fire, sitting and spinning, singing; or
In Moorish-style arcade, beneath a sky
Of blue... It matters not; for, by and by,
Our thoughts will ever fly to her; and all
Our moments, swiftly flown, lie in her thrall,
Are hers alone. And if, aloft, there flies
A dream steeped in young joy, grazing our eyes,
Lying in sleep—like shadow of a swan
That, winging past, goes gliding free upon
The mirrored lakes—ever it beckons us,

La jeune fille!—elle est un souvenir des cieux,
Au tissu de la vie une fleur d'or brodée,
Un rayon de soleil qui sourit dans l'ondée!

Calls us to join her with miraculous,
Magic words, murmured... Lo! Just one can be
All our woes' cure, so sure its sorcery!
Her gayety dispels our wakened fears.
And when our pain wrenches from us our tears
Untold, it is her gentle kiss that dries
Them straightaway, and wipes them from our eyes.
Maiden fair! Life's gold-flower embroidery,
Heaven-wrought sunbeam smiling in the sea!

LE LUXEMBOURG

> Enfant, dans les ébats de l'enfance joueuse...
> —J. Delorme

Au Luxembourg souvent, lorsque dans les allées
Gazouillaient des moineaux les joyeuses volées,
Qu'aux baisers d'un vent doux, sous les abîmes bleus
D'un ciel tiède et riant, les orangers frileux
Hasardaient leurs rameaux parfumés, et qu'en gerbes
Les fleurs pendaient du front des marronniers superbes,
Toute petite fille, elle allait du beau temps
A son aise jouir et folâtrer longtemps,
Longtemps, car elle aimait à l'ombre des feuillages
Fouler le sable d'or, chercher des coquillages,
Admirer du jet d'eau l'arc au reflet changeant
Et le poisson de pourpre, hôte d'une eau d'argent;
Ou bien encor partir, folle et légère tête,
Et, trompant les regards de sa mère inquiète,
Au risque de brunir un teint frais et vermeil,
Livrer sa joue en fleur aux baisers du soleil!

THE LUXEMBOURG

> Child, in the happy games of childhood's joy...
> —J. Delorme

Often, when, in the Luxembourg's expanse,
Sparrows would warble their exuberance
In joyous flight; and when the orange trees—
Still chill, despite the tender-kissing breeze
Over a laughing, warming sun's deep blue
Abyss—risked fragrant boughs in gentle to
And fro... And when the chestnuts, oh so proud
To hang their flower bouquets, stood haughty-browed,
She—little tot—would frolic in the sun,[5]
Long, long... For it was oh such pleasant fun,
There in the leafy shade, to tread the park's
Gold sands in search of shells; to watch the arc's
Changing reflections as the jet shot free,
And, in the silver pool, watch lovingly
The crimsoned fish at play... Or, naughty child,
Scamper away, as mother stands beguiled,
Fearing the tot's fresh blush go all amiss,
Bloom-bereft, tanned by many a sunshine kiss!

LE SENTIER

> En une sente me vins rendre
> Longue et estroite, où l'herbe tendre
> Croissait très drue.
> —*Le Livre des quatre Dames*

> Un petit sentier vert, je le pris...
> —Alfred de Musset

Il est un sentier creux dans la vallée étroite,
Qui ne sait trop s'il marche à gauche ou bien à droite.
—C'est plaisir d'y passer, lorsque Mai sur ses bords,
Comme un jeune prodigue, égrène ses trésors;
L'aubépine fleurit; les frêles pâquerettes,
Pour fêter le printemps, ont mis leurs collerettes.
La pâle violette, en son réduit obscur,
Timide, essaie au jour son doux regard d'azur,
Et le gai bouton d'or, lumineuse parcelle,
Pique le gazon vert de sa jaune étincelle.
Le muguet, tout joyeux, agite ses grelots,
Et les sureaux sont blancs de bouquets frais éclos;
Les fossés ont des fleurs à remplir vingt corbeilles,
A rendre riche en miel tout un peuple d'abeilles.
Sous la haie embaumée un mince filet d'eau
Jase et fait frissonner le verdoyant rideau
Du cresson.—Ce sentier, tel qu'il est, moi je l'aime
Plus que tous les sentiers où se trouvent de même
Une source, une haie et des fleurs; car c'est lui,
Qui, lorsque au ciel laiteux la lune pâle a lui,

THE LANE

> The grass was growing thick upon
> A lane I chanced to happen on,
> Narrow and long.
> > —*The Book of the Four Ladies*
>
> I took a path, a little green-grown lane...
> > —Alfred de Musset

A sunken lane winds through the valley, quite
Unsure whether it ambles left or right.
—A joy it is to walk its length, when May—
Young spendthrift—casts his treasured wealth away,
Thither and yon... The hawthorn blooms; the frail
Daisies, that donned their collars fine to hail
The spring and celebrate its coming; shy,
The violet—timid, pale—stands meekly by
In shaded corner, yet will try, anon,
To work its azure charms gently upon
The day... The golden bud lights up the scene,
Pricking bright yellow sparks on grassy green.
The lilies of the valley shake their tinkling
Little bells; and the elders spread their sprinkling
Of fresh white blooms; the ditches overflow
With buds to fill a score of baskets! Lo!
Enough to make a swarm of honeybees
Grow rich in nectar... And, midst all of these
Pleasuredoms' treasure troves, within
The fragrant hedges' modest reach, a thin,

A la brèche du mur, rendez-vous solitaire
Où l'amour s'embellit des charmes du mystère,
Sous les grands châtaigniers aux bercements plaintifs,
Sans les tromper jamais, conduit mes pas furtifs.

Muttering trickle, and a quivering veil
Of watercress, deep green… I never fail
To love this lane just as it stands: more yet
Than other paths with hedge, flowers, rivulet;
For here it is—when, in the milky sky,
The pallid moon has shone—that, by the by,
Through a breach in the wall. I keep
My tryst with this place, where the landscape's deep,
Mysterious charm beautifies love, and which
Draws me stealthily to this lonely niche—
Never unfaithful to love's mysteries—
Beneath the swaying, sighing chestnut trees.

CAUCHEMAR

> Bizoy quen ne consquaff a maru garu ne marnaff.
> Jamais je ne dors que je ne meurs de mort amère.
> —Ancien proverbe breton

Les goules de l'abyme,
Attendant leur victime,
        Ont faim :
Leur ongle ardent s'allonge,
Leur dent en espoir ronge
        Ton sein.

Avec ses nerfs rompus, une main écorchée,
Qui marche sans le corps dont elle est arrachée,
Crispe ses doigts crochus armés d'ongles de fer
Pour me saisir; des feux pareils aux feux d'enfer
Se croisent devant moi; dans l'ombre, des yeux fauves
Rayonnent; des vautours, à cous rouges et chauves,
Battent mon front de l'aile en poussant des cris sourds;
En vain pour me sauver je lève mes pieds lourds,
Des flots de plomb fondu subitement les baignent,
A des pointes d'acier ils se heurtent et saignent,
Meurtris et disloqués; et mon dos cependant,
Ruisselant de sueur, frissonne au souffle ardent
De naseaux enflammés, de gueules haletantes :
Les voilà, les voilà! dans mes chairs palpitantes
Je sens des becs d'oiseaux avides se plonger,
Fouiller profondément, jusqu'aux os me ronger,
Et puis des dents de loups et de serpents qui mordent

NIGHTMARE

Bizoy quen ne consquaff a maru garu ne marnaff.
Never I sleep but that I die a bitter death.
—Old Breton proverb

Chasm-ghouls wend their way,
And, famished, stalk their prey,
Obsessed:
They reach with yearning claw
As, hopeful, their teeth gnaw
Your breast.

A hand scuttles in bodiless parade,
Torn from its former flesh, skin raw and flayed,
Nerves rent, its fingers, iron-nailed, claw-bent
To seize me; to my awed bewilderment,
Flames like the fires of hell flare, zigzagging
Before my gaze; beast-eyes emblazoning,
Flash in the shadows; vultures—reddish-necked
And bald—grunt, lash my brow... I would protect
Myself, flee, lift my heavy feet... In vain!
Suddenly, floods of molten lead splash, rain
Upon them as, bloodied and bruised, they fall
To bits, against steel spikes; my back, withal,
Sweat dripping, shudders in the moon-bathed huff
Of fire-exhaling nostrils, throats a-puff
With smoke... Here they come! Here they come! I sense
Vast beaks lunge, bent on foul malevolence,
And plumbing to the bone my quivering flesh...

Comme une scie aiguë, et des pinces qui tordent;
Ensuite le sol manque à mes pas chancelants :
Un gouffre me reçoit; sur des rochers brûlants,
Sur des pics anguleux que la lune reflète,
Tremblant, je roule, roule, et j'arrive squelette.
Dans un marais de sang; bientôt, spectres hideux,
Des morts au teint bleuâtre en sortent deux à deux,
Et, se penchant vers moi, m'apprennent les mystères
Que le trépas révèle aux pâles feudataires
De son empire; alors, étrange enchantement,
Ce qui fut moi s'envole, et passe lentement
A travers un brouillard couvrant les flèches grêles
D'une église gothique aux moresques dentelles.
Déchirant une proie enlevée au tombeau,
En me voyant venir, tout joyeux, un corbeau
Croasse, et, s'envolant aux steppes de l'Ukraine,
Par un pouvoir magique à sa suite m'entraîne,
Et j'aperçois bientôt, non loin d'un vieux manoir,
A l'angle d'un taillis, surgir un gibet noir
Soutenant un pendu; d'effroyables sorcières
Dansent autour, et moi, de fureurs carnassières
Agité, je ressens un immense désir
De broyer sous mes dents sa chair, et de saisir,

Then wolves and serpents ravage me afresh,
Biting with saw-sharp teeth, ripping asunder
My limbs in savage wise... All at once, under
My faltering feet, the earth yawns, opens wide
A deep abyss, sucking me in... Inside,
I tumble headlong, down... down... over burning,
Craggy peaks, moon-bathed cliffs, till, twisting, turning,
Plunging, I fall—mere bones!—into a pool
Of gore and blood... Soon, many a hideous ghoul—
Spectral cadaver-pairs, pale-skinned—rise, hand
In hand, lean over me... Their ghastly band
Would teach me all Death's mysteries, that he
Reveals to his drear vassals... Presently,
By some spell, some enchantment, what had been
Myself, rises aloft, flies from within
The chasm, passes slowly, higher, higher,
Through a mist cloaking every slender spire
Of a church, Gothic, decked in Moorish lace...
A crow, his meal clutched in his maw's embrace,
Tears at his prey, filched from a tomb; and, when
He spies me, joyously this denizen
Of gloom goes winging off to the Ukraine's
Dismal steppes, and, by some legerdemain's
Magical powers, he deigns to drag me there
As well... Soon I see, dangling in mid-air—
Hard by an old chateau, its hedgerow jutting
Sidewise—rising high, a black gibbet cutting
Its silhouette; and, from a noose there hangs

Avec quelque lambeau de sa peau bleue et verte,
Son cœur demi-pourri dans sa poitrine ouverte.

A corpse, while gruesome witches dance... My fangs,
In frenzy, thirst to crush his flesh between
My jaws, to shred his skin, sallow blue-green,
In feverish ecstasy; to rip apart
His gaping breast and seize his rotting heart...

PROMENADE NOCTURNE

> Allons, la belle nuit d'été.
> —Alfred de Musset

> C'était par un beau soir, par un des soirs que rêve
> Au murmure lointain d'un invisible accord
> Le poète qui veille ou l'amante qui dort.
> —Victor Pavie

La rosée arrondie en perles
Scintille aux pointes du gazon;
Les chardonnerets et les merles
Chantent à l'envi leur chanson;

Les fleurs de leurs paillettes blanches
Brodent le bord vert du chemin;
Un vent léger courbe les branches
Du chèvrefeuille et du jasmin;

Et la lune, vaisseau d'agate,
Sur les vagues des rochers bleus
S'avance comme la frégate
Au dos de l'Océan houleux.

Jamais la nuit de plus d'étoiles
N'a semé son manteau d'azur,
Ni, du doigt entr'ouvrant ses voiles,
Mieux fait voir Dieu dans le ciel pur.

NIGHT STROLL

> Ah! What a lovely summer night.
> —Alfred de Musset

> One lovely night, when sleepless poet dreams
> To sounds of distant murmur's chord unseen,
> Or mistress dreaming in her sleep serene.
> —Victor Pavie

Dew drops, as round as pearls, I see
Twinkling the ground's grass firmament,
As wrens and blackbirds joyously
Sing their songs to their hearts' content;

White sequin-flower embroideries
Edge the green path in brisk array;
Their boughs bent lightly in the breeze,
Jasmine and woodbine gently sway.

And the moon—agate vessel—plies
Her course on rock-blue waves; and she—
Frigate-like, as they fall and rise—
Lights her way on the rolling sea.

Night's azure cloak was never sown
With more stars strewn than here it is;
Nor—veils drawn—has it better shown
God in that flawless sky of his.

Prends mon bras, ô ma bien-aimée,
Et nous irons, à deux, jouir
De la solitude embaumée,
Et, couchés sur la mousse, ouïr

Ce que tout bas, dans la ravine
Où brillent ses moites réseaux,
En babillant, l'eau qui chemine
Conte à l'oreille des roseaux.

Arm in arm, then, shall you and I
Go off, O mistress mine, from here,
In balm-spread solitude to lie
Upon the moss, there to give ear

To brooklet's babble as it proceeds
Through the vale's tangle, moist-aglow:
Things that the water tells the reeds
In secret, as it whispers low...

SONNET II

> Amour tant vous hai servit
> Senz pecas et senz failhimen,
> Et vous sabez quant petit
> Hai avut de jauzimen.
> —Peyrols

> Ne sais-tu pas que je n'eus onc
> D'elle plaisir ni un seul bien?
> —Marot

Ne vous détournez pas, car ce n'est point d'amour
Que je veux vous parler; que le passé, madame,
Soit pour nous comme un songe envolé sans retour,
Oubliez une erreur que moi-même je blâme.

Mais vous êtes si belle, et sous le fin contour
De vos sourcils arqués luit un regard de flamme
Si perçant, qu'on ne peut vous avoir vue un jour
Sans porter à jamais votre image en son âme.

Moi, mes traits soucieux sont couverts de pâleur :
Car, dès mes premiers ans souffrant et solitaire,
Dans mon cœur je nourris une pensée austère,

Et mon front avant l'âge a perdu cette fleur
Qui s'entr'ouvre vermeille au printemps de la vie,
Et qui ne revient plus alors qu'elle est ravie.

SONNET II

> So well have I served you, Love
> Without reproach and faithfully,
>   And you know how slight thereof
> The joys you have bestowed on me.
>   —Peyrols
>
> Know you not that I never had
> Even the merest boon from her?
>   —Marot

Turn not your head aside, madame, I pray.
I would not speak of love; the past is past;
May it be like a fleeting dream; so lay
No blame on me for wrongs I rue, aghast.

Let man gaze on your beauty but one day:
Beneath your eyebrows' arch your glance will cast
A flame so piercing sharp that never may
Your image quit his soul, held ever fast.

As for me, dour my features' pallid gloom;[6]
For, from my earliest years—alone, distraught,
In pain—my heart harbors a single thought,

And my brow, age-unbowed, has lost the bloom
That, scarlet, spreads its petals in life's spring,
With no return beyond its vanishing.

L'OISEAU CAPTIF

> Car quand il pleut et le soleil des cieux
> Ne reluit point, tout homme est soucieux.
> —Clément Marot

> . . . yet shall reascend
> Self raised, and repossess its native seat.
> —Lord Byron

Depuis de si longs jours prisonnier, tu t'ennuies,
Pauvre oiseau, de ne voir qu'intarissables pluies
De filets gris rayant un ciel noir et brumeux,
Que toits aigus baignés de nuages fumeux.
Aux gémissements sourds du vent d'hiver qui passe
Promenant la tourmente au milieu de l'espace,
Tu n'oses plus chanter; mais vienne le printemps
Avec son soleil d'or aux rayons éclatants,
Qui d'un regard bleuit l'émail du ciel limpide,
Ramène d'outre-mer l'hirondelle rapide
Et jette sur les bois son manteau velouté,
Alors tu reprendras ta voix et ta gaîté;
Et si, toujours constant à ta douleur austère,
Tu regrettais encor la forêt solitaire,
L'orme du grand chemin, le rocher, le buisson,
La campagne que dore une jaune moisson,
La rivière, le lac aux ondes transparentes,
Que plissent en passant les brises odorantes,
Je t'abandonnerais à ton joyeux essor.
Tous les deux cependant nous avons même sort,

THE CAPTIVE BIRD

> For, when it rains, and when the heavens' sun
> Fails to shine, then morose is everyone.
> —Clément Marot

> . . . yet shall reascend
> Self raised, and repossess its native seat.
> —Lord Byron

Poor bird, so long you languish, prisoner pent,
Day upon endless day, in anguish spent,
Watching the ceaseless rains streaking the sky's
Dark fog with gray, on gabled roofs that rise,
Pointed, through smoke clouds... Now, no more you dare
Sing in the morning wind that fills the air
With squall and storm. But, come the sun-borne spring—
Bursting with beams of gold, emblazoning—
Whose limpid look casts its unblemished blue
Over the heavens' pure enameled hue,
And summons back from far beyond the seas
The swift-winged swallow, and spreads on the trees,
In forest deep, its velvet cloak... Ah, then
Will you find that sweet voice of yours again,
And know once more your gay refrain. But, should
Your soul—still, sullen, pained—pine for the wood,
The stately elm, the cliff, the brooklet-glade,
The meadow with its harvest-tinted shade
Of gold, the lake's clear waters that the fair

Mon âme est comme toi : de sa cage mortelle
Elle s'ennuie, hélas! et souffre, et bat de l'aile;
Elle voudrait planer dans l'océan du ciel,
Ange elle-même, suivre un ange Ithuriel,
S'enivrer d'infini, d'amour et de lumière,
Et remonter enfin à la cause première.
Mais, grand Dieu! quelle main ouvrira sa prison,
Quelle main à son vol livrera l'horizon?

And fragrant breezes, gently passing there,
Waft into billows... Then would I, by right,
Let you go off, un-caged, in joyous flight.
Yet I, no less than you, suffer your very
Fate; for my soul, shut tight in solitary
And deathly cage, wings drooping, would be free
To soar the skies' ocean-immensity,
And rise, led by Ithuriel, no less[7]
Than he an angel, gorged on drunkenness
Of love, light, and the infinite's pure laws,
To stand at last before the Primal Cause.
But who, great God, will, from its prison-place,
Let my soul fly horizonward through space?

REVE

> Et nous voulons mourir quand le rêve finit.
> —A. Guiraud

> Toute la nuict je ne pense qu'en celle
> Qui ha le cors plus gent qu'une pucelle
> De quatorze ans.
> —Maître Clément Marot

Voici ce que j'ai vu naguère en mon sommeil :
Le couchant enflammait à l'horizon vermeil
Les carreaux de la ville; et moi, sous les arcades
D'un bois profond, au bruit du vent et des cascades,
Aux chansons des oiseaux, j'allais, foulant des fleurs
Qu'un arc-en-ciel teignait de changeantes couleurs.
Soudain des pas légers froissent l'herbe; une femme,
Que j'aime dès longtemps du profond de mon âme,
Comme une jeune fée accourt vers moi; ses yeux
A travers ses longs cils luisent de plus de feux
Que les astres du ciel; et sur la verte mousse
A mes lèvres d'amant livrant une main douce,
Elle rit, et bientôt enlacée à mes bras
Me dit, le front brûlant et rouge d'embarras,
Ce mot mystérieux qui jamais ne s'achève...
O nuit trompeuse! Hélas! pourquoi n'est-ce qu'un rêve?

DREAM

> And we would choose to die when done the dream.
> —A. Guiraud

> I muse all night upon the fairest belle,
> With body like a virgin demoiselle
> Of fourteen years.
> —Maître Clément Marot

Recently, in my sleep I saw, outspread,
The sunset flaming the horizon red,
Framing the city's windowpanes; and I—
In forest arbors, mid their sough and sigh,
And waterfall cascading free... I heard
The coos and chirping call of many a bird,
As I trod over flowers in bloom, and whose
Colors shone with the rainbow's changing hues.
All at once, footsteps graze the grass: I see
A woman I have loved passionately
Run to me with young fairy tread; her eyes
Dart more fire through long lashes than the skies'
Legions of stars... She lays a soft caress
Upon my lips, on the green moss... I press
Her, laughing, to my breast; and she laments,
With burning brow and modest reticence,
The ever-endless mystery: "Wherefore,
False night, is this a dream and nothing more?"

PENSEES D'AUTOMNE

> La rica autouna s'es passada
> L'hiver suz un cari tourat
> S'en ven la capa ementoulada
> D'un veû neblouz enjalibrat.
> —*Son autounous*

> J'entends siffler la bise aux branchages rouillés
> Des saules qui là-bas se balancent mouillés.
> —Auguste M.

L'automne va finir : au milieu du ciel terne,
Dans un cercle blafard et livide que cerne
Un nuage plombé, le soleil dort ; du fond
Des étangs remplis d'eau monte un brouillard qui fond
Collines, champs, hameaux dans une même teinte ;
Sur les carreaux la pluie en larges gouttes tinte ;
La froide bise siffle ; un sourd frémissement
Sort du sein des forêts ; les oiseaux tristement,
Mêlant leurs cris plaintifs aux cris des bêtes fauves,
Sautent de branche en branche à travers les bois chauves,
Et semblent aux beaux jours envolés dire adieu.
La pauvre paysan se recommande à Dieu,
Craignant un hiver rude ; et moi, dans les vallées
Quand je vois le gazon sous les blanches gelées
Disparaître et mourir, je reviens à pas lents
M'asseoir, le cœur navré, près des tisons brûlants,
Et là je me souviens du soleil de septembre
Qui donnait à la grappe un jaune reflet d'ambre,

AUTUMN THOUGHTS

The Autumn, richly hued, has fled.
In frigid tumbril, veiled and shrouded,
Winter draws round, hiding his head,
In the chill fog and mist beclouded.
—*Autumn Song*

I hear the whistling wind rustle the boughs
Of willows swaying low their dripping brows.
—Auguste M.

Autumn draws to a close: a dull sun lies
Sleeping amid the pallid, sallow sky's
Encircling leaden cloud; from deep within
The watery marsh, fog rises, cloaking in
One selfsame tint, hills, hamlets, fields; the rain's
Thick drops tinkle against the window panes;
The frigid north wind whistles; a faint groan
Sighs from the forest's shuddering breast; birds moan
Their low laments, that mingle with the cry
Of feral beasts, as, fluttering on high
From bough to leafless bough, they seem to tell
Fair day—now flown—one final, sad farewell.
The lowly peasant prays God grant His grace,
Fearing fell winter's chill; and, to this place
Come I, when, in the valley's deep, I see
Grass vanish, dead, frost-whitened... As for me,
With slow and measured pace I sit, heart-sore,
Before the burning embers, and, once more

Des pommiers du chemin pliant sous leur fardeau,
Et du trèfle fleuri, pittoresque rideau
S'étendant à longs plis sur la plaine rayée,
Et de la route étroite en son milieu frayée,
Et surtout des bleuets et des coquelicots,
Points de pourpre et d'azur dans l'or des blés égaux.

Remember the September sun , whose shine
Dappled an amber glow on grape and vine;
The apple-trees, beside the road, bent low
Beneath their load; the clovers, row by row,
Spread drape-like, picturesque; and the ill-mown,
Narrow path through the thickets, overgrown;
And poppies and cornflowers, most of all—
Crimsons and azures midst grains reaching tall...

INFIDELITE

> Bandiera d'ogni vento
> Conosco que sei tu.
> —Chanson italienne

> La volonté de l'ingrate est changée.
> —Antoine de Baïf

Voici l'orme qui balance
Son ombre sur le sentier;
Voici le jeune églantier,
Le bois où dort le silence,
Le banc de pierre où, le soir,
Nous aimions à nous asseoir.

Voici la voûte embaumée
D'ébéniers et de lilas,
Où, lorsque nous étions las,
Ensemble, ô ma bien-aimée!
Sous des guirlandes de fleurs,
Nous laissions fuir les chaleurs.

Voici le marais que ride
Le saut du poisson d'argent,
Dont la grenouille en nageant
Trouble le miroir humide;
Comme autrefois, les roseaux
Baignent leurs pieds dans ses eaux.

FALSEHEARTEDNESS

> O you, breeze-blown, and ever
> Faithless, but faithful never.
> —Italian song

> The faithless maiden's heart's desires have changed.
> —Antoine de Baïf

Here, the swaying elm, that sweeps
Now its shade over the lane;
Here, the young dog-rose again,
And the wood where silence sleeps,
And the bench of stone, where it
Pleasured us, by night, to sit.

Here, the fragrant arch, where twine
Lilacs round, and ebonies,
Where we rested by the trees—
You and I, O mistress mine!
Flower-garlanded retreat,
Refuge from the fleeting heat.

Here, the placid marsh, the bog's
Mirror-surface, wrinkling when
Silver fish leaps from the fen—
Waters churned up by the frogs;
And the rushes, by the shore,
Bathe their feet, just as before.

Comme autrefois, la pervenche,
Sur le velours vert des prés
Par le printemps diaprés,
Aux baisers du soleil penche
A moitié rempli de miel
Son calice bleu de ciel.

Comme autrefois, l'hirondelle
Rase, en passant, les donjons,
Et le cygne dans les joncs
Se joue et lustre son aile;
L'air est pur, le gazon doux...
Rien n'a donc changé que vous.

And, as then, on velvet greens
Of the meadow—mottle-hued,
Sun-kissed in most festive mood—
Periwinkle bows and preens,
Gently lading honey's dew
In its cup of heaven-blue.

And, as then, the flitterings
Of the swallow skim the towers;
And the swan passes the hours
In the reeds, smoothing his wings...
Soft grass, pure the air above...
Nothing changed... Save you, my love.

A MON AMI AUGUSTE M***

> For yonder faithless phantom flies
> To lure thee to thy doom.
> —Goldsmith

> C'est, dit-il, d'autant que j'ay veu plusieurs bouteilles qui
> avoient la robe toute neufve et le verre estoit cassé dedans;
> et plusieurs pommes desquelles l'écorce estoit vermeille et
> reluisante dont le dedans estoit mangé de vers et tout pourry.
> —*Le Vagabond*

Par une nuit d'été, quand le ciel est d'azur,
Souvent un feu follet sort du marais impur.
Le passant qui le voit le prend pour la lumière
Qui scintille aux carreaux lointains d'une chaumière;
Vers le fanal perfide il s'avance à grands pas,
Tout joyeux; et bientôt, ne s'apercevant pas
Qu'un abîme est ouvert à ses pieds, il y tombe,
Et son corps reste là sans prière et sans tombe.
Aux lieux où fut Gomorrhe autrefois, et que Dieu
En courroux inonda d'un déluge de feu,
Sur la grève brûlée, asile frais et sombre,
Des orangers touffus s'élèvent en grand nombre,
Chargés de fruits riants dont la tunique d'or
Ne livre que poussière à la dent qui les mord :
Dans ma pensée, ami, je trouve qu'une femme
Qui sous de beaux semblants cache une vilaine âme,

TO MY FRIEND AUGUSTE M***

> For yonder faithless phantom flies
> To lure thee to thy doom.
> —Goldsmith

> The fact is, he said, I have seen many a bottle with
> perfectly new wicker casings but whose glass inside was
> cracked, and many an apple whose peel was a shining
> scarlet but whose insides were worm-eaten and rotten.
> —*The Vagabond*

On summer nights, when azure-blue the sky
Above the swamp, it happens by and by
That, from the dank, murky morass, arises
Saint Elmo's fire... The passerby surmises
That it must be the sparkling window-glow
Of distant cottage, and off he will go
To join the faithless beacon, joyously
And swift of step... But never does he see
The chasm at his feet; down will he fall,
There to remain, unmourned, for good and all...
On the spot where Gomorrah stood, years past,
And where an angry God of vengeance cast
A flood of flame, now an oasis stands,
Shaded and cool amidst the once-fired sands;
And there, many an orange tree—their boughs
Heavy with smiling fruits, whose tunics rouse
Sweet lust for gold—yields naught but tasteless dust
To biting tooth... Alas, dear friend, I must

Pour ceux que sa beauté décevante a séduits,
Pareille au feu follet, l'est encore à ces fruits.

Confess that, to my mind, the woman whose
Beauty lures man who ardently pursues,
But beauty that hides crabbèd soul, dissembles,
And, mere will-o'-the-wisp, those fruits resembles.

SONNET III

> L'homme n'est rien qu'un mort qui traîne sa carcasse.
> —Du May

> Fronti nulla fides.

Quelquefois, au milieu de la folâtre orgie,
Lorsque son verre est plein, qu'une jeune beauté
Endort son désespoir amer par la magie
D'un regard enchanteur où luit la volupté,

L'âme du malheureux sort de sa léthargie;
Son front pâle retrouve un rayon de gaîté,
Sa prunelle mourante, un reste d'énergie;
Il sourit, oublieux de la réalité.

Mais toute cette joie est comme le lierre
Qui d'une vieille tour, guirlande irrégulière,
Embrasse en les cachant les pans démantelés;

Au dehors on ne voit que riante verdure,
Au dedans, que poussière infecte et noire ordure,
Et qu'ossements jaunis aux décombres mêlés.

SONNET III

> A corpse dragging his carcass: such is man.
> —Du May

> Fronti nulla fides.

At times, in orgiastic revelry
Gaily consumed, when full his glass, and when
A young belle, with voluptuous sorcery,
Stares at him with a gaze beyond his ken,

The wretch's soul casts off its lethargy;
His pale brow finds a ray of joy again;
His deathly eye, a remnant of esprit;
He smiles, forgets the world's dour regimen!

But all that joy is like the ivy vine,
Whose garlands, round an ancient tower, entwine
And hide its ruins' utter disrepair;

Without, one sees naught but the smiling green;
Within, the black remains of what had been:
Fetid bones, yellowed, midst the dust laid bare.

IMITATION DE BYRON

Il est doux de raser en gondole la vague
Des lagunes, le soir, au bord de l'horizon
Quand la lune élargit son disque pâle et vague,
Et que du marinier l'écho dit la chanson;

Il est doux d'observer l'étoile qui rayonne,
Paillette d'or cousue au dais du firmament,
L'étoile qu'une blanche auréole environne,
Et qui dans le ciel clair s'avance lentement;

Il est doux sur la brume un instant colorée
De voir, parmi la pluie, aux lueurs du soleil,
L'iris arrondissant son arche diaprée,
Présage heureux d'un jour plus pur et plus vermeil;

Il est doux, par les prés où l'abeille butine,
D'errer seul et pensif, et, sous les saules verts
Nonchalamment couché près d'une onde argentine,
De lire tour à tour des romans et des vers;

Il est doux, quand on suit une route inégale
Dans l'été, vers midi, chargé d'un lourd fardeau,
Et qu'on entend chanter près de soi la cigale,
De trouver un peu d'ombre avec un filet d'eau;

IMITATION OF BYRON

How sweet to skim the waves of the lagoon,
Gondola-swept, by night, devil-may-care,
Beneath the pale haze of the swelling moon,
As echoes croon the *gondoliere*'s air;

How sweet to watch that star's rays—darting beams—
Gold sequin-star sewn on sky's canopy;
Star haloed all in white, bright orb that seems
To tread the heavens slowly, steadily.

How sweet to see, one moment, through the dark
Rain-mist with starlight tinged, piercing its way,
The rainbow thrust its mottled, curving arc,
Omen of a more pure and radiant day;

How sweet, in meadows where bees filch their prize,
Gently to wander and, beneath green willows
Lying alone, nonchalant, pensive-wise,
Read novels, poems, by the silver billows.

How sweet—when one trudges with weighty load
On heat-drenched path, by summer noons beset,
Hearing cicadas chirping by the road—
To find a bit of shade, a rivulet...

Il est doux, en hiver, lorsque la froide pluie
Bat la vitre, d'avoir, auprès d'un feu flambant,
Un immense fauteuil gothique, où l'on appuie
Sa tête paresseuse en arrière tombant;

Il est doux de revoir avec ses tours minées
Par le temps, ses clochers et ses blanches maisons,
Ses toits rouges et bleus, ses hautes cheminées,
La ville où l'on passa ses premières saisons;

Il est doux pour le cœur de l'exilé malade,
Par le regret cuisant et la douleur usé,
D'entendre le refrain de la vieille ballade
Dont sa mère au berceau l'a jadis amusé :

Mais il est bien plus doux, éperdu, plein d'ivresse,
Sous un berceau de fleurs, d'entourer de ses bras
Pour la première fois sa première maîtresse,
Jeune fille aux yeux bruns qui tremble et ne veut pas.

How sweet, in winter, with the chill rain falling,
Lashing the windowpane, to sit at rest
Before a flaming fire, lazily lolling,
Head heavy, to great Gothic armchair pressed;

How sweet to see once more—its towers worn
By time, high chimneys, steeples, roofs blue, red,
Its houses white—the town where one was born
And where he spent his childhood years, home-bred;

How sweet for suffering exile's heart, in pain
And long undone with longing's biting woe,
To listen to the old ballade's refrain
His mother sang, cradling him long ago:

But sweeter far, in drunken swoon, to press,
Cradled in flowered arms—O joy fulfilling!—
One's own first mistress, in a first caress:
Maiden with eyes of brown, trembling, unwilling...

SOLEIL COUCHANT

> Notre-Dame,
> Que c'est beau!
> —Victor Hugo

En passant sur le pont de la Tournelle, un soir,
Je me suis arrêté quelques instants pour voir
Le soleil se coucher derrière Notre-Dame.
Un nuage splendide à l'horizon de flamme,
Tel qu'un oiseau géant qui va prendre l'essor,
D'un bout du ciel à l'autre ouvrait ses ailes d'or;
—Et c'étaient des clartés à baisser la paupière.
Les tours au front orné de dentelles de pierre,
Le drapeau que le vent fouette, les minarets
Qui s'élèvent pareils aux sapins des forêts,
Les pignons tailladés que surmontent des anges
Aux corps raides et longs, aux figures étranges,
D'un fond clair ressortaient en noir : l'Archevêché,
Comme au pied de sa mère un jeune enfant couché,
Se dessinait au pied de l'église, dont l'ombre
S'allongeait à l'entour mystérieuse et sombre.
—Plus loin, un rayon rouge allumait les carreaux
D'une maison du quai.—L'air était doux, les eaux
Se plaignaient contre l'arche à doux bruit, et la vague

SUNSET

> How beautiful
> Is Notre Dame!
> —Victor Hugo

One day, crossing the Pont de la Tournelle[8]
I stopped a moment, as the evening fell,
To watch the setting sun sinking behind
Notre Dame. There, a cloud majestic lined
Swatches of splendorous flame across the sky,
End to end, like some great bird poised to fly,
Its golden talons clenched to rend the air.
—So bright the sight that one could scarcely bear
To open wide an eye... The towers' lace
Embroidery of stone dazzling their face;
The wind-whipped flag, blown free; the steeple-tall
Minarets, like forest of firs; and all
About the walls, angle-cut gables, and
Atop them, angels—long, stiff, odd-faced—stand,
Jutting out in the darkness; and below,
At the cathedral's base—pianissimo—
Sleeps the archbishop's palace, like a child
Tucked at its mother's feet in manner mild,
Mid spreading shadows' somber mystery.
—Beyond, a ray lights red, above the quai,
A house's windowpanes... There, gently waft
The winds; the river's billows, lapping, soft,
Against the arch, moaned low lament, as they

De la vieille cité berçait l'image vague;
Et moi, je regardais toujours, ne songeant pas
Que la nuit étoilée arrivait à grands pas.

Cradled the haze-enshrouded old Cité...[9]
And I gazed blithely as dull daylight shone
Its last, and star-strewn night came loping on...

DECLARATION

> Mais toujours fust mon opinion telle
> Que toute amour doict estre mutuelle;
> Qui son cœur donne, il en merite autant
> —*Les loyalles et pudicques amours de Scalion*
> *de Virbluneau, à madame de Boufflers*

Je vous aime, ô jeune fille!
Aussi, lorsque je vous vois,
Mon regard de bonheur brille,
Aussi tout mon sang pétille
Lorsque j'entends votre voix.

Douce à mon amour timide,
Vous en accueillez d'aveu,
Mais sans qu'un rayon humide
Argente votre œil limpide,
Lac pur où dort le ciel bleu.

Pourquoi cette retenue?
Entre nous, rien de caché.—
Enfant! votre âme ingénue
Peut se montrer toute nue
Comme Eve avant le péché.

AVOWAL

This, my opinion, ever was it such;
That he who gives his love deserves as much;
Who yields his heart deserves one in return.
—*The loyal and proper loves of Scalion de
    Virbluneau for Madame de Boufflers*

How I love you, maiden mine!
Thus I see you and rejoice,
And my eyes with gladness shine,
And my blood sparkles like wine
Every time I hear your voice.

You accept the love that I,
Timid-hearted, proffer you,
Yet your eye stands ever dry—
Limpid lake, unsilvered: Why?—
Wherein sleeps a sky of blue.

Why that shy reserve, my child?
Nothing more concealed is there
'Twixt us two: your soul—pure, mild—
Like Eve's, not yet sin-beguiled—
May shine forth unhidden, bare.

C'est un amour sans mélange
Que l'amour que j'ai pour vous,
Frais comme au cœur la louange,
Ardent à toucher un ange,
Pur à rendre Dieu jaloux.

And so true my love, taint-free—
Never false or counterfeit,
Fresh its heart-praised purity—
That an angel touched would be,
And God too would covet it!

SONNET VII

> Liberté de juillet! Femme au buste divin,
> Et dont le corps finit en queue!
> —G. de Nerval

> E la lor cieca vita è tanto bassa
> Ch'invidiosi son d'ogn'altra sorte.
> —*Inferno*, canto III

Avec ce siècle infâme il est temps que l'on rompe;
Car à son front damné le doigt fatal a mis
Comme aux portes d'enfer : Plus d'espérance!—Amis,
Ennemis, peuples, rois, tout nous joue et nous trompe.

Un budget éléphant boit notre or par sa trompe;
Dans leurs trônes d'hier encor mal affermis,
De leurs aînés déchus ils gardent tout, hormis
La main prompte à s'ouvrir et la royale pompe.

Cependant en juillet, sous le ciel indigo,
Sur les pavés mouvants, ils ont fait des promesses
Autant que Charles dix avait ouï de messes!

Seule, la poésie incarnée en Hugo
Ne nous a pas déçus, et de palmes divines,
Vers l'avenir tournée, ombrage nos ruines.

SONNET VII

> July-born liberty! Bosom divine,
> But foul her body, tailing off to naught!
> —G. de Nerval

> Fallen so low, so blind now is their life,
> That jealous of all other fates are they.
> —*Inferno*, canto III

Now must we break with this foul century;
Its cursèd brow bears fate's foul lettering,
As on hell's gates: "Abandon hope..." No king,[10]
People, friend, foe, but treats us scurvily!

Their elephant-trunked budget snorts, makes free,
Sucks up our gold; they hold the tottering
Thrones of their elders, copy everything
Save generous hands and royal pageantry.

Yet, oaths they swore beneath a purpling sky,
On July's pavement chaos sans surcease,
Frequent as masses sung before Charles Dix![11]

Poetry... Hugo's! His alone kept high
Our hopes, deceived us not: its palms sublime
Waft us, in ruins, toward a better time.

DEBAUCHE

Buvons du grog et cassons-nous les reins.
—Chanson des marins

Tu as Dieu dans la bouche et dans le cœur Satan.
—Du Bartas

Je hais plus que la mort cette débauche prude
    Qui n'ose sortir que de nuit,
Et retourne la tête avec inquiétude
    Tout empourprée au moindre bruit,
Et joue à la vertu comme une honnête femme,
    N'ayant pas la force qu'il faut
Pour être hardiment et largement infâme,
    Pour porter sa honte front haut.
Aussi le cœur me lève, à ces sobres orgies
    Faites dans un salon étroit,
Aux discrètes lueurs de quatre à cinq bougies
    Et dont chacun retourne droit;
A ce vice bourgeois, mesquin, suant la prose,
    Comme le font les boutiquiers,
Gens qui savent ôter le galbe à toute chose,
    Les dandys, avec les banquiers;
Ce vice, homme rangé qui ne l'est qu'à ses heures,
    Qui sort calme d'un mauvais lieu,
Comme l'on sortirait des plus chastes demeures
    Ou de quelque église de Dieu,

DEBAUCH

> Let's drink our grog and break our backs in sport.
> —Sailors' song

> God's in your mouth and Satan's in your heart.
> —Du Bartas

I detest more than death the would-be prude's
    Debauch, she who takes mincing care
To roam only by night; whose attitudes
    Belie her lust; who turns to stare
At slightest sounds with panicked blush; who plays
    At honest woman's morals; who
Has not the strength of will to spend her days
    Doing as all frank harlots do,
Bearing her shame, proud head held high, unbowed.
    And I am sickened quite as much
By tepid salon orgies, never loud
    Or harsh, but ever deft of touch;
That vice bourgeois, discreet, sweating in prose,
    Good merchant-style, by candlelight;
People who cheapen everything, like those
    Bankers and dandies; vice upright,
Like the man well-positioned, and who will
    Indulge only as suits his whim;
Who ventures calmly from places of ill
    Repute, looking all tidy, trim,

La cravate nouée et les cheveux en ordre,
    Le frac boutonné jusqu'au cou,
Pas le plus petit pli sur quoi l'on puisse mordre,
    Rien de débraillé, rien de fou,
Rien de hardi, de chaud, de bon viveur, qui fasse
    Au reproche mollir la voix
Et dire au père : « Il faut que jeunesse se passe, »
    Comme l'on disait autrefois.
J'aime trente fois mieux une débauche franche,
    Jetant son masque de satin,
Le coude sur la nappe et la main sur la hanche.
    Criant, buvant jusqu'au matin,
Qui laisse, sans corset, aller sa gorge folle,
    Rose encor des baisers du soir,
Qui tord lascivement sa taille souple et molle,
    Sur tous les genoux va s'asseoir,
Et, bleuissant sa joue au punch qui siffle et flambe
    Au fond du cratère vermeil,
Rit de se voir ainsi, danse et montre sa jambe,
    Et ne veut pas qu'on ait sommeil :
—C'est une poésie au moins, une palette
    Où brillent mille tons divers,

Cravatted, hair combed, as if from some chaste
    Holy of Holies, primly decked
In frock-coat buttoned to the brim, with taste;
    No wrinkles that one might expect
To carp and rail against; nothing that could
    Seem passionate or uncontrolled,
Or even mad; —yes—not a thing that would
    Bespeak the bon vivant—rash, bold—
Or make a father, though loath to condone
    His son, say: "Youth must have its way,"—
Albeit tweaking in a gentle tone—
    As yesteryear they used to say.
I prefer thirtyfold a candid, pure
    Debauch, who casts her satin mask
Aside, and sits in posture staunch and sure,
    Arms on the table, by the cask
Of flowing wine, arrogant, hand on hip,
    Drinking the night away till morn,
Un-corseted, cries rising to her lip
    From wanton bosom brashly born,
Still pink from night's mad kisses; who swirls, twists
    Her supple waist lasciviously
To slowly sensuous rhythms, and insists
    On flitting, lap to lap, as she
Goes sitting on each one's in turn; and who
    Sees her cheek in the flaming, steaming
Crater of punch flambé's vague haze of blue,
    And, dancing with wild laughter, beaming,

Un type net et franc, une chose complète,
De la couleur! des chants! des vers!

Reveals her leg, lest any sleep! Ah, what
    A poem is this debauchery:
Palette of hues diverse, an utter glut
    Of color, song, and poetry!

LE BENGALI

A une jeune fille créole

> Les bengalis dont le ramage est si doux.
> —Bernardin de Saint-Pierre

> La France et ses printemps, ses hivers inconnus
> Où la bise gémit, où les arbres sont nus,
> Où l'on voit voltiger ces blancs flocons de neige
> Que je désirais voir, et la glace,—que sais-je?
> —Mlle. L. A.

Oiseau dépaysé, qui t'amène vers nous?
Notre soleil est froid, notre ciel en courroux;
    Nos bois sont chauves; à nos haies,
A nos buissons armés de dards aigus, au lieu
Des beaux fruits blonds mûris à vos midis de feu,
    Pendent à peine quelques baies.

Comme nos passereaux hardis, pauvre étranger,
Bengali du désert, sauras-tu voltiger
    Dans nos forêts de cheminées?
Parmi les tuyaux noirs qui fument, sauras-tu
Accrocher ton nid frêle à quelque toit pointu,
    Entre deux pierres ruinées?

Entends-tu, bel oiseau, le rauque sifflement
De la bise du nord qui râle incessamment
    Et fait chanter la girouette,
Le bruit confus des chars, des cloches, le frisson

THE BENGALI

For a Creole Maid

> The waxbills, whose chatter is so sweet.
> —Bernardin de Saint-Pierre

> France and her springs, her winters little known,
> When growls the wind, when bare the trees, when blown
> Those snowflakes white that flutter in the air,
> Dear to my sight... The ice... What more is there?
> —Mlle. L. A.

Bird far from home, what brings you here to us?
Our sun is cold; our sky, dull, ominous.
      Bald, our woods; from our bushes, or
Our spike-armed shrubs, instead of lush fruit fair
And blond, warm-ripened by your noondays, there
      Hang a few berries, little more.

Will you, poor stranger, like our sparrows stout,
Bird of the Bengal desert, flit about
      On chimney-forest roofs? What art
Will build your fragile nest? Will you be able
To hang it, by black smokestacks, from some gable,
      'Twixt old stones fallen quite apart?

Lovely bird, do you hear the North wind blast
In raucous rattles, as it whistles past
      And sets the weathercock a-swinging;
The muddled noise of wagons, bells; the pounding

De la pluie aux carreaux qui pleurent, et le son
  Des tuiles que la grêle fouette?

Ouvre ton aile et pars, retourne-t'en là-bas,
Au bois des goyaviers, reprendre tes ébats;
  Dans la savane aux grandes herbes,
Avec les colibris va becqueter les fleurs,
Boire à leurs coupes d'or, te baigner dans leurs pleurs,
  Bâtir ton hamac sous leurs gerbes!

Shudder of rain on weeping panes; resounding
    Tiles that the hailstones whip, a-winging?

Go, spread your wings, return home whence you flew,
Mid guava groves play as you waxbills do;
    In deep grass loll away your days;
With hummingbirds, peck at the flowers' face,
Bathe in their tears, sip from their gold cups; place
    Your hammock under their bouquets.

Emaux et Camées, 1852–1872

Gautier's original text is found in René Jasinski, *Poésies complètes de Théophile Gautier,* 3 vols. (Paris: Nizet, 1970), 3:3–130.

"Preface"

1. As the rest of the prefatory sonnet explains, Gautier is suggesting that just as Goethe took refuge in Weimar from the political upheavals of the Wars of the Empire by writing his Orient-inspired *Westöstlicher Divan*—a collection of philosophical poems published in 1819—he is doing likewise during the Paris unrest of 1848 and the Second Republic by writing his often exotically inspired *Emaux et Camées.* Goethe's work had been translated into French in 1843.

2. Nisami (or Nizami, Nesami, et al, 1141?–1209) was considered Persia's most eminent romantic poet of his period. As for the "hudhud," it is the rather exotic hoopoe, a bird that figures a number of times in the Goethe work.

3. Still today the most popular poet of Iran, Hafiz (1324–1391) was a native of Shiraz, known as the city of roses and nightingales. The rose plays a prominent part in his inspiration.

"Hidden Affinities"

4. I assume the reference to Venus's farewell is an allusion to the famous Botticelli canvas *The Birth of Venus,* painted ca. 1482, and showing the goddess, known as Venus Anadyomenes—that is, "rising from the sea"—standing fully grown on a large open seashell.

5. The Generalife gardens, part of the Alhambra palaces, were the summer residence of the Moorish kings of Granada. Boabdil is a Spanish corruption of the name of Abu Abdullah, the last of them (1460?–1533?). It

is said that the gardens, begun in the thirteenth century, were planned to resemble paradise on earth, as described in the Qur'an.

6. My wordplay is an attempt to produce something of the effect of the original's repetition: "*se re*spire et *se re*connaît."

"The Poem of Woman"

I opt for the universal "woman"-in-general for my version's title, although there are a few possibly specific references to women of Gautier's acquaintance throughout. (See Claudine Gothot-Mersch's edition of *Emaux et Camées* [Paris: Gallimard, 1981], 229–30.) The Greek island of Paros, one of the Cyclades in the central Aegean, had long been known for its fine white marble. Gautier refers to it several times in his poetry.

7. Nacarat is a shade of pale reddish orange, often with opalescent glints suggested by its etymological relationship with the French *nacre*, mother-of-pearl.

8. One of the suggested specific inspirations for the present poem is the colorful marquise de La Païva (1819–1884). Born in Moscow as Esther Lachmann, she later assumed the names Pauline and Thérèse, eventually adding a number of others, legal and otherwise. As wife of Portuguese marquis Albino Francesco de Païva-Araujo, she acquired a title, a fortune, and her nickname, La Païva. Following the marquis's suicide, she married her final conquest, the Prussian count Guido Henckel von Donnersmarck, continuing her life as one of the most "successful" French nineteenth-century courtesans, counting as her admirers not only Gautier but Richard Wagner and others. Gautier, who alludes to her often, mentions her specifically as a devotee of the Théâtre des Italiens—now the Opéra Comique—built at the end of the seventeenth century.

9. Apelles of Kos was a fourth-century BCE Greek portraitist of the court of Alexander the Great. One of his paintings, none of which has survived, was the Venus (or Aphrodite) Anadyomenes. (See note 75, to "Winter Fantasies," below.) Cleomenes, easily confused with others of that name, appears to have been a third-century BCE Athenian sculptor, thought to have executed the Venus de' Medici.

10. According to Madeleine Cottin, the Ingres odalisque referred to is the painter's second, known as the *Odalisque à l'esclave*. (See "*Emaux et*

camées," avec une iconographie rassemblée et commentée par Madeleine Cottin [Paris: Lettres modernes, 1968], 10.)

11. Gothot-Mersch (*Emaux et Camées*, 231) goes to some pains to explain—successfully, I think—the unexpected ending, conflating sexual climax with death.

"Study in Hands, I. Imperia"

Imperia, the "professional" name of Lucrezia de Paris, was a prominent Venetian courtesan born in Ferrara in 1485 and active during the sixteenth century as a favorite of men of both state and church. She is the subject of a Balzac short story "La Belle Impéria" in his *Contes drôlatiques* and was often praised by the Romantics for her beauty and other physical qualities.

12. Aspasia ("the desired one"), one of the most famous women of ancient Athens, was a citizen of Miletus. Possibly (though not unquestionably) a *hetaira*—a well-educated and socially adept high-class companion rather than a mere prostitute—she eventually became the mistress of Pericles (fifth century BCE), with whom she became the butt of frequent satire.

13. "A courtesan's? A queen's? . . . " The reference would seem to be to Aspasia and Cleopatra, of the first quatrain.

"Study in Hands, II. Lacenaire"

Pierre-François Lacenaire (1800–1836), a celebrated murderer-cum-poet, after a career of petty crimes, was executed for a notorious double murder. We are told that he became an instant celebrity in prison, and that "he was swamped with messages and gifts from ladies of the best society." (See Gordon Wright, *Insiders and Outliers: The Individual in History* [San Francisco: W. H. Freeman and Co., 1981], 31.) He attracted the attention of none other than Baudelaire, and the murder for which he paid with his life supposedly furnished the plot of Dostoyevsky's *Crime and Punishment*. Maxime Du Camp (1822–1894), in his biography *Théophile Gautier* (Paris: Hachette, 1890), claimed to own Lacenaire's mummified hand, the sight of which, according to him, inspired the present poem.

14. The "Caesar" referred to is the emperor Tiberius, who reigned from 14 to 37 CE. Disillusioned with affairs of state and having virtually abandoned power to Sejanus, he spent his later years on the island of Capri—early known as "les Caprées"—where, according to Suetonius and generally accepted belief, he rid himself of the cares of the empire by hosting and indulging in an array of erotic and bizarre excesses.

15. Manfred is the eponymous hero of Byron's dramatic poem, published in 1817 and popular among the Romantics, thanks to its inclusion of supernatural elements and, especially, to the character's exaggerated Faustian angst. With murderous proclivities and poetic pretensions, Lacenaire, despite his would-be elegance and bravado, was, for Gautier, no more than a low-class Manfred with none of the noble hero's genuine panache.

"Variations on the Carnival of Venice, I. In the Street"

The inspiration for this group of poems can be traced to a recital, attended by Gautier on January 29, 1843, by the brilliant young Italian violinist Camillo Sivori, pupil of the flamboyant—many would even say diabolical—virtuoso Niccolo Paganini, at which he had played his recently deceased master's variations on the popular Venetian song "Le Carnaval de Venise." Gautier expressed his boundless enthusiasm for the performance in a review in *La Presse* two days later.

16. Though the noun has long had a pejorative meaning, my translation interprets "les serins," for which the tune was "classique," as the twirling canaries atop music-boxes rather than as bourgeois "boobies" whose musical taste didn't rise above the banal.

17. My translation attempts to preserve the play on the English "crochet," a small hook, and, in musical terms, a quaver or quarter-note, "tail" and all. It accords also with a typical bit of dramatic showmanship that Paganini, "the Devil's consort," is said to have displayed at many of his own recitals, where a double of his, in satanic cloak, hooves, and horns, would pretend to use his long tail to guide his bow.

18. I have had to resort to an apostrophe—"crochet'd"—to maintain the pronunciation of the past tense of the verb "to crochet," which would be lost if spelled out correctly: "crocheted."

"Variations on the Carnival of Venice, II. On the Lagunes"

19. Venetian painter Giovanni Antonio Canal (1697–1768), known as Canaletto, was especially famous for his *vedute*—views—of Venice and, by a delightful coincidence, her canals.

"Variations on the Carnival of Venice, III. Carnival"

20. Harlequin (Arlecchino in Italian), along with the others mentioned in the succeeding quatrains, was a stock character of the sixteenth-century commedia dell'arte, the largely improvisational theater that developed into the farce and situation comedy of later generations. A wily, skillful, physically and mentally agile servant, not without a healthy dose of self-interest, he would, under a variety of names, spawn many descendants, most notable among them Beaumarchais's and Mozart's famous Figaro.

"Variations on the Carnival of Venice, IV. Sentimental Moonlight"

21. The "chanterelle" is the highest string on a violin. In referring to the harmonica, Gautier, I imagine, means the now-common handheld wind instrument, which, originally invented in China, had been manufactured in Germany in the early nineteenth century. He may also mean the glass harmonica, in either of its two incarnations: the original water-filled wineglass version known since the Renaissance and popularized in the 1740s, or the more mechanical crank-turned version developed by Ben Franklin and others.

"Symphony in White Major"

22. The object of Gautier's admiration was Maria Kalergis(-Muchanow) (1822–1874), née Comtesse Nesselrode, a talented pupil of Chopin and socially prominent Polish beauty, to whom the poem was originally dedicated, and whose portrait had been painted by Delacroix. (See Maria Rubins, *Crossroads of Arts, Crossroads of Cultures: Ecphrasis in Russian and French Poetry* [New York: Palgrave, 2000], 70–71.)

23. See "The Poem of Woman."

24. Melancholy heroine of Balzac's fantastic 1834 novel that bears her name, Séraphita is the female element of a perfect androgyne, sharing her body with Séraphitüs in a model of complete humanity in the philosophy

of theologian-mystic Emanuel Swedenborg (1688–1772). Their confused romantic adventures with their respective lovers, Wilfrid and Minna, are played out on the gloomy but no less sheer white landscape of Norway's Stromfjord.

"Posthumous Coquettishness"

The flesh-and-blood inspiration for this poem was shown to be Marie Mattei, Gautier's companion during a memorable stay in Venice in 1850. (See Jasinski, *Poésies complètes*, 1:lxxxv.) A more generally allegorical interpretation has been advanced, however, by Constance Gosselin Schick in her study *Seductive Resistance: The Poetry of Théophile Gautier* (Amsterdam: Rodopi, 1994), 130.

"Diamond of the Heart"

25. Jasinski (*Poésies complètes*, 1:c) and Cottin (*Emaux et camées*, 32), among others, cite a letter from Marie Mattei to Gautier in which she claims to have shed a tear of joy at the thought of him. Cottin substantiates the claim by stating that, in examining the manuscript of "Coquetterie posthume," she actually saw the tear stain in question.

26. The allusion to the pearl dissolved in a "cup of love" is explained by a passage from Pliny's *Natural History*, explaining how Cleopatra proved to Antony that she was going to toast him with a drink of inestimable value: "There have been two pearls that were the largest in the whole of history; both were owned by Cleopatra. . . . In accordance with previous instructions, the servants placed in front of her only a single vessel containing vinegar, the strong rough quality of which can melt pearls. She was at the moment wearing in her ears that remarkable and truly unique work of nature. Antony was full of curiosity to see what in the world she was going to do. She took one earring off and dropped the pearl in the vinegar, and when it was melted swallowed it" (IX.59.119–21).

27. Ophyr (or Ophir) was an Oriental land of fabulous wealth referred to in several books of the Old Testament, with numerous and widely divergent suggestions as to its location, some even positing Atlantis. Legend has it that it paid regular tribute to King Solomon, in the form of gold, silver, jewels, sandalwood, ivory, and exotic beasts.

"Contralto"

Gothot-Mersch (*Emaux et Camées*, 237) details the dual inspiration of the present poem: the person of opera singer Ernesta Grisi, Gautier's wife—daughter of an eminent musical family of the time—and the frequent Romantic theme of hermaphroditism, comparing the perfectly dual-sexed beauty of a Greek statue to the masculine-like timbre of the female contralto voice.

28. In Greek mythology, the naiad Salmacis, quite unlike her typically virginal sister-nymphs, attempted the rape of Hermaphroditus. In Ovid's *Metamorphoses*, IV, 372 ff., the gods allow their two bodies to blend perfectly into one.

29. The allusion to Cinderella is no doubt to her operatic incarnation in the Rossini opera *La Cenerentola*, which had enjoyed considerable success after its premiere in 1817, not only in Italy but throughout the musical world.

30. The heroines named here by Gautier—and even the heroes, in days of operatic gender-switching—were all sung by contraltos: Rossini's Arsace, Tancrede, Malcolm, and Desdemona, in *Semiramide*, *Tancrede*, *La Donna del lago*, and *Otello*, respectively, and Mozart's Zerlina, in *Don Juan*. At least one of them, the Scot Malcolm, had been a triumph for Ernesta Grisi. (See Gothot-Mersch, *Emaux et Camées*, 238.)

31. The somewhat abstruse references to Gulnare and Kaled come from two Oriental tales by Lord Byron, *The Corsair* (1814) and its immediate sequel, *Lara*. In the first, Gulnare, a beautiful slave-girl of Seyd's harem, is rescued from the flaming palace by the corsair, Lord Conrad, eventually releasing him in turn from his own imprisonment and going off with him to his island. In the second, Kaled, Lord Lara's page boy, is revealed to be a woman in disguise. The two were assumed by readers to be the original Conrad and Gulnare after their precipitous disappearance at the end of *The Corsair* and are now interpreted by some as an example of Byron's own sexual ambivalence.

"Cærulei Oculi"

For a detailed explanation of the probable shades of blue intended by Gautier in his title and the succeeding quatrains, see Gothot-Mersch,

Emaux et Camées, 242. It might be added parenthetically that the phrase was used by Tacitus in his description of the Germans, as cited by Isaac Taylor in his pre-Nazi anthropological study of the Aryans. (See *The Origin of the Aryans: An Account of the Prehistoric Ethnology and Civilisation of Europe* [London: Walter Scott Publishing Co., 1906], 109.)

32. In Goethe's poem "The King of Thule," translated into French by Gérard de Nerval (see note 133, to "The Castle of Memory," below) and appearing also in Gounod's *Faust*, as sung by Marguerite, the eponymous monarch, upon the death of his beloved, receives a golden goblet. Sensing his own death approaching, he flings it into the sea, never to drink again. Thule, in a variety of spellings and suggested locations, was considered by ancient and medieval navigators to be the northernmost point in Europe —*ultima Thule*—hence of the world.

33. Regarding Cleopatra's "other pearl," see note 26, to "Diamond of the Heart," above.

34. Solomon's legendary ring was said to possess the power to make him invisible, to rule over genies, and even to speak to animals. According to one Arabic source, the demon Sakhr stole the ring and replaced Solomon on the throne while the king, destitute, wandered the countryside. In time, however, Sakhr threw the ring into the sea. A fish that swallowed it was eventually caught and, as coincidence would have it, served up to the king himself.

35. The Schiller ballad in question is *The Diver*, in which a king hurls a golden goblet into the whirling waters of Charybdis, promising a reward to any one of his knights who will dive in and retrieve it. They all hang back, but a young page accepts the challenge. When the tide flings him back to the shore, he gives the king not only the goblet, but also a chilling account of the waters' mysteries. The king, wanting still more, promises him his beautiful daughter if he dives in again. Despite the princess's pleadings, he does so, and is never seen again.

36. According to Gothot-Mersch (*Emaux et Camées*, 243), among the many completely and partly legendary exploits of Harald Harfagar ("the fair-haired"), who became king of Norway in 859, the one referred to here is the subject of a poem bearing his name, by Heinrich Heine, and translated into French by Nerval. (See note 133, to "The Castle of Memory,"

below.) It relates his purported two-hundred-year undersea liaison with a beautiful mermaid, whose enchanting eyes so captivated him that he was unable to tear himself away from her. (Less completely legendary is the report that he had about eighteen wives, none of whom was the mermaid, however.)

"Rondalla"

A *rondalla* is a typically Spanish—Aragonese—under-the-window serenade. Gautier's was often set to music, notably by Jacques Offenbach.

37. As Gothot-Mersch explains (*Emaux et Camées*, 243–44), it was customary for the gallant in question to post confederates at both ends of the street to keep others from attempting to serenade his lady as well, thus giving rise to frequent spirited and even bloody disputes.

38. By the time Gautier himself was traveling in Spain, the violence of these *rondallas* had abated considerably, despite the bloodthirsty quatrains that follow. At least so he tells us in his 1843 travelogue, *Tra los montes:* "In the olden times, two serenades would not have been tolerated in the same street; the first arrival counted upon being left alone and would not allow the thrum of any guitar but his own to break the silence of the night. These pretensions were upheld at the point of the rapier or the knife." In his day, however, "(t)he touchiness of serenaders has been greatly mollified, and everyone may *rascar el jamón* (scrape the ham) with tranquil mind under the walls of his fair one." (The original 1843 edition was republished in 1845 as *Voyages en Espagne* [Paris: Charpentier, 1845], translated into English ten years later, apparently anonymously, as *Wanderings in Spain* [London: Ingram, Cooke, and Co., 1853], and subsequently by Catherine Alison Phillips in 1926 as *A Romantic in Spain.* The quote is from the latter's 2001 republication [Oxford: Signal Books Ltd., 179].) As for the French *râcler le jambon*, the equivalent of the Spanish expression, it appears to have originated in military slang and is found at least as late as the 1940s, referring to guitars, violins, and mandolins.

39. The *capitans* of the original refer to the swaggering stock character of the commedia dell'arte (see note 20, to "Variations on the Carnival of Venice, III. Carnival," above) inherited from the Latin *miles gloriosus* (braggart warrior).

"Obelisks' Longings, I. The Paris Obelisk"

Gothot-Mersch (*Emaux et Camées,* 245–46) relates in detail the genesis of this two-part poem as told by Maxime Du Camp (see the unnumbered headnote to "Study in Hands, II. Lacenaire," above) and fantasizing the despair of the two Luxor obelisks when they were separated from each other. Both were given to the French in 1829 by the viceroy of Egypt, Mehemet Ali, but only one was ever delivered. It arrived in Paris on December 21, 1833. On October 25, 1836, King Louis-Philippe had it placed in the center of Place de la Concorde, where a guillotine had stood during the Revolution. The other one stayed in Egypt, too difficult to move, and in the 1990s President François Mitterrand officially "returned" it to the Egyptians.

40. The pyramidion, originally the capstone of a pyramid, is the miniature pyramid-shaped apex of an obelisk. During Egypt's Middle Kingdom, it would usually be covered with gold leaf to reflect the sun's rays, and was frequently inscribed with religious symbols or royal titles.

41. See the unnumbered headnote to this poem, above.

42. The sparrows referred to ("moineaux francs") are the European domestic house sparrows that Gautier's nostalgic obelisk seems eager to differentiate from his (or her?) own country's variety.

43. The "pschent" of the original is the double-crown of upper and lower Egypt—the red and the white, joined together to represent the unified country—originally assumed by Narmer (Menes), the founder of the First Dynasty around 3100 BCE, and subsequently worn by the priests guiding the "bari" (funeral boat) in its course to the afterlife.

44. Gautier uses the name of the Greek lawgiver Solon because of the proximity of the obelisk to the Assemblée Nationale. As for the name Arthur, it was used for affected young men who often frequented women of easy virtue, and continued with that meaning into the twentieth century with even more pejorative connotations.

"Obelisks' Longings, II. The Luxor Obelisk"

45. The great god Thot (or Thoth), the "master of the hieroglyphs," was one of the most important of the Egyptian deities. He was usually portrayed with the head of an ibis, the common bird of the Nile valley,

whose white and black feathers were thought to represent both day and night. The Egyptians believed that, thanks to the ibis's very long, thin beak, Thot had the power to delve into souls and unearth buried secrets.

46. Similar to Baudelaire, though perhaps to a lesser extent, Gautier too was bedeviled by the ennui that the early Romantics had called the *mal du siècle* and that his generation, for misinformed anatomical reasons, termed *spleen*. In an article cited by Gothot-Mersch (*Emaux et Camées*, 246–47), Marc Eigeldinger calls attention to the characteristic difference between Baudelaire's and Gautier's, however; the former being gloomy and dark—*brumeux*—and the latter marked rather by an often oppressive sun.

47. A fellah is an Egyptian peasant. As Gothot-Mersch (*Emaux et Camées*, 270) points out in a later note to the poem of that name, the noun is rarely used—as here and in that poem—to refer to a female.

48. The cangia was one of several types of Egyptian riverboats, with forward lateen sails and oars. At the beginning of his short story "Une Nuit de Cléopâtre" (1838), Gautier himself gives a description of an especially luxurious one: "This cangia was narrow, long, elevated at both ends in the form of a new moon . . . the figure of a ram's head, surmounted by a golden globe, armed the point of the prow, showing that the vessel belonged to some personage of royal blood."

49. Syene was the original name of Aswan, well known for the pink granite used in the sculpting of its famous monuments.

"Veterans of the Old Guard"

The expression used as the poem's title seems to have first appeared in 1847 in Balzac's novel *Le Cousin Pons* and refers to the surviving old troopers of Napoleon's "garde impériale," assembled in a nostalgic reunion on May 5, 1848. (See Jasinski, *Poésies complètes*, 1:civ.)

50. In his mini-tableau of nocturnal horrors, Gautier—rather than referring to the generic semidivine mischief-making Elves of pre-Christian Germano-Scandinavian lore—is evoking the Willies or Willie-Sprites. Nymphs originally known by their Slavic name—Vila or Wili—these denizens of clouds, waters, and woods, who lived on the mist, were known for their often fierce temperament and their ability to assume shapes of

various beasts, birds, and—especially—beautiful maidens. As the latter, they would lure gullible young men into frenetic and exhausting dances, as in the present quatrain, usually with unhappy results. It will be remembered that, in 1841, Gautier collaborated with the prolific Henri Vernoy de Saint-Georges (1799–1875) on the libretto of the ballet *Giselle*—subtitled *Les Willis*—inspired by a poem of Heinrich Heine, to music of Adolphe Adam (1803–1856), with the principal role created by Carlotta Grisi. (See note 112, to "The Little Dead Girl's Toys," below.) The word is probably the source of the English expression "to have the willies."

51. Baron Joseph Christian von Zedlitz (1790–1862) was an Austrian Romantic poet and playwright. The ballade referred to is his best known, "Die nächtliche Heerschau," first published in 1829 and included in his collection *Gedichte* (1832). It presents a spectral Napoleon in a nostalgic nocturnal review of his soldiers fallen at the battle of Austerlitz.

52. The Gymnase and the Variétés are two prominent Parisian theaters. The first was built in 1820 and was, for a long time, second in importance only to the national theaters of the Comédie-Française and the Odéon, presenting especially the social realism of dramatists Scribe, Augier, Dumas *fils*, Becque, et al. The Variétés, despite rocky beginnings on Boulevard Montmartre in 1807, marked by professional in-fighting, has maintained its importance over the years and was declared a *monument national* in 1975.

53. There is some question here whether Gautier intended the English word "mob" or the name of the supernaturally endowed Mab, queen of the fairies. The latter sprite is referred to in numerous works, from Shakespeare's *Romeo and Juliet*, I, iv (where she is said to ride in a walnut-shell carriage), to Berlioz's famous "Queen Mab Scherzo" in his 1839 *Roméo et Juliette*, as well as in Shelley's first lengthy work, *Queen Mab: A Philosophical Poem*, of 1813. The second interpretation, halfheartedly defended by Gothot-Mersch (*Emaux et Camées*, 248), strikes me as more in keeping with the tenor of the passage.

54. Gautier refers specifically to a lithograph executed in 1836 by the eminent historical painter and engraver Denis-Auguste-Marie Raffet (1804–1860), entitled *La Revue nocturne*, inspired by the Zedlitz poem (see note 51 above). The lithograph gave rise also to a watercolor of similar

subject, showing a ghostly Napoleon on horseback in the midst of his tattered phantom-troops eerily lighted by a cloud-veiled moon.

55. Napoleon's *grand retour* refers to the transfer of his ashes to the Invalides in 1840. Considering his military defeat, the adjective in "grand return" is probably to be taken with not a little sarcasm.

56. The *poussa(h)* is the French name for the figurine, weighted at its semi-spherical base, that refuses to stay down when pushed. The toy, supposedly inspired by the sitting Buddha, originated in China. Likewise its name, whose seeming etymological relationship with the verb *pousser*, "to push," is only accidental.

57. The Battle of Berezina (November 26–29, 1812) was a stunning defeat for some forty thousand of Napoleon's troops when they attempted to cross the river of that name in White Russia (Belarus) on their ill-fated retreat. The expression *c'est la bérézina* is still used in French to express an utter disaster.

58. The column at which the "vieux de la vieille" assembled to honor their emperor's ashes is the one topped with his statue, on Place Vendôme.

"Sadness at Sea"

59. The reference to England as the "land of coal, of fog" speaks for itself. As for its being the land of suicide, Jasinski discusses the stereotype of English *spleen*, no doubt fostered by the early Romantics (Jasinski, *Poésies complètes*, 1:cix). Gautier himself would refer to England as "the native land of the spleen and of suicide" in his *Voyages en Italie*, published in 1852, the year when "Tristesse en mer" first appeared in the *Revue de Paris*, June 1. (See the English translation, *Travels in Italy*, trans. Daniel Vermilye [New York: Brentano's, 1902], 338.)

60. Gautier alludes here to the Feast of Our Lady of Sorrows, celebrated on the Sunday after the first Friday after Easter. Mary is frequently portrayed in paintings with seven blades piercing her heart, each representing one of her seven sorrows: the prophecy of Simeon over the infant Jesus (Luke 2:34); the flight into Egypt of the holy family (Matthew 2:13); the loss of the child Jesus, in the temple for three days (Luke 2:43); the meeting of Jesus and Mary along the Via Dolorosa (Luke 23:26); the

crucifixion, as Mary stands at the foot of the cross (John 19:25); the descent from the cross, as Mary receives the body of Jesus in her arms (Matthew 27:57); and the burial of Jesus (John 19:40).

"To a Pink Dress"

61. The inspiration for this poem, Apollonie-Aglaé Sabatier (born Joséphine Savatier [1822–1889]), was a beautiful model-cum-courtesan whose Parisian literary and artistic salon hosted many prominent admirers and would-be lovers. Among the former were the likes of Hugo, Musset, Flaubert, Berlioz; among the latter, notably Baudelaire, with whom she would have a brief affair in 1857, and who would dedicate to her a number of the poems in *Les Fleurs du mal*. A seminude recumbent statue of Madame Sabatier, sculpted by devotee Auguste Clésinger in 1847, entitled *Femme piquée par un serpent*, caused a major scandal in the Parisian art world. But the specific painting of her and her pink dress was in all likelihood done by another admirer, Napoleonic artist Jean-Louis-Ernest Meissonier (1815–1891), entitled *A l'ombre des bosquets chante un jeune poète*, painted in 1852–1853, in which she is thought to be the figure wearing a dress of that color.

62. Napoleon's sister Pauline, wife of Prince Camille Borghese, had posed nude for a reclining marble statue in neoclassical style sculpted in 1808 by Italian master Antonio Canova (1757–1822). Gautier had already noted this fact in passing in the celebrated and controversial preface to his transvestite novel, *Mademoiselle de Maupin*, published in 1835.

"Inès de Las Sierras"

Gautier, who was born in Tarbes, close to the Spanish border, likely came by his admiration for Spain and things Spanish naturally. It would be evident not only in his travelogue *Voyages en Espagne* (see note 38, to "Rondalla," above) but also in a number of disparate poems, like this one, as well as in the collection *España*. One can believe the sentiment, commonly attributed to him, that discovering Spain was like discovering his true home, the native land of his spirit. More specifically, his admiration for the tale of "Inès de Las Sierras," which inspired this poem, stems from the pervasive influence of its author, Charles Nodier (1780–1844), a champion of the Gothic tale and author of a number of *contes fantastiques* that enjoyed considerable vogue among the young Romantics, and of which "Inès de Las Sierras" (1838) is a typical example.

Petra Cámara was a celebrated Spanish dancer of the period, much admired by Gautier, who mentions her several times in his works. Cottin (*Emaux et camées*, 92–93) quotes one of two reviews that he wrote for the journal *La Presse*, August 18, 1851, praising her performance at the Théâtre du Gymnase as a perfect incarnation of the Nodier heroine, "fantôme de la vieille Espagne."

63. English novelist Ann Radcliffe (1764–1823) was one of the pioneers of the Gothic novel in Britain, especially admired for her descriptions of ghostly landscapes, haunted castles, and the like. It is said that, despite their vivid qualities, she seldom if ever actually visited her settings. Her best-known novel is *The Mysteries of Udolpho* (1795). (It should be noted that Gautier conveniently—though no doubt accidentally—spells her first name with an *e*, thereby providing a necessary vowel to flesh out his octosyllable.)

64. Venetian architect-engraver Giovanni Battista (Giambattista) Piranesi (1720–1778), known as Le Piranèse, was especially famous for his *Carceri d'invenzione* (Imaginary Prisons), a series of sixteen labyrinthine engravings, predating the Kafkaesque convolutions of M. C. Escher by two centuries, and masterpieces of fantastic, tortuous, almost surreal, imagination.

65. The cachuca is a Spanish—especially Andalusian—solo dance in 3/4 time, similar to the bolero, and usually accompanied with castanets.

66. In bullfighting, the *divisa* is the rosette that shows the distinguishing colors of the ranch where the bull was bred. After the kill it might be given as a token to the torero's lady friend.

67. In his review of Petra Cámara's performance (see unnumbered headnote regarding the poem's dedication, above), Gautier alludes to the fatal knife-wound inflicted on Inès three centuries earlier by a "meurtrier pâle et morne."

"Apollonie"

This poem was inspired by, and dedicated to, Madame Sabatier. (See note 61, to "To a Pink Dress," above.)

68. See unnumbered headnote to "Veterans of the Old Guard," above.

69. The Oracle at Delphi, which flourished in Greece during the eighth century BCE, was presided over by Apollo's priestess Pythia (or Pithia), who, with semicomprehensible mutterings, dispensed her prophecies to those who came to consult her. It is said that she did so while seated on a golden tripod.

"The Blind Man"

70. The Venetian jail alluded to was a subterranean dungeon situated under the canals.

"Lied"

There doesn't seem to be any particular reason why Gautier chose to give this Romantic lyric a German title—the noun for "song"—though one might posit his admiration for Heine, the poet as well as the man, whom he described as "a German Apollo" and "a charming god," an admiration shared by many of his literary contemporaries: Hugo, Balzac, Sand, Lamartine, Musset, and many others. (See Amos Elon, *The Pity of It All: A Portrait of the German-Jewish Epoch, 1743–1933* [New York: Henry Holt, 2002], 141.)

71. Cottin (*Emaux et camées*, 110) calls attention to the apparent inspiration for the third quatrain: a painting in the Louvre entitled *Bacchante* by (Louis-Antoine-)Léon Riesener (1808–1878), showing a reclining nude playing with a tiger and holding a bunch of grapes. Gautier, whose portrait Riesener had done in 1850, would have been able to admire the painting even before its completion in 1855.

"Winter Fantasies"

72. Though it cannot be proved, Gothot-Mersch (*Emaux et Camées*, 256) offers the possibility that Gautier's image of an immobilized swan might have suggested to Mallarmé the subject of his famous sonnet "Le vierge, le vivace, et le bel aujourd'hui." While Gautier's original does not specify in so many words that ice is the culprit, I think the surrounding scenario justifies the addition of "ice-bound" in my version.

73. The reference is to a statue of Athenian statesman and general Phocion (or Phokion) (402?–318? BCE), often called "the Good" thanks to

his reputation for outstanding honesty. One of Plutarch's *Parallel Lives* is devoted to him.

74. Claude Michel (1738–1814), known as Clodion, was a French rococo sculptor. Though he executed many commissions for Louis XVI, he is best remembered for his bas-reliefs and small-figure groups of mythological inspiration: nymphs, fauns, and the like. As for his statue supposedly entitled "La Frileuse," there appears to be some confusion. Clodion's work does not seem to include any sculpture by that title, and Gautier is obviously not referring to the bronze statue *La Frileuse* by his more famous contemporary Jean-Antoine Houdon (1741–1828), sculpted in 1787. It has been suggested that the reference to "La Frileuse" is, rather—despite the capitals—a simple description of the marble Venus alluded to, whitened by the winter snows (and, I would add, all the more *frileuse* given her scant attire). My translation does not attempt to solve the problem, though I do suppress the capitals.

75. The parade of flesh-and-blood women, fantasized into mythological and statuary heroines, begins with the Venus Anadyomenes (see note 4, to "Hidden Affinities," above), more warmly—and less revealingly—dressed than her painted counterpart.

76. As her name implies, Flora was a Roman fertility goddess associated with flowers, springtime, and the renewal of life. Though a rather minor mythological personage, she figures quite prominently in literary, and especially poetic, allusion.

77. Nicholas Coustou (1658–1733), Guillaume Coustou (1677–1746), and their uncle (Charles-)Antoine Coysevox (1640–1720) were baroque sculptors of mythological and pastoral inspiration, all of whom are represented in the Tuileries. Coysevox's *Flore et l'Amour* may have inspired Gautier's reference in the previous quatrain.

78. Vetiver (or vetyver, in the original) is an aromatic grass (*vetiveria zizanioides*) found especially in India, Java, and Tahiti, used in medicines and perfumes. The cosmetic properties of its essential oil are said to reduce wrinkles and heal wounds, while as a medication it is thought to have a calming effect on the hormonal system and to be useful against hysteria. Also dubbed the "oil of tranquility," it is known under a variety of

other native names, one of the more common of which is "khuskhus," as in my version.

79. Palmyre was an ultrafashionable Parisian modiste of the period. She is frequently alluded to in contemporary works, not the least among them a curious four-sided epistolary novel, *La Croix de Berny*, jointly authored by Gautier, Delphine Gay (Mme Emile de Girardin) (1804– 1855), Jules Sandeau (1811–1883), and Joseph Méry (1797–1866). The original text—considered something of a literary spoof and rarely mentioned in Gautier bibliographies—appears to date from around 1845 and was republished several times. In it, Gautier, in the person of one Edgar de Meilhan, explains, describing a beauty's dress: "the secret of its making was preserved by the modiste. It was tight and easy at the same time, a perfect fit attained by Palmyre in her moments of inspiration." (See *The Cross of Berny; or Irene's Lovers*, trans. Florence Fendall and Florence Holcomb [Philadelphia: Porter and Coates, ca. 1873], 71.)

80. I cannot say if scholarship has suggested an identity for the apparently Andalusian lady—real or imagined—whom Gautier apostrophizes here, and whom he warns against leaving incriminating footprints in the snow, as explained in the following quatrain. Biographical chronology permitting, one could suggest Eugénie Fort. (See note 123, to "The Castle of Memory," below.)

81. The use of Cupid and Psyche as prototypical lovers refers to the tale in the second-century CE *Metamorphoses* of Apuleius (frequently ascribed to Ovid), in which the young god, disobeying his mother Venus's spiteful orders to make the beautiful mortal fall in love with a monster, falls in love with her himself. Given Gautier's frequent sculptural allusions, this one may well have been inspired by the famous statue *Psyché ranimée par le baiser de l'Amour*, completed in 1793 by Antonio Canova (see note 62, to "To a Pink Dress," above) and prominently displayed in the Louvre.

"The Spring"

82. Gothot-Mersch (*Emaux et Camées*, 257) cites biographical support for Georges Matoré's assertion (*Emaux et Camées*, ed. [Geneva: Droz, 1947], 158) that the lake in question was Lac de Neuchâtel.

"Pyres and Tombs"

83. According to the *Natural History* of Pliny the Elder (23–79 CE), the *ægipans* were Pan-like satyrs believed to inhabit the mountains of North Africa. Other sources suggest that they were fish-tailed goats. (See David A. Williams, *Deformed Discourse: The Function of the Monster in Medi-aeval Thought and Literature* [Montreal: McGill-Queen's University Press, 1996], 179.) Another less recent but seemingly authoritative source identifies them as followers of Dionysus: "Those curious and elusive beings, called Pans or Aegipans, swarm in every Bacchanalian rout. . . . The Aegipans of Dionysus did not wear horns and hoofs for naught, since they appear to have bequeathed these appendages to the devil of many a modern legend." (See Louis Dyer, *Studies of the Gods in Greece at Certain Sanctuaries Recently Excavated* [London: Macmillan, 1891], 98–99.)

84. The reference is to the "memento mori" theme in the episode of Trimalchio's feast, in the *Satyricon*, xxxiv, of Petronius (27–66 CE), at which a servant brings in a silver skeleton—not quite the "ivory mask (*larve*)" of Gautier's version—to encourage the guests to eat, drink, and be merry.

85. According to a legend related by Plutarch, in the reign of Tiberius (14–37 CE), an Egyptian sailor, Thamus, sailing to Italy, heard voices announcing the death of Pan. He was told to spread the news that "the great god Pan is dead." He did so, thus supposedly symbolizing the beginning of the Christian era. Oscar Wilde immortalized the event in his poem "Santa Decca" (whose title is a misinterpretation of the Greek for "Ten Saints"):

> The Gods are dead: no longer do we bring
> To grey-eyed Pallas crowns of olive-leaves!
> Demeter's child no more hath tithe of sheaves,
> And in the noon the careless shepherds sing,
> For Pan is dead, and all the wantoning
> By secret glade and devious haunt is o'er:
> Young Hylas seeks the water-springs no more;
> Great Pan is dead, and Mary's son is King.
> And yet—perchance in this sea-trancèd isle,

> Chewing the bitter fruit of memory,
> Some God lies hidden in the asphodel.
> Ah Love! if such there be, then it were well
> For us to fly his anger: nay, but see,
> The leaves are stirring: let us watch a while.

86. Cottin (*Emaux et camées*, 121) is probably correct in suggesting that this quatrain may have been inspired by one of Goya's plates in *Los Caprichos*, entitled "Y aún no se van." Gautier, who is generally credited with popularizing Goya in France, seems specifically to describe that etching in his *Voyages en Espagne* (121), though in considerably more detail: "puis une grande pierre, une dalle de tombeau qu'une figure souffreteuse et maigre s'efforce de soulever.—La pierre, trop lourde pour les bras décharnés qui la soutiennent, et qu'on sent près de craquer, retombe malgré les efforts du spectre et d'autres petits fantômes."

87. The woodcuts of the *Simulacre de la mort* of Hans Holbein the Younger (1497–1543), published in Lyon in 1538, graphically detail the medieval topos of the *danse macabre*, in which no element of society is spared from taking part in the deathly sarabande described in Gautier's several preceding quatrains.

88. In the decorative arts, the rococo *style Louis XV*, characterized by its lush curves, was also known as the *style Pompadour* after the king's celebrated mistress (1721–1764).

89. See the unnumbered headnote to "The Poem of Woman," above.

"The Armors' Supper"

Gothot-Mersch (*Emaux et Camées*, 259) notes Gautier's fascination with a watercolor entitled "Sir Bjorn aux yeux étincelants," by English aquarellist George Cattermole (1800–1868). The painting was shown at the Salon of 1855; its typically Gothic scenario was discussed in voluminous detail in Gautier's *Les Beaux-Arts en Europe*, published in the same year.

90. Given the description of Bjorn as a hermit, Matoré (*Emaux et Camées*, 186) posits a confusion here between Gautier's "cénobite," a monk living in a monastic community, and a more expected term, like "anachorète," all questions of meter being equal.

91. Curiously, Gautier does not give the usual German spellings of the trio of titles, compounds of the noun "Graf" (count) with the nouns for land, Rhine, and town.

92. The "guivre" was a legendary and particularly ferocious beast in medieval French folklore, which usually inhabited lakes and forests. Part serpent and part dragon, its mere breath was noxious enough to kill its victims. Gautier seems to be confusing it here with Celtic heraldry's wyvern, to which it was similar in both etymology and anatomy, except that the latter beast was often represented with eagle-type wings and claws, and occasionally with two heads, as here.

93. The "morion" was a type of light helmet.

94. Church cantors are often mocked for their snoring, as in the comparison "ronfler comme un chantre" (to snore like a cantor), but their drinking habits are also turned to metaphor, as in the expression "gris (drunk) comme un chantre." Gautier had already used it at the end of chapter two of his lengthy short story "Le Petit Chien de la Marquise," even adding the Swiss to his metaphor: "Avec cela, Franfreluche, qui n'a pas la tête forte, est gris comme un Suisse et deux chantres d'église." (See Théophile Gautier, *Nouvelles* [Paris: Charpentier, 1845], 233.)

95. The French heraldic term *lampassé*—"langued" in equally obscure English terminology—is used to refer to an animal's tongue, especially a lion's, when hanging out of its mouth and usually of a color different from the rest of its body.

"The Pocket Watch"

96. As its etymology suggests, the mythical hippogryph (or hippogriff) is a cross between the horse and the also variously spelled gryphon, itself a legendary creature with lion's head and tail and eagle's wings and claws. It was said to be the result of the mating of a male gryphon with a female horse, with the head, wings, and forelegs of the former, and the hind legs of the latter, and was able to fly at incredible speeds. For that reason it was used as a mount by a number of Charlemagne's knights, appearing also in Ariosto's *Orlando furioso* (1516, 1532). Gautier's specific metaphorical intention is a little unclear. He must have had one, however, since the present quatrain, not originally in the poem, was eventually added in 1868.

"The Nereids"

In Greek mythology, the Nereids were the fifty beautiful daughters of Nereus, who, along with Proteus, was one of the two "Old Men of the Sea." As sea goddesses and patrons of sailors and fishermen, they lived with their father at the bottom of the Aegean and, often pictured riding on the backs of dolphins, were charged with protecting seamen in distress. Though usually represented as fully or partially clothed, the Nereids occasionally sported mermaid's tails, which would explain why Gautier's poem, according to Gothot-Mersch (*Emaux et Camées*, 261), was originally to be entitled "Les Sirènes." Cottin (*Emaux et camées*, 90) cites artworks, entitled "Les Sirènes" and "Les Néréides," discussed by Gautier in his *Salons* of 1846, 1848, and 1851, the first of which, apparently now lost, was the work of Polish artist Théophile Kuwiatkowski, whose name, understandably, is found in several spellings. (See *Artistic Relations: Literature and the Visual Arts in Nineteenth-Century France*, eds. Peter Collier and Richard Lethbridge [New Haven: Yale University Press, 1994], 188–91.)

97. In Greek mythology, Triton was the messenger of his parents, sea gods Poseidon and Amphitrite. Carrying a trident, he was known to raise and calm the waves by blowing on a conch shell.

98. Collier and Lethbridge (*Artistic Relations*, 190) cite "Les Néréides" by Ernest-Augustin Gendron (1817–1891) (see the unnumbered headnote to this poem, above) as the possible inspiration for the steamboat motif of the Gautier poem, with its clash of ancient and modern cultures. Cottin (*Emaux et camées*, 99) suggests another: the painting by (Emile-Jean-)Horace Vernet (1789–1863) entitled *La Vapeur mettant en fuite les dieux marins*, which shows a mermaid astride a vicious-looking dolphin about to be struck by the paddle-wheels of a steamboat. (See Henri Gourdon de Genouillac, *Paris à travers les siècles: histoire nationale de Paris et des Parisiens depuis la fondation de Lutèce jusqu'à nos jours* [Paris: F. Roy, 1879–1882], 3:133.) The Vernet work, dating from 1847 and clearly at odds with Gautier's, was commissioned to adorn the ceiling of the Salon de la Paix of the Palais Bourbon, in honor of the era's technological advances. It would not be Vernet's only encomium to the steam engine.

99. The Greek lyric poet Arion is said to have lived around 625 BCE.

Legend has it that when about to be forced by pirates to jump into the sea, he began to sing. His song so charmed the dolphins following the boat that when he finally hurled himself overboard, one of them took him on its back and led him to safety.

100. In Roman mythology, Venus, the goddess of beauty, was obliged to marry the ugly fire god Vulcan. But Gautier's allusion does not imply that the latter was a wife beater, despite his mate's infidelities, especially with the handsome Mars. The conditional tenses of "souffletterait" and "meurtrirait" only compare the paddlewheel's doubtless depredations to those that Vulcan would inflict were he ever to vent his anger.

101. If Gautier's Nereids are of the mermaid variety, the "membres nus" of the original must refer, ipso facto, to their arms, not their legs.

"The Love Locks"

102. See note 53, to "Veterans of the Old Guard," above.

"The Tea-Rose"

103. The supposed beauty apostrophized here was Princess Ludovica Teresa Maria Clotilde of Savoy, daughter of Vittorio Emanuele II, king of Sardinia (and eventually of Italy), teenage wife of Napoléon-Joseph-Charles-Paul Bonaparte ("Prince Napoléon"), son of the emperor's youngest brother, the colorful Jérôme Bonaparte. Contemporary portraits of the royal spouse cast doubt on Gautier's taste in beauty or his sincerity, if not on both.

"Carmen"

104. It is impossible to know which of the various paintings showing Venus rising from the waves inspired Gautier's allusion here. I suspect it might well be the most famous, Botticelli's *The Birth of Venus*. (See note 4, to "Hidden Affinities," above.)

"What the Swallows Say"

105. "Hajji" is the title given to Muslims who have gone on the hajj, the required pilgrimage to Mecca.

106. The "chibouch" or "chibouk" is the characteristic, long-stemmed Turkish pipe, sometimes reaching four feet in length. Its sociological and artistic significance has long been noted. In a study of Turkish-motif

paintings, for example, it is described as a symbol of masculinity: "In several harem pictures the chibouk functions as a scepter to the powerful male." And the author, describing one painting, refers to it as "one pleasure he holds in his left hand" and "the half-naked woman a pleasure in his right." In another, "A reclining odalisque offers wine to a huge master puffing on an extraordinarily long, arching chibouk, symbolizing his virility." Other examples are more blatantly phallic. (See Joan delPlato, *Multiple Wives, Multiple Pleasures: Representing the Harem, 1800–1875* [London: Associated University Presses, 2002], 112–13.) In the present poem, dating from September 1859, why Gautier used the chibouch, instead of the equally exotic and more generally known hookah, is an open question. Was it to out-Baudelaire Baudelaire, who had used the latter in his "Au lecteur" of *Les Fleurs du mal* some two years earlier? Or, avoiding the alternate spelling "chibouk," simply to take advantage of a convenient rhyme with the equally exotic "tarbouch"? As for the latter, he might also have chosen the more common fez as a typical headdress—as do I in my version—basically the same as the tarbouch, though differing slightly in detail.

107. Balbec, usually spelled Baalbek, was originally the Roman city of Heliopolis, literally "Sun City," not to be confused with another, similarly named city in Egypt. In the Bekaa valley of Lebanon, it got its name from Alexander the Great after his conquests in the Near East in 334 BCE, and is famous for its many impressive and well-preserved ruins, including some of the largest temples of the empire, which attest to the city's vast wealth in its day.

108. The architectural term "triglyph" refers to a raised stone block in a Doric frieze consisting of three vertical channels, any one of which would have provided enough room for the swallow to cling to as she hung down over her brood.

109. See note 40, to "Obelisks' Longings, I. The Paris Obelisk," above.

110. Friedrich Rückert (1788–1866) was an important German poet, Orientalist, and polyglot. Many of his lyrics, in a variety of forms—over a hundred and twenty, we are told—were set to music by such composers as Schubert, Schumann, Brahms, and others of more modern periods, the best-known work being Mahler's *Kindertotenlieder*. Gautier clearly knew

Rückert's verse, well enough at least to be moved to publish in *Le Moni-teur universel* of June 9, 1856, his translation of the ten-stanza apostrophe to wings referred to here, of which I cite the first two quatrains in both the original and his version:

Flügel! Flügel! um zu fliegen	Des ailes, des ailes pour voler
Über Berg und Tal,	Par montagne et par vallée!
Flügel, um mein Herz zu wiegen	Des ailes pour bercer mon cœur
Auf des Morgens Strahl!	Sur le rayon de l'aurore!
Flügel, übers Meer zu schweben	Des ailes pour planer sur la mer
Mit dem Morgenrot,	Dans le pourpre du matin!
Flügel, Flügel übers Leben,	Des ailes au-dessus de la vie!
Über Grab und Tod!	Des ailes par-delà la mort!

"Noel"

111. As a Francophile I have to admit my discomfort at rhyming "non-pareil" with "Noel." But the word has been in the language for many centuries, from the Middle English "nounparalle," and all the diction-aries consulted give only the non-French pronunciation.

"The Little Dead Girl's Toys"

112. The child in question was the three-year-old Maria, daughter of Giulia Grisi, cousin of Gautier's wife, beautiful diva Ernesta, and her no-less-beautiful sister Carlotta, virtuoso dancer (whom he had unsuccess-fully courted and for whom he co-wrote the scenario of *Giselle* in 1841). Also a prima donna, Giulia was the third star of the Grisi musical con-stellation. According to Gothot-Mersch (*Emaux et Camées*, 265) the poem's manuscript is dated October 1860. (See also the unnumbered headnote to "Contralto," above.)

113. The horse-and-rider dolls were inspired by the Franconi dynasty of equestrian circus performers, male and female, begun by Antonio (1738–1836), founder of the popular Cirque Olympique in Paris. The last of the famous family was Laurent Franconi, who died in 1849.

114. Reams have been written about the supposed nursery rhyme "Ah! vous dirai-je, maman," probably dating from the early eighteenth century.

Its story is not as innocent as it appears, recounting a young girl's seduction by one Silvandre and, in one version, even a beating by Love himself. Gautier is justified in characterizing it as he does. As for its tune—the nearly universal "Twinkle, Twinkle, Little Star"—not only has it been a nursery favorite, but it was also used by Mozart and many other composers, especially as a theme for variations.

115. The elegant "Quadrille des Lanciers" is said by some sources to have been developed in 1818 in Dublin by a dancing master named Olivier Metra. Others credit French composer of waltzes and popular dance music, (Jules-Louis-)Olivier Métra (1830–1889). Origin aside, it is clear that Gautier chose its bouncy melody—anything but "triste comme un enterrement"—to show that even a typically cheerful tune was colored by the sadness of the poem's scenario.

116. "La Donna è mobile," one of opera's best-known arias, is from Act 3 of Verdi's *Rigoletto.* The reference to "Le rouleau qui tourne et joue" (the "revolving cylinder" of my translation) may cause readers to assume that Edison's early phonograph is intended. His invention, however, dates from almost two decades after the 1860 date given in the manuscript of the poem. What is referred to is no doubt the music box. Though musical clocks had entertained the aristocracy as early as the sixteenth century, legend has it that the first cylinder-driven music box was made for Marie Antoinette. Developed from the musical snuff box popular in the eighteenth century, it was the work of Swiss watchmaker Antoine Favre in 1796. The industry flourished until the late 1880s, when the cylinder was eclipsed by flat disc, ancestor of the phonograph record.

"After the Article"

To help support himself, his wife and several of her relatives, two daughters, two younger sisters, and eventually a son, Gautier devoted much of his time and talent as an art and theater critic, especially for *La Presse,* to which he contributed articles from 1836 to 1854. He also served as director of the *Revue de Paris* from 1851 to 1856, and, after leaving *La Presse,* wrote for *Le Moniteur universel* from 1855 to 1870, ultimately serving as editor of the important review *L'Artiste* from 1856 to 1859. It is not surprising that a number of his poems first appeared in those reviews, among others. Especially influential were his editorials in *L'Artiste*, in which he articulated his celebrated theory of "Art for Art's Sake." But despite his prominence and success as a critic, Gautier could never come to terms with his bourgeois acceptance of having to write for money, as this poem clearly and somewhat sardonically shows. Nor was it the only time he would complain about it.

"The Castle of Memory"

This dramatic poem is an excellent example, in verse, of the macabre atmosphere, typical of the Romantic inspiration, that had come to color many of Gautier's prose tales.

117. The allusion is to the famous Greek myth of Ariadne—Ariane in French—daughter of King Minos of Crete. When Theseus went to slay the deadly Minotaur, she saved him from Daedalus's intricate labyrinth by giving him a ball of thread to help him find his way out.

118. The first of Apollo's "escapades" pictured on the tapestry describes the randy god's pursuit of the beautiful Daphne and her subsequent transformation by her river-god father into a laurel tree to save her from his lubricious designs. The episode is recounted in Ovid's *Metamorphoses*, I, 525–52: " 'Help me father! If your streams have divine powers change me, destroy this beauty that pleases too well!' Her prayer was scarcely done when a heavy numbness seized her limbs, thin bark closed over her breast, her hair turned into leaves, her arms into branches, her feet so swift a moment ago stuck fast in slow-growing roots, her face was lost in the canopy. Only her shining beauty was left" (trans. A. S. Kline).

119. Admetus was a mythical king of Thessaly known for his hospitality. When Apollo was condemned by Zeus for killing the Cyclops and sentenced to serve a mortal for one year, he chose the realm of Admetus and became his herdsman.

120. The nine Muses, daughters of Zeus and Mnemosyne, were the goddesses of the arts and sciences. The Pindus mountain range of northern Greece was their bailiwick when not cavorting with Apollo on their favorite Mount Helicon or Mount Parnassus. Gautier's description of them as a "troupe hagarde" does not speak to their mythological characters but rather to the threadbare condition of the tapestry.

121. La Cydalise (or Cidalise) was one of the early Romantics' female divinities, many of whom were known only by their noms de guerre, and most of whom, like her, frequented the "headquarters" in the Impasse du Doyenné. Gautier was said to be madly in love with her and insanely jealous—like many of his confreres—of her liaison with artist Camille Rogier (1810–1896), who, at twenty-five, was the patriarch of the group, causing many to wonder what she could see in someone so ancient. Richard Holmes describes her as "a pale young seamstress with a tiny wasp-waist, who took up permanent residence in the Doyenné, but tragically died there of consumption." (See the introduction to his selection of translations, *My Fantoms: Théophile Gautier*, 2nd ed. [New York: New York Review of Books (Random House), 2008], xvii.)

122. A sketch of La Cydalise by Rogier—modern tastes as to her beauty might differ—serves as the frontispiece in Orlo Williams, *Vie de Bohème: A Patch of Romantic Paris* (Boston: Gorham Press, 1913). Though the details of her dress in these two quatrains do not quite match that portrait, the author does give a colorful description of the extravagances of female attire of the period: "Cydalise . . . would have kicked a little cross-laced foot out from ethereal folds of flowered muslin and gathered a gauzy scarf enticingly round bare shoulders. . . . (T)here were bows everywhere, on the bosom, on the sleeves, and, with long dazzling streamers, round the waist" (257).

123. Gothot-Mersch (*Emaux et Camées*, 267) identifies the "Andalouse" as Eugénie Fort (1812–1881), Gautier's mistress as La Cydalise lay dying, and mother of his son Théophile (1836–1904). (See note 80, to "Winter Fantasies," above.) The Murillo referred to is the Spanish Baroque painter Bartolomé Esteban Murillo (1617?–1682).

124. See the unnumbered headnote to "Inèz de Las Sierras," above.

125. Jasinski declares in *Les années romantiques de Théophile Gautier* (Paris: Vuibert, 1929, 295) that the "beauté robuste" was another of the denizens of the Impasse du Doyenné, Gautier's hot-blooded sometime mistress known as "La Victorine." Richard Holmes borrows a description of her from Arsène Houssaye's *Confessions, souvenirs d'un demi-siècle, 1830–1890* (Paris: Dentu, 1885–1891). In it the author often called "the last

of the Romantics" described her as "a beautiful girl with dark brown hair, a big scarlet mouth, and hell-fire eyes . . . who pounced on Théo like some lioness, and subdued him with her great mane of hair and her terrible claws" (Houssaye, *Confessions*, xix). The description is echoed by Gautier in the succeeding quatrains.

126. What follows is Gautier's tongue-in-cheek self-portrait, emphasizing his famous garish vest that caused quite a stir at the premiere of Hugo's romantic drama *Hernani* in 1830, and the typically French literary battle that ensued. Many readers of French who may not know a word of Gautier's poetry are familiar at least with his vest.

127. It is hard to be sure to which of the two Devéria brothers— Eugène(-François-Marie-Joseph) (1805–1865), and Achille(-Jacques-Jean-Marie) (1800–1857)—Gautier refers. Both were historic portrait painters of the period. If the former was the better known, the latter was praised by Gautier as virtually his equal: "Si les nécessités de la vie ne l'eussent forcé à une production incessante, il eût sans doute laissé un grand nom, car il n'était pas bien moins doué que son frère." The poet goes on to name the many Romantics who frequented the Devéria household, among them the second portraitist mentioned, Louis(-Candide) Boulanger (1806–1867). (See Gautier's *Histoire du romantisme*, second edition [Paris: Charpentier, 1874], 221.)

128. Gautier compares the young Romantic rebels of 1830, whose number had dwindled dramatically over the years, to the Turks who sacked the southern Italian town of Otranto in 1480, beheading hundreds of martyrs who refused to renounce Christianity.

129. Cottin (*Emaux et camées*, 159) and Gothot-Mersch (*Emaux et Camées*, 268) disagree on the probable identity of this red-bearded Romantic, the former opting for Camille Rogier (see note 121, above), the latter, more convincingly, for the stunningly hirsute Jules Vabre, enigmatic pro-*Hernani* battler to whom Gautier devoted chapter IV of his *Histoire du romantisme*, entitled "Le compagnon miraculeux" (34–42), and whose only claim to fame among his contemporaries was his inordinate love of Shakespeare and the supposed manuscript—never completed or at least never published—of an "Essai sur l'incommodité des com-

modes." The reference to Barbarossa "dans son roc" is an allusion to the legend according to which the celebrated red-beard cheated death by taking centuries-long refuge in a cave with his soldiers.

130. The mustachioed, cigarette-puffing dandy is Pétrus Borel (1809–1859), born Joseph-Pierre Borel (d'Hauterive). Charismatic eccentric, who adopted the nickname "Le lycanthrope" (the werewolf), Borel was the acknowledged soul of the Romantic movement in its early incarnations. As Gautier describes him, "Pétrus, qui était le plus parfait spécimen de l'idéal romantique et eût pu poser pour le héros de Byron, se promenait suivi de sa troupe, admiré de tous . . . le coin de son manteau jeté sur l'épaule" (*Histoire du romantisme*, 22). True to form, some of the poems in his collection *Rhapsodies* (1831)—intended, like his personal life, to shock the bourgeoisie—seem to prefigure the work of the Surrealists. In his destitute later years, Gautier and other friends of his youth were obliged to come to his rescue.

131. Gothot-Mersch is no doubt correct in identifying this concocter of intricate and usually horrific Boulevard melodramas—artistically slim but financially successful—as Joseph Bouchardy (1810–1870), whom Gautier discusses at length, poking gentle fun at his exaggerated stagecraft: "couloirs secrets, escaliers en spirale, salles voûtées, cabinets mystérieux, cachettes dans l'épaisseur des murs, oubliettes, caveaux mortuaires, chapelles cryptiques où ses héros et ses héroïnes devaient plus tard se rencontrer, s'aimer, se haïr . . . s'assassiner ou s'épouser" (*Histoire du romantisme*, 26). The quatrain, comparing him to Molière and the profound Spanish playwright Pedro Calderón de la Barca (1600–1681), is flattering, to say the least, though not insignificant, since much of Bouchardy's box-office success came from productions in Spain, where they apparently struck a responsive chord.

132. One of the lesser-known "vaillants de dix-huit cent trente," Napoléon Tom, according to Cottin (*Emaux et camées*, 161), was the illustrator of Borel's *Rhapsodies*. (See note 130, above, regarding Pétrus Borel.)

133. In the early Romantics' get-togethers, mystical poet Gérard de Nerval (1808–1855)—born Gérard Labrunie—who was to become one of Gautier's lifelong friends, would frequently adopt pseudonyms. "Il a signé

successivement Fritz, Aloysius et d'autres noms, et il sera difficile au-jourd'hui de reconnaître ses œuvres dans les catacombes poudreuses du journalisme" (*Histoire du romantisme*, 74). The passage from Goethe's *Faust* that he explicates for La Cydalise (see note 121, above) relates Faust's dream of characters from Shakespeare's *Midsummer Night's Dream* fol-lowing his and Mephistopheles's participation in the demonic witches' sabbath of Walpurgisnacht (Walpurgis Night), the eve of May 1, feast day of the eighth-century Saint Walpurgis (or Walpurga). Nerval would have known whereof he spoke. At the age of twenty, he had already published a translation of *Faust*, which was praised by Goethe himself.

"The Fellah"

See note 47, to "Obelisks' Longings, II. The Luxor Obelisk," above.

134. An illustration of the watercolor in question, by Princess Mathilde (-Laetitia-Wilhelmine Bonaparte) (1820–1904), daughter of Napoleon's brother Jérôme, can be seen at the Agence photographique de la Réunion des Musées Nationaux Web site http://216.139.227.103/CorexDoc/RMN/Media/TR1/DL13X7/01–001703.jpg.

"The Loft"

135. Rigolette was a character in the immensely popular and socially influential novel *Les Mystères de Paris*, by Eugène Sue (1804–1857), pub-lished serially in *Le Journal des Débats* from June 19, 1842, to October 15, 1843. Her name, like Margot in the next quatrain, was typical for the *grisette*.

136. The prestigious furniture firm, founded by Georges-Marie Mon-bro (1774–1841) and continued by his son, also named Georges (1807–1884), was synonymous with elegance.

137. The area around the then Rue Bréda—known to Anglophiles of the period (like Monsieur Homais in chapter 6 of *Madame Bovary*) as Bréda Street—was celebrated for its streetwalkers. One is reminded of a passage in Somerset Maugham's *Of Human Bondage*: "'Oh, I love Paris,' sighed Miss Wilkinson. . . . 'I had a tiny apartment in the Rue Breda, on the cinquieme: it wasn't at all respectable. You know about the Rue Breda—ces dames, you know.'"

"The Cloud"

Gothot-Mersch (*Emaux et Camées*, 271) informs us that this poem was written during a trip Gautier took to Geneva in 1866 to visit Carlotta Grisi. (See note 112, to "The Little Dead Girl's Toys," above.)

138. The painting *Antiope Sleeping* or *Jupiter and Antiope* (ca. 1523) by Antonio Allegri, known as Correggio (1494?–1534), depicts one of Zeus's not uncommon seductions, that of Antiope, princess of Thebes.

139. Ixion was a king of Thessaly, guilty not only of the unpardonable crime of murdering a family member—his father-in-law—but also of attempting the less unusual seduction of Zeus's wife, Hera. To test him, the god shaped a cloud in the goddess's likeness, with which Ixion promptly had his way. To punish him Zeus chained him to a wheel of fire, to turn for all eternity.

"The Blackbird"

140. The Arve River rises in the Alps, near Savoy, and merges with the Rhone south of Geneva. It was apparently on his trip to that city that Gautier wrote this poem and the preceding. (See the unnumbered headnote to "The Cloud," above.) According to Cottin (*Emaux et camées*, 187), it was dedicated to Carlotta Grisi's and Prince Radziwill's daughter Léontine.

"The Flower That Makes the Spring"

According to Gothot-Mersch (*Emaux et Camées*, 272) this poem, like the two preceding, also dates from Gautier's stay in Geneva at the Villa Grisi.

141. Gothot-Mersch (*Emaux et Camées*, 272) cites a variant of the final quatrain, of interest in that it specifically names Carlotta, Gautier's passion of the moment:

> Sous le ciel d'azur ou de brume,
> Une fleur rare s'ouvre ici,
> Qui toujours rayonne et parfume;
> Son nom est Carlotta Grisi.

She points out also that, appropriate to the text, Adolphe Boschot recalls that Gautier nicknamed Carlotta "la dame aux yeux de violette."

(See Boschot's *"Emaux et Camées": Texte definitif (1872), suivi de Poésies choisies* [Paris: Classiques Garnier, 1954], 334.)

"Last Wish"

142. Gothot-Mersch (*Emaux et Camées*, 272–73) presents a number of chronological problems posed by this poem, discussed in detail by Jasinski, Boschot, and others, of academic interest to biographers and researchers.

"The Pleasant Evening"

143. Gautier's admiration for Heine is well documented. (See the unnumbered headnote to "Lied," above.) The poet's famous *Lyrisches Intermezzo*, comprising a prologue and sixty-five of his finest lyrics, appeared in 1822–23.

144. *Thomas Grain-d'Orge* (or *Graind'orge*, or *Graindorge*) is a socially sardonic novel by Hippolyte Taine (1828–1893), whose fanciful description in chapter XI, "A Ball at the English Embassy," illustrates Gautier's tongue-in-cheek assessment of British decorum: "Une étuve, un entassement de têtes serrées, pêle-mêle, qui essaient de remuer et grimacent patiemment le meme sourire. . . . Etuve et bouillie. Tous les quarts d'heure la bouillie s'épaissit; la double porte ouverte verse un nouveau liquide humain, qui se mélange au reste, parmi des tournoiements et des remous. . . . Onze heures. La colle est faite, rien ne coule plus; les deux premiers salons sont arrivés à cet état des pâtes visqueuses qu'une cuiller qu'on enfonce reste debout; impossible d'avancer ni de reculer." (See Hippolyte Taine, *Notes sur Paris: Vie et opinions de M. Frédéric-Thomas Graindorge*, seventh edition [Paris: Hachette, 1877], 127.)

145. The brothers de Goncourt—Edmond (1822–1896) and Jules (1830–1870)—formed an inseparable literary partnership that produced not only several Naturalist novels but also, and especially, their celebrated *Journal*. In it, beginning in 1851, they chronicled, with not a little sarcasm and even personal enmity, what they considered to be the literary, artistic, and social vulgarities of their age.

"Art"

Jasinski (*Poésies complètes*, 1:cxxviii) quotes a similar poem,"Odelette," by Théodore de Banville (1823–1891)—similar even in form—in response to which Gautier dedicated to him, in 1857, this capstone of his collection.

Preaching an avoidance of the ethereal, often vaporous lyricism of the earlier Romantics, "L'Art" is considered the *ars poetica* of the Parnassians' "Art for Art's Sake" movement in French poetry.

146. In the Greek and Roman theater, the cothurn (or cothurnus) was a high boot laced up the calf, worn by actors of tragedy, hence symbolizing the tragic muse.

147. Like its counterpart from the Greek isle of Paros (see the unnumbered headnote to "The Poem of Woman," above), marble from Carrara, in Italy, was (and is) much prized for statuary.

148. Gautier's sculpturally incisive imperatives—"Sculpte, lime, cisèle . . ."—make this frequently cited final quatrain the ne plus ultra of the Parnassian poetic credo.

From *España*, 1845

Gautier's original text is found in Jasinski, *Poésies complètes*, 2:251–320.

"*Leave-taking*"

1. The Escurial (El Escorial in Spanish) is the complex of royal buildings—palace, church, mausoleum, monastery, and library—erected between 1563 and 1584 by Philip II, some thirty miles northwest of Madrid.

2. Like the biblical Canaan, "land flowing with milk and honey," the legendary utopia of El Dorado, familiar to readers of Voltaire's *Candide* (1759), became a metaphor for a land overflowing with great treasure. The legend began in the practice of the Chibcha people of Colombia to choose a tribal chieftain each year, ceremonially cover his body in gold dust, and eventually wash it off in a sacred lake. In time, the tale of *el dorado*—the gilded one—lured various Spanish conquistadors down the Amazon in fruitless searches. One, especially disastrous, occurred in 1541. Though Francisco de Orellana and Gonzalo Pizarro failed in their quest for gold, their expedition was the first to sail to the mouth of the Amazon. Another hopeful but unsuccessful adventurer was Sir Walter Raleigh, in 1595.

"*The Pine of the Landes Country*"

3. The *département* of Les Landes, in southwestern France, close to the Spanish border, was originally a broad area of sandy marshland, in which

great pine forests were planted early in the nineteenth century to minimize soil erosion.

"Saint Casilda"

4. Saint Casilda (died ca. 1050) was a Spanish martyr (though some accounts have her living to the age of one hundred). A native of Toledo, born to Moorish parents, she was known for her kindnesses to Christians and eventually converted to Christianity, becoming a hermitess near Briviesca. Casilda is venerated in Burgos and Toledo. The painting of her martyrdom, mistakenly attributed to Fra Diego de Leyva (1580?–1637), a specialist in martyrdom canvases, hangs in the cathedral of Burgos. According to Jasinski (*Poésies complètes*, 1:lxxiii), it is the work of Juan Rizi (1595?–1675?). The canvas is described by Gautier in chapter IV of his *Voyages en Espagne* (see note 38, to "Rondalla," from *Emaux et Camées*, above), in a passage detailing the saint's gory image, her two amputated breasts lying by her side, with blood gushing from two red spots on her bosom as she gazes with an expression of "feverish and convulsive ecstasy" at an angel bearing her a comforting palm leaf. Gautier goes on to point out that he found such graphic paintings rather common in Spain.

"On the Way to the Miraflores Charterhouse"

5. Of the supposedly difficult ascent to reach the Charterhouse, Schick (*Seductive Resistance*, 95) remarks: "The reader should not be surprised when Jasinski asserts that the climb to this monastery at Miraflores is not as arduous as the poem pretends, that the olive trees growing in the poem do not grow in the geographical vicinity of Miraflores, and that the church which contained the tomb of the Cid is not visible from the monastery." (See the unnumbered headnote to "Posthumous Coquettishness," from *Emaux et Camées*, above.) For her, many (if not most) of the physical descriptions in *España* are Gautier's pretexts for mimetic metaphor, or, in her words, "mock-referentiality effecting a mock-metaphoricity."

6. The bones of Ruy (Rodrigo) Díaz de Vivar, known to history and literature as El Cid Campeador (1040–1099), Spain's national hero—though some feel he was more a mercenary than a patriot—repose with those of his wife, Doña Jimena (Ximena) (1054–1115), not in just an ordinary "église," but in the majestic cathedral of Burgos, to which they were

moved in 1921 after lying in a monastery outside the city, and, according to some sources, even, for a time, in the less than impressive town hall. Be that as it may, his exploits are glorified in the famous epic, *El Cantar de Mío Cid,* dating probably from the fourteenth century.

"The Cemetery Fountain"

7. Though in my version I have preferred couplets to Gautier's somewhat arbitrary rhyme scheme (which some editions separate into sestets), for the climactic conclusion I do choose a more dramatic *abbacddc*.

"The Blue Eyes of the Mountain"

8. Ithuriel was one of the two archangels sent by Gabriel to find Satan in the Garden of Eden. Archangels were the highest order of angel in the heavenly hierarchy; winged spirits able to change shape at will, but not without some human attributes and failings. They were said to protect man and to battle the rebel angels in God's behalf. It will be remembered that Ithuriel figures, along with others of the archangelic host, in John Milton's *Paradise Lost* (ca. 1665).

9. Guadarrama is one of the more important towns of the mountain range in central Spain, bearing its name. High and cool, it has long been a favorite summer retreat for the residents of Madrid, in Gautier's day no less than in our own.

"In Madrid"

This poem, among others of the art-inspired poems in *España,* is cited by Kathleen Koestler to support her thesis that Gautier the critic was not comfortable with realism in art, and especially Spanish art, with religion's emphasis on the horrors of the flesh: what she terms "the leaden rhetoric of martyrdom": "Gautier condemned realism in Spanish painting." And, speaking of "A Madrid" in particular: "The poet criticizes realism in Spanish art more obliquely here than in other poems, but his bitter and heavy-handed ironies still overshadow the poem's playfulness" (Kathleen Koestler, *Théophile Gautier's "España"* [Huntsville, Ala.: Summa Publications, 2002], 67–70.) And this, somewhat paradoxically, at a time when realism—though not of the often brutal Spanish variety—was beginning to dominate Gautier the poet's aesthetic in the form of "Art for Art's Sake."

10. Gautier is alluding here to the eminent baroque sculptor Juan (de) Martínez Montañés (1568–1649), who, born in Granada, spent most of his artistic life in Seville, dying there at the height of his celebrity. He was especially known for his elegant carved wood altarpieces and statuary, often painted in gold and bright colors, which earned him the sobriquet "el dios de la madera" (the god of wood).

"On the Prometheus in the Madrid Museum"

11. José Ribeira (or Ribera) (1588–1652), also known as "Lo Spagnoletto," especially during his lengthy stay in Naples, was a typical example of a painter whose lurid realism Gautier scorned. "The tone of 'Sur le Prométhée du Musée de Madrid' . . . is unequivocal. Bitterness permeates this transposition . . . as it does Gautier's other critiques of Spanish realism" (Koestler, *Gautier's "España,"* 67). Famous for the chiaroscuro effects with which he rendered it early in his career, Ribeira eventually tempered his style in keeping with the more devotional spirit of the Counter-Reformation.

"The Escurial"

See also note 1, to "Leave-taking," above.

12. The elephant comparison may have been at least prompted by an anecdote concerning Abada, the king's "pet" rhinoceros, and a joke he played on the friars at El Escorial. In the autumn of 1584, "among the trophies he had brought from Portugal were an Indian elephant and a rhinoceros. In October he arranged for the elephant . . . to saunter round the cloister, up the steps and into the cells of the astonished Jeronimites. A week later it was the turn of the rhinoceros, which was not quite so cooperative." (See Henry Kamen, *Philip of Spain* [New Haven: Yale University Press, 1997], 249.)

13. Gautier likens Philip II, builder of the Escurial mausoleum, not only to Egyptian pharaohs, but also, more accusatorily, to the Roman emperor Tiberius, known for his excesses, both governmental and personal. (See note 14, to "Study in Hands, II. Lacenaire," from *Emaux et Camées,* above.) His architectural "débauche"—to use Gautier's ungenerous term—was equaled only by his inquisitional zeal: "But Philip II, the rival of Tiberius, of Nero, and of Caligula . . . encouraged accusa-

tions, and rewarded the accusers; and thus the cells of the Holy Office were crowded with illustrious victims: inquisitional fury delivered to the flames, indiscriminately, the bodies of ecclesiastics, of the nobility, the gentry, and principal people of Spain." (See Adolfo de Castro, *The Spanish Protestants and Their Persecution by Philip II: A Historical Work*, trans. Thomas Parker [London: Charles Gilpin, 1851], 217–18.)

"The Solitary King"

Inspired by the Escurial, Gautier imagines a monologue by Philip II, dramatically recalling the poet's Romantic roots in the midst of his foray into objective Parnassianism. (See the unnumbered headnote to "Art," from *Emaux et Camées*, above.) Specific details aside, the angst-ridden message is that of the typical Romantic hero, exiled from humanity by his greatness, whose prototype is Moses in the poem "Moïse," one of the *Poèmes antiques et modernes* (1826–1837) of arch-Romantic Alfred de Vigny (1797–1863).

"In Deserto"

14. The site of the village of La Guardia, in the province of Toledo, appears, from archaeological remains, to date back to the Bronze Age, with its more recent history beginning in 1164. Its location on a mountainous outcropping contributed to its strategic importance in the defense against the Moors, as well as to the arid climate that Gautier describes, perhaps exaggeratedly.

"Stanzas"

15. We can assume, I think, that the original's phrase "travailleur noir" refers not to the miner's race but to the result of his digging in the mines.

16. The plateau of Don Quixote's La Mancha, in the very center of the Iberian peninsula, is both barren in the mountains and fertile on the plains. It is perhaps for the former quality—if for any at all—that Gautier found in it the inspiration for this rather morbid poem.

"Passing by a Cemetery"

If the metaphor of this single quatrain is easily explained by critic Gautier's devotion to the theater, its length—the shortest in *España*—is less so. I tend to think that its startling brevity is inversely proportional to the profundity of the subject: to wit, the very meaning of life. Is Gautier giving a wink to the reader, as if to ask: "What more need I say?" Especially in death-obsessed Spain...

"Higher I climbed..."

17. One wonders if Gautier's claim to have climbed "plus haut que l'aigle et le nuage" was literally true. The Sierra Nevada (Spanish for "snowy range") is the principal mountain chain of southern Spain, reaching heights of over 11,000 feet. As such it would present a challenge, except in the lowest foothills, to climbers as portly as one knows him to have been. But his possible exaggeration does nothing to dull the poetry, here and in the poems that follow.

18. The similarities, differences, and eschatological functions of the biblical beasts, Behemoth and Leviathan, have often given rise to lengthy scriptural discourse. Since Gautier's allusion does not appear based on prophetic "end of the world" considerations, suffice it to remind the reader that the former, from a Hebrew word, perhaps originally Egyptian, refers to a huge land creature, possibly the rhinoceros, cited in Job 40:15–24. The latter, a sea monster thought to have been a huge crocodile, is mentioned at least a half dozen times in the Old Testament.

"In the Sierra"

19. Apart from his own possible abilities as a climber, Gautier's love of the mountains was beyond question, such that in many effusive passages he would justify it by waxing philosophical, sounding more the early Romantic than the Parnassian. For example, in a feuilleton dating from 1867, writing from Zermatt, he would say: "Quoique la raison y puisse objecter, cette lutte de l'homme avec la montagne est poétique et noble. La foule qui a l'instinct des grandes choses environne ces audacieux de respect et à la descente toujours leur fait une ovation. Ils sont la volonté protestant contre l'obstacle aveugle, et ils plantent sur l'inaccessible le drapeau de l'intelligence humaine." (See the posthumous collection *Vacances du lundi* [Paris: Charpentier, 1881], 285.)

"The Poet and the Masses"

20. Details aside, Gautier seems, in this couplet, to be echoing the beginnings of many a French fable—no doubt deeply entrenched in schoolboy memory—not a few of which personified elements of nature rather than the more usual animals and even occasional human beings. "The Oak and the Reed" of Jean de La Fontaine (1621–1695) comes immediately to mind: "Le Chêne un jour dit au Roseau / 'Vous avez bien sujet d'accuser la nature; / Un roitelet pour vous est un pesant fardeau'" (See my translation in *The Complete Fables of Jean de La Fontaine* [Urbana: University of Illinois Press, 2007], 25–26.)

21. As for Gautier's "moral" here, it is typical of the Romantic cliché of the civilizing mission of the poet and the glory that accrues to him despite his frailties.

"The Hunter"

22. The animal denizen referred to is the mountain antelope known as the "chamois" in French and English, native to the Alps and Appenines, and also to the Pyrenees, where it is called the "isard" (or "izard"). An herbivore, its Latin species name is *rupicapra pyrenaica* ("Pyrenees cliff goat"). Its skin is prized and often made into soft chamois leather.

"Serenade"

Much less vigorous, even savage, in spirit than "Rondalla"—the serenade-inspired poem in *Emaux et Camées* (see notes to "Rondalla," above)—this one is no less Spanish in atmosphere, though lacking a specific place of composition, and though reminiscent of a fairy tale of Germanic rather than Spanish origin. The tale of Rapunzel—she of the long locks, let down from a tower for the prince charming to scale—has been traced back to the fifteenth century. Its best-known version, properly sanitized for children, was included by the Brothers Grimm in their *Children's and Household Tales* in 1812 and subsequent collections. A French version, entitled *Persinette*, had been published by Charlotte-Rose de La Force in 1698.

"In the depths of my heart..."

23. The word "carte" is ambiguous here, since the text offers no specifics. Several different kinds of carte spring to mind: maps, cartes du jour

(bills-of-fare), calling cards, or playing cards. I have finally settled on the last, given the card games that Gautier obliquely mentions at the social gatherings he attended. (See note 24.)

24. As for a possible specific love-affair, none of Gautier's various amours, platonic or otherwise, seems to fit the situation. I suspect, rather, that, carried away by Granada's sensual milieu, he is fantasizing—and a little tongue-in-cheek, at that—about any of the señoritas that enlivened his visit. "We could not have had a more cordial, open-hearted and amiable reception. . . . According to the Spanish usage, we were called by our Christian names . . . while we were allowed the liberty of calling the women and girls of the families in which we were received by theirs: Carmen, Teresa, Gala, etc. . . . So we went to a *tertulia* every evening, in one home or another, from eight o'clock till midnight. . . . Guitars lie here and there; the piano stands in one corner, and the card-tables are set up in another." (*A Romantic in Spain*, 176.)

25. Though the detail that this poem, dating from 1841, was written in Granada—the picturesque Moorish city in Andalusia—may seem rather arbitrary, I am tempted to explain the poem's effusive outpourings either as playful exaggeration (see note 24), or, if utterly sincere, as the effect of Granada on Gautier's ever-Romantic soul, "conversion" to Parnassianism notwithstanding. Several years after his visit, he would confess in his Spanish memoirs (see note 38, to "Rondalla," from *Emaux et Camées*, above) that the several days and nights he spent in Granada "were without doubt the most delicious moments of my life," going on to lament: "A few days later we left Granada, heaving a sigh no less profound than that of King Boabdil." (See *A Romantic in Spain*, 180, 211; for King Boabdil, see note 5, to "Hidden Affinities," from *Emaux et Camées*, above.)

"The Oleander of the Generalife"

See also note 5, to "Hidden Affinities," from *Emaux et Camées*, above.

26. Koestler (*Gautier's "España,"* 70) suggests that this poem "is one of the few happy poems of *España*. . . . The poem is a variation on the myth of Pygmalion, the illusion being that of a statue come to life. In embracing it, the poet embraces his own creation." I might add that, were this roman-

tic fiction true, Gautier would have been much the worse for it. One has to assume that he did not know that, for all its delicate beauty, the olean-der (or rose laurel) is one of the most poisonous plants in nature, able to cause not only a variety of disagreeable symptoms, but even coma and, in some cases, death.

"The Moon"

In this example of Gautier's many-stringed bow, I have intentionally tried to duplicate the lighthearted lilt of the seven-syllable lines through-out. Here the *impair* (that is, odd-number) meter suggests almost a kind of nursery-rhyme quality, or even something of a fable coloration—though rhythmically quite different from that of "Le Poète et la foule." (See note 20, to "The Poet and the Masses," above.) It is this lilting rhythm that leads Koestler to quote Serge Fauchereau: "On veut tellement voir le peintre en Gautier qu'on oublie de remarquer la musicalité des vers." This was far from a spontaneous musicality, however. We are told that the manuscript of the poem reveals seven reworkings of one of the stanzas. (See Koestler, *Gautier's "España,"* 76–78.)

27. Gautier is playing here with a common proverb: "Le soir (*or* la nuit) tous les chats sont gris (*or* noirs)," usually rendered in English as "all cats are gray in the dark."

"As I no longer would remain..."

As Koestler points out (Koestler, *Gautier's "España,"* 78), there is, in this poem, and in "La Lune" as well, "less emphasis upon color and texture and more upon the effects of rhythm and sound. . . . Both are essentially theatrical." I try to suggest these several qualities in my translation.

"A red carnation... My snow breast..."

This brief poem, dating from 1845, is Gautier's free translation of a Spanish *copla*, the typically hot-blooded and amorous genre native to Andalusia. Similar to the romance, it is often set to music. Though essen-tially popular in nature and typical of its Andalusian roots, the copla is not limited in scope and has been practiced by well-lettered Spanish poets throughout the Hispanic world.

"The Moor's Last Sigh"

28. After the final days of the reconquest of Andalusia by Ferdinand and Isabel, the Moorish king, Boabdil (see note 5, to "Hidden Affinities," from *Emaux et Camées*, above), fleeing south with his mother and his retinue, stopped briefly on Mount Padul to look back longingly over his lost kingdom. The spot where, according to legend, he voiced his lament became known in Spanish as "El Suspiro del Moro" (The Moor's Sigh). The French pre-Romantic writer and statesman François-René de Chateaubriand (1768–1848) recounted the event in his novella *Les Aventures du dernier Abencerrage* (1826): " 'Weep now like a woman, for the loss of a kingdom, which thou hast been unable to defend like a man.' They descended the mountain and Granada disappeared from their eyes for ever" (trans. William Evans Burton, in *The Gentleman's Magazine*, no. 4 [Philadelphia: Charles Alexander, 1838], 233.) Details of the story were also recounted in Part 17 of *Tales of the Alhambra* (1832), by American author Washington Irving (1783–1859). In our own day, author Salman Rushdie has used the tale to analogize elements of his personal "exile," in *The Moor's Last Sigh* (New York: Random House, 1995).

29. The Darro River is a tributary of the Genil (or Jenil), itself a tributary of the Guadalquivir (from the Arabic *wadi-al-kabir*, "great river"), the major river of southern Spain and the country's only navigable waterway. The Darro was important to Moorish Granada in that it supplied water to the Alhambra through a series of aqueducts.

30. Sierra d'Elvire (or Sierra Elvira, in Spanish) is a range of moderate mountains in the vicinity of Granada, few of which reach heights over 3,000 feet.

"View"

31. On the Guadalquivir (see note 29, to "The Moor's Last Sigh," above), the majestic city of Seville (or Sevilla, in Spanish), fourth largest in Spain, is the capital of Andalusia.

32. The cathedral's bell tower, La Giralda, built between 1184 and 1196, was originally a minaret. It was considered such a work of art that when the besieged city was about to be reconquered in 1248, King Ferdinand III of Castile demanded that not a single stone be harmed despite the Moors'

intention to destroy it rather than let it fall into Christian hands. The angel referred to is a life-size head adorning the breast of a bronze female figure, standing on a great globe some six feet in diameter, that serves as the tower's weather vane, dominating the skyline.

"By the Seashore"

Koestler (*Gautier's "España*," 46–47) suggests that this poem, along with several others written around the same time, were imitations of Spanish verse forms. "Though virtuoso pieces, they are primarily exercises in adaptation." I do not think, however, that as simple octosyllables they necessarily owe much to Spanish versification.

33. Difference between mountain-climbing and flying aside, the last lines recall Gautier's Romantic "yearning for the heights," voiced in "J'étais monté plus haut... ." (See note 17, to "Higher I Climbed... ," above.)

34. Clearly, Gautier's progress toward Parnassian objectivity had not lulled the early Romantic in him. What better background against which to express it than the lush, sub-tropical Málaga, on the Mediterranean's Costa del Sol, in the shadow of Gibraltar? Founded by the Phoenicians and today a modern metropolis, Andalusia's second-largest city was in Gautier's time even more the "City of Paradise."

"Saint Christopher of Ecija"

Known as both "The Frying Pan of Andalusia" and "The City of Sun and Towers," the ancient Moorish village of Ecija, on the Genil River (see note 29, to "The Moor's Last Sigh," above) between Seville and Córdoba, had to be largely rebuilt after a devastating earthquake in 1757. It is still, as it was in Gautier's day, an architectural treasure of brilliantly tiled churches, bell towers, flamboyantly shaped mansions, and assorted magnificent monuments.

35. One of the monuments, the subject of his poem, is detailed in his *Wanderings in Spain* (see note 38, to "Rondalla," from *Emaux et Camées*, above), in which he describes the two "rather strange monuments" that ornament the village square: "The first is a gilt statue of the Holy Virgin, placed upon a column, the pedestal of which evidently forms a kind of chapel. . . . The second is a gigantic Saint Christopher, also of gilt metal,

with his hand resting upon a palm-tree, a sort of walking-stick in keeping with his immense size; on his shoulder he bears, with the most prodigious contraction of all his muscles . . . an exceedingly small infant Jesus, of the most delicate and charming style." Gautier claims that the "powerful colossus" was the creation of Michelangelo's antagonist, Florentine sculptor Pietro Torregiano (or Torrigiano) (1474–1522), and goes on to explain that the figure "is stuck upon a Solomonic column (as wreathed columns are here called) . . . the spiral wreaths of which end half-way up in a mass of volutes and extravagant flower-work" (Théophile Gautier, *Wanderings in Spain* [London: Ingram, Cooke and Co., 1853], 241–42).

36. The "vieux Crotoniate" would appear to be Pythagoras, often referred to as "The Sage of Croton (or Crotona)," the town on the heel of Italy where, around 540 BCE, he founded his school of philosophy and taught his disciples. The comparison with Samson and Hercules is, however, curious. Though Pythagoras's power and influence were considerable—he is said to have transformed the morals of the townspeople in no time at all—they were hardly of the physical variety. One could also be tempted to see in the line "Mon poignet vaut celui du vieux Crotoniate" a convoluted reference to Torregiano (see note 35), "who flattened, with a blow of his fist, Michael Angelo's nose" (Gautier, *Wanderings*). But there seems to be no evidence that the irascible sculptor ever lived in Crotona, and the similarity is probably coincidental.

"During the Storm"

37. There is nothing unusual in poets' dramatizing sailors' prayers for safe passage in the midst of stormy seas. I have no doubt that world literature presents any number of such poetic pleadings to a variety of gods and goddesses. What one finds charming in Gautier's example, however, is the pleasantly naïve, almost childlike manner in which the speaker promises the Virgin that she will be rewarded. We are reminded, across a cultural and geographical divide, of the similar bribes (a silk scarf and assorted sweets) offered by storm-tossed Haitian fishermen to their voodoo divinity—the "loa" Agwè—in the 1930s poem "Vœu" by Carl Brouard (1902–1965):

Le ciel est noir,
le vent siffle, et les vagues furieuses
ballottent çà et là le frêle boumba.
Puissant Agouey,
loa à la chevelure glauque,
aie pitié de nous!
Si tu nous délivres du peril,
nous te donnerons un foulard vert,
des sirops onctueux,
de succulents gateaux faits à Port-au-Prince.

38. Cadiz (or Cadix in French), reputed to be the oldest city in Europe, was founded by the Phoenicians in about 1100 BCE and was subsequently settled by the Carthaginians and the Romans. On a long, narrow peninsula, it is surrounded by water and was an important commercial port in Spain's flourishing trade with much of the world during the seventeenth century. As such, it was an appropriate background for the present poem.

"Farewell to Poetry"

With all of *Emaux et Camées* yet ahead of him, Gautier's leave-taking of poetry was premature, to say the least (unless he meant it as a temporary hiatus—the relaxation of a "moment," as line 8 of the original might allow us to infer). He had already hinted at it in "Le Poète et la foule" (see note 21, to "The Poet and the Masses," above); and if he was to "fall into prose," he had, in fact, as a journalist, never really left it. (See unnumbered note to "After the Article," from *Emaux et Camées*, above) Such poetic farewells were something of a cliché, especially among the Romantics, disillusioned with the public's scorn for their emotional superiority and their civilizing mission. Gautier would have had one wordy model in the twenty-sixth of the *Méditations poétiques* (1820) of Alphonse de Lamartine (1790–1869), also entitled "Adieux à la poésie," and another in the more personal and less antibourgeois (but no less premature) "farewell" of his contemporary Louise Ackermann (1813–1890), who, in her last stanza, complains:

J'irai seule et brisant ma lyre,	Breaking my lyre, off will I go
Souffrant mes maux sans les chanter;	In pain, alone, yet not declare it;
Car je sentirais à les dire	For suffer will I more my woe,
Plus de douleur qu'à le porter.	Singing it, than if I but bear it.

(See my *French Women Poets of Nine Centuries: The Distaff and the Pen* [Baltimore: The Johns Hopkins University Press, 2009], 674–75.) While Gautier chose "Adieux à la poésie," appropriately, as the final poem in *España*, he actually wrote it before two others of the collection: "J'ai laissé dans mon sein de neige..." (see unnumbered note to "A red carnation... My snow breast...," above) and "Letrilla," not translated here. (See Koestler, *Gautier's "España*," 80.)

From "Pièces diverses" in *Poésies nouvelles*, 1845
Gautier's original text is found in Jasinski, *Poésies complètes*, 2:219–50.

"You crave my verse..."
This poem is entitled "Sur un album" in Jasinski (*Poésies complètes*, 2:219), who assures us that the "vous" in question is unknown.

1. However uncertain the identity—real or fictitious—of the lady addressed, the subject of Gautier's diatribe against the critics and criticism, and his own humiliating need to participate in it, is clear. (See unnumbered note to "After the Article," from *Emaux et Camées*, above.) Two decades later, Arsène Houssaye (1815–1896), "the last of the Romantics," writing under one of his many pseudonyms—René de la Ferté—would quote its first twenty-two lines in his journal *L'Artiste: revue du XIXe siècle*, to buttress his own similar condemnation. (See "Le Monde et le théâtre," in no. XXXVII, July 1, 1867, 147–48.) Its opening lines would also be cited by (Jean-Baptiste-Joseph-)Emile Montégut (1825–1895) a decade after Gautier's death, chronicling the "tyranny of the feuilleton" in his artistic existence and its intrusion into his life as a poet. (See *Nos morts contemporains*, 2e série [Paris: Hachette, 1884], 45–46.)

2. In Greek mythology, Aonia, in Boeotia, at the foot of Mount Helicon, was the home of the Muses.

3. Gautier clearly had reason to feel optimistic, as we have seen from

his lengthy poetic career, other supposed leave-takings notwithstanding. (See unnumbered note to "Farewell to Poetry," from *España*, above.)

"Prayer"

Along with Faith and Hope, Charity, the third (and according to Saint Paul, the most important) of the trio of Christian virtues, has long figured in theological iconography. A typical example, and one that, incidentally, echoes Gautier's text in its broad lines, would be found decades after his poem in one of the three stained glass windows designed by pre-Raphaelite artist Sir Edward Burne-Jones (1833–1898) for St. Martin's Church in Brampton, England, in 1889. Analogous with the Virgin, the figure of Charity, in a flowing robe, is seen with a yellow flame rising from her right hand, and with her left arm supporting an infant. Two other young children stand close by, clutching her knees as if for protection.

"For an Italian Miss"

This poem, first appearing in the *Revue de Paris*, May 21, 1843, was written for Carlotta Grisi. (See note 112, to "The Little Dead Girl's Toys," from *Emaux et Camées*, above.)

"Kissing the shore, the suffering sea…"

Almost six decades after the composition of this poem, it was quoted as a fitting summation for an encomium to Constantinople. In the final chapter of his *Constantinople: The Story of the Old Capital of the Empire* (London: J. M. Dent, 1900), William Holden Hutton concludes his description of the city's antiquities with a look at the imperial museum: "The museum, with its treasures scattered about the rooms and in the gardens . . . may not unfitly serve to represent the endless interests of the great city, its associations with every phase of the historic life of East and West. But the fascination of the imperial city which lies 'betwixt two seas' lies in something besides her history. And the poets have known it." He then proceeds to prove his point by citing Gautier's poem in toto. What remains curious, however, is that Gautier's own travels to Turkey did not take place until 1852, seven years after the date usually given for the composition of this poem.

4. Gautier's firsthand description of the Hagia Sophia is rather less

enthusiastic than the present one, possibly culled from secondary sources. (See the unnumbered headnote to this poem, above.) In his travelogue, *Constantinople* (Paris: M. Lévy, 1853), he describes the famous mosque as "the most ancient and most important building of Constantinople," not without a dose of disillusionment, however. "After having once seen . . . the back—enriched with delicate carvings and inscriptions—of the fountain of Achmet III, Saint-Sophia presents but an ill-assorted mass of misshapen constructions. The original plan has disappeared, beneath an aggregation of excrescences and additions, which have obliterated the primitive outlines and rendered it almost impossible to discover them." (See the rather turgid translation of Robert Howe Gould [London: David Bogue, 1854; New York: Henry Holt and Co., 1875], 265.)

"*Sultan Mahmoud*"
Gautier appears here to be referring to Mahmoud II, though that sultan reigned from 1808 to 1839, and the poet's own travels would have taken him to Constantinople in 1852, under the rule of Mahmoud's son Abdul-Medjid (1839–1861). (See unnumbered headnote to "Kissing the shore, the suffering sea... ," above.) There would, however, have been no dearth of secondary sources describing Mahmoud, given the fashionable popularity of Turkish subject matter at the time. While his son was seen as something of a brooding romantic, Mahmoud himself had been described as a rather lackluster Ottoman potentate: "sa physionomie ne révèle point l'énergie qu'il a déployée dans certaines circonstances; il a le regard terne et sans expression, il ne manque cependant pas de dignité dans son maintien; on dit généralement que Mahmoud est l'idole des harems." (See Joseph Michaud and Joseph Poujoulat, *Correspondance d'Orient* [1833–1835], 3 vols. (Brussels· Grégoirs, Wouters, et Cie, 1841), 3:12.)

"*Mid the wild-growing forest filigree...*"
This poem, even more obviously indebted to the fable genre than some of the preceding (see note 20, to "The Poet and the Masses," and the unnumbered headnote to "The Moon," both from *España*, above), is entitled "Le Puits mystérieux" in Jasinski (*Poésies complètes*, 2:240).

5. The text, specifically echoing Aesop's fable of the crow and the water jug, differs in that, in the original, the stratagem was successful.

From "Poésies diverses," published with
La Comédie de la mort, 1833–1838

Gautier's original text is found in Jasinski, *Poésies complètes*, 2:51–215.

"The Last Leaf"

1. Gautier's final quatrain is engraved on his tombstone in the Montmartre cemetery where he is buried.

"The Spectre of the Rose"

Many of Gautier's lyrics have been set to music over the years as art songs and choral pieces, in French as well as other languages; this is one among them. The present poem is also famous for the ballet that it inspired. Set to music of Carl Maria von Weber (1786–1826) and choreographed by Michel Fokine (1880–1942) for Diaghilev's Ballets Russes, it was first danced in 1911 by the legendary Vaslav Nijinsky (1890–1950), and subsequently by Rudolf Nureyev (1938–1993) and Margot Fonteyn (1919–1991) numerous times between 1979 and 1987, the final year of their celebrated artistic collaboration. The ballet depicts a rose's love for a young girl, who, through no fault of her own, wears the dead flower to her first ball. Returning, she dreams that the ghost of the rose invites her to dance. When she awakes she can only wonder if the dance was, indeed, a dream.

"The Hippopotamus"

One of Gautier's rare forays into humorous verse—though not without a semiserious moral at the end—this poem served as an inspiration for a similar work by T. S. Eliot (1888–1965), entitled "The Hippopotamus," also replete with moral, in this case a religious one. I quote the first two of its nine quatrains:

> The broad-backed hippopotamus
> Rests on his belly in the mud;
> Although he seems so firm to us
> He is merely flesh and blood.
>
> Flesh-and-blood is weak and frail,
> Susceptible to nervous shock;

> While the True Church can never fail
> For it is based upon a rock.

(See T. S. Eliot, *Poems* [New York: Alfred A. Knopf, 1920], 27–28. The original publication was in *Little Review*, 4.3 [July 1917], 8–11.)

2. The imperviousness of Gautier's hippopotamus to the kris—a traditional Malay dagger—and the bullets made famous by the Sepoy War of 1857 against the British in India, recalls a less moralistic bit of nonsense verse by Franco-British poet Hil(l)aire Belloc (1870–1953), also entitled "The Hippopotamus," from his collection *The Bad Child's Book of Beasts* (1896), which includes tributes of varying lengths to the yak, the whale, the dromedary, the marmozet (*sic*), the dodo, et al. Its single quatrain, for which I would not suggest any influence of the Gautier poem, reads:

> I shoot the Hippopotamus
> With bullets made of platinum,
> Because if I use leaden ones
> His hide is sure to flatten 'em.

From *Premières Poésies*, 1830–1845

The rubric "Premières poésies" can be deceiving. The chronology of Gautier's collections is frequently complicated by the fact that successive editions often included poems from previous collections but with a change of rubric. As for his earliest work, in 1830 Gautier published a collection of forty-two poems, composed when he was eighteen. Its title was simply *Poésies*. When no copies were sold—thanks at least in part to the political turmoil of the July Revolution—the volume was taken off the market. It was reprinted two years later, revised and expanded, along with Gautier's lengthy poem *Albertus*. A definitive version eventually appeared at the end of his *Poésies complètes* (Paris: Charpentier, 1845), subsequently reedited by Jasinski (*Poésies complètes*, 1:1–126). It is from the latter that the present texts are taken (including a few epigraph inconsistencies).

"Meditation"

The epigraph is taken from "Consolation à M. du Périer sur la mort de sa fille," by François de Malherbe (1555–1628), classical reformer of French poetry, not at all in the generally Romantic spirit of the Gautier poem, which was clearly inspired by Lamartine's *Méditations poétiques* (see unnumbered note to "Farewell to Poetry," from *España*, above). Schick (*Seductive Resistance*, 12) cites Harry Cockerham's attempt to explain the contradiction "by maintaining that the poem was probably a very early poem written when Gautier had not yet fully renounced or overcome his classical education."

"*Elegy I*"

Alain Chartier (1385?–1433?) was a medieval poet and prose writer of stature, court poet of Charles II, and praised as "the father of French eloquence" by poet/*Rhétoriqueur* Jean Bouchet (1476–1577). His celebrated *La Belle Dame sans merci* inspired John Keats's poem of the same title published in 1820.

Despite the rather specific details offered throughout the text, the inspiration for Gautier's encomium appears to have eluded researchers.

1. Besides Goethe's Romantic icon, *The Sorrows of Young Werther* (1774), which influenced over a generation of youth—and by no means all pallid English maidens, to be sure—Gautier alludes here (notwithstanding the erroneous double "s") to the earlier *History of Charles Grandison*, the sentimental epistolary novel of 1753 by Samuel Richardson (1689–1761), author of the even more popular *Pamela, or Virtue Rewarded* (1740) and *Clarissa, or The History of a Young Lady* (1748). As for the "Creole" identity of the shadowy figure, Gautier seems to be using the term as it was (and is) frequently misused to suggest a person of mixed race. Baudelaire would use it correctly in his "A une dame créole" to identify a person of European ancestry born in the colonies. (See my *Selected Poems from "Les Fleurs du Mal"* [Chicago: University of Chicago Press, 1998], 107–8, 198.)

"*Landscape*"

The epigraph quotes Virgil's *Georgics*, I, 371–72.

2. I think Gautier may have intentionally chosen the *impair* (odd-number) seven-syllable line to suggest something of the breathless quality of the storm-drenched landscape, though in other contexts it can also give other colorations. (See unnumbered note to "The Moon," from *España*, above.) In any event, whatever his reasons, I choose to follow his poetic lead.

"Oath"

The influence—for good or ill—of the monumental medieval poem *Le Roman de la Rose*, source of the epigraph, hardly begs discussion here. A work in two very asymmetrical parts, it began as a rather conventional allegory of a "courtly" love affair by Guillaume de Lorris (1210?–1237?), lay incomplete, for whatever reason, in about 1230, and was taken up again around 1275 by Jean de Meun(g) (1240?–1305?) as a vehicle for his encyclopedic, philosophical, rationalistic ideas enlivened with not a little bawdy misogynism. It was probably the most widely read work of medieval French literature and extended its influence over generations and well beyond the borders of France in the persons of Chaucer, Dante, Petrarch, and others. The couplet in question quotes lines 85–86.

3. Again, the specific source of Gautier's inspiration is a mystery, though his broad hints at a seventeen-year-old señorita limit the field; that is, assuming—given his fondness for all things Spanish, even before his travels through Spain—that she is not merely an idealized imaginary construct. (See unnumbered headnote to "Inès de Las Sierras," from *Emaux et Camées*, above.)

"Maiden Fair"

The first epigraph is from the work of (Pierre-Marie-Jeanne-)Alexandre(-Thérèse) Guiraud (1788–1847), prolific but rather banal early Romantic poet and playwright. One of the founders of *La Muse française* in 1823–1824, he was named a baron by Charles X and was elected to the Académie Française in 1826 over Lamartine. Four volumes of his *Œuvres complètes* were published three years before his death. The quote—not particularly related to Gautier's text except in its pithy cliché—is from Canto IV, "La Mort," of his "Isaure, Poëme Elégiaque en cinq chants," one of his rather saccharine *Poëmes et chants élégiaques* (Paris: A. Boulland, 1824), 79:

> La vierge est un ange d'amour
> Qui sème sur ses pas d'ineffables délices,
> Qui sait pour nos douleurs des paroles propices,
> Et belle, à son matin, sourit comme un beau jour.
>
> Mais le jour quelquefois se voile, dès l'aurore:

> L'ange, échappé du monde, à Dieu se réunit:
> Et lorsqu'il a passé, nous le cherchons encore...
> Et nous voulons mourir quand le rêve finit.

One might wonder if friendship and perhaps the general fashionability of Guiraud's work, rather than genuine artistic admiration, prompted Gautier to quote him.

Jasinski (*Poésies complètes*, 1:xix) identifies "M*****" as referring to Auguste Maquet (1813–1888), a classmate of Gautier's at the Collège Charlemagne and eventually one of the major collaborators of prolific novelist Alexandre Dumas *père* (1802–1870), but offers no suggestions as to the line's (never published?) source.

4. The mythological sylphs were minuscule, airborne elves of Celtic, Germanic, and Gallic tradition. Kindly toward humans, they were transparent and sweet smelling and able to become invisible or even to change into human form. The peris, their Oriental relatives, who acted as immortal messengers of the spirit, were not always so pleasant. Gautier collaborated with choreographer Jean Coralli (Peracini) (1779–1854) on the libretto for the popular ballet *La Péri*, in 1843, to music by (Johann-Friedrich-)Franz Burgmüller (1806–1874). It tells of the poet Sultan Achmet, who, in an opium-dream, falls in love with the Fairy Queen. We know that this would not be Gautier's only work inspired by the Orient. (See unnumbered note to "Sultan Mahmoud," from "Pièces diverses" in *Poésies nouvelles*, above.) Nor was it his only ballet libretto. (For his many writings on the dance, see Ivor Guest's collection of translations, *Gautier on Dance* [London: Dance Books, 1986].)

"The Luxembourg"

The Luxembourg is a well-known park in the middle of Paris, a favorite haunt of young children and young (and not-so-young) lovers.

Gautier's epigraph cites Joseph Delorme, the poetic alter ego of Charles-Augustin Sainte-Beuve (1804–1869), known primarily as the first major professional literary critic, author of weekly reviews in the *Globe* that were eventually collected in fifteen volumes as his *Causeries du lundi* (Paris: Garnier Frères, 1851–1862). After abandoning medical studies, he began his literary career, however, with two collections of poetry in the then-avant-garde Romantic vein: *Vie, poésies, et pensées de Joseph Delorme* (Paris: Dangle Frères, 1829) and *Les Consolations: poésies* (Paris: U. Canel, 1830). The line of verse chosen by Gautier is the second line of a poem in the former collection: "Toujours je la connus . . .":

Toujours je la connus pensive et sérieuse:
Enfant, dans les ébats de l'enfance joueuse.
Elle se mêlait peu, parlait déjà raison;
Et, quand ses jeunes sœurs couraient sur le gazon,
Elle était la première à leur rappeler l'heure . . .

There is no way of knowing if Gautier, in 1830—the original date of *Poésies*—was aware that "J. Delorme" was, in fact, Sainte-Beuve.

5. Sources do not definitely identify the level-headed young child in question.

"The Lane"

The text of the present poem dates from Gautier's republication in 1845 (see unnumbered note introducing *Premières Poésies*, above). It differs almost entirely from the original 1830 version, given by Jasinski in his introduction (*Poésies complètes*, 1:xx–xxi).

Le Livre des quatre Dames was the earliest work of medieval poet-moralist Alain Chartier. (See unnumbered note to "Elegy I," above.) Dating from around 1415 or 1416, it is a dialogue among four ladies, all of whom lost their lovers in France's stunning defeat at the hands of the English at the battle of Agincourt. The epigraph is taken from lines 149–51.

The second epigraph, from the pen of Romantic poet and playwright Alfred de Musset (1810–1857), is from scene V of his one-act closet drama *Les Marrons du feu*, in *Contes d'Espagne et d'Italie* (1830). It is spoken by the swaggering Rafael Garuci, explaining how he began his ill-fated liaison with the beautiful ballerina La Camargo:

Un beau soir, je ne sais comment se fit l'affaire,
La lune se levait cette nuit-là si claire,
Le vent était si doux, l'air de Rome est si pur:—
C'était un petit bois qui côtoyait le mur,
Un petit sentier vert,—je le pris . . .

One wonders how Gautier happened to hit upon the line for his epigraph. He could not have heard it on stage since the play was not performed in his lifetime. Is it reasonable to assume that it was so striking—even to an eighteen-year-old Romantic—that it stood out in a reading of the text as appropriate to his poem?

"*Nightmare*"

I cannot vouch for the authenticity—and, less, for the accuracy—of Gautier's "old Breton proverb." Nor can I offer a cogent reason for his choosing it especially, except, perhaps, from a desire—typical of the Romantic Jeunes-France cohort to which he belonged—to "épater le bourgeois" with a bit of esoteric exotica.

As for the second epigraph, also characteristic of early Romantic macabre inspiration, Gautier does not identify it. Neither I nor sources consulted can do so either, though I happily translate it.

"*Night Stroll*"

Musset's line is taken from the ninth (and last) quatrain of his poem "L'Andalouse," from his *Contes d'Espagne et d'Italie* (see unnumbered headnote to "The Lane," above):

> Allons, mon page, en embuscades!
> Allons! la belle nuit d'été!
> Je veux ce soir des sérénades
> A faire damner les alcades
> De Tolose au Guadalété.

Even this early in his career Gautier was much taken with everything Spanish. (See unnumbered headnote to "Inès de Las Sierras," from *Emaux et Camées*, above.) The similarity of this scenario and that of "Rondalla" is especially striking; and the physical description of Musset's "Andalouse" will echo in many later Gautier works. One example among many is "Carmen," in *Emaux et Camées*.

The reference to the lines by Victor Pavie is rather enigmatic. Pavie (1808–1886) was director of an important publishing house and champion of the early Romantics, many of whom were his close friends. A poet and *littérateur* himself, his published works date from no earlier than 1846, however, well after the composition of *Poésies*. Though he is not mentioned in Gautier's *Histoire du romantisme*, it is hard to believe that the two did not at least know one another, and Gautier may well have been offering him a bit of friendly tribute by citing his—unpublished?—lines in this epigraph.

"*Sonnet II*"

Peirol (or Peyrol[s]) was a Provençal (that is, Occitan) troubadour from Auvergne, born around 1160 and dying in the 1220s. Thirty-four rather traditional "courtly love" lyrics have been attributed to him, most of them *cansos* (songs) for some of which the melodies have been preserved. The one cited by Gautier—a typical piece of evidence of the Romantics' fascination with the Middle Ages in general and troubadour literature in particular—is from eight debate-poems, or *tensos*, a common Provençal genre of alternating stanzas, the debate here being between Peirol and Love. Curiously, the quoted lines differ from the usually cited version, but not enough to change the cliché. Again, one wonders at young Gautier's motivation for an epigraph in Occitan:

> Amors, tan vos ai servit,
> E nulhs pechatz no.us en pren,
> E vos sabetz quan petit
> N'ai avut de jauzimen.

Clément Marot (1496–1544) was a leading Renaissance poet, in and out of trouble with the Church, but usually protected by Marguerite, the sister of François I and eventually queen of Navarre. More graceful than his medieval predecessors and often more elegant than his contemporaries and followers, much of his verse has been characterized as "elegant badinage," though not without its more somber—and even devotional—elements. (See my *Lyrics of the French Renaissance: Marot, Du Bellay, Ronsard* [New Haven: Yale University Press, 2002; Chicago: University of Chicago Press, 2006].) The lines cited, in "modernized" spelling, are from his "Dialogue de deux amoureux," one of his *Opuscules:*

> Ne sçais-tu pas que je n'euz onc
> D'elle plaisir n'y un seul bien?

(See *Œuvres choisies de Clément Marot* [Paris: P. Didot l'Aîné, An X (1801)], 39.)

6. Jasinski (*Poésies complètes*, 1:xxii) explains, with no elaboration, that Gautier, at the time of writing, was apparently emaciated and sickly.

"The Captive Bird"

Gautier quotes from Number 43 of Marot's seventy rondeaux, "D'un délaissé de s'Amye":

> Tout à part soy est melancolieux
> Le tien servant, qui s'élongne des lieux
> Là où l'on veut chanter, danser, et rire:
> Seul en sa chambre il va ses pleurs escrire,
> Et n'est possible à lui de faire mieux.
> Car quand il pleut, et le soleil des Cieux
> Ne reluit point, tout homme est soucieux,
> Et toute beste en son creux se retire
> > Tout à part soy. . . .

The editor of an eighteenth-century collection of his works, *Œuvres de Clément Marot, valet-de-chambre de François I, Roy de France* (The Hague: P. Gosse & J. Neaulme, 1731), appends a quaint note, to the effect that Marot must have been inexperienced in love if he failed to realize that tears unseen by the lady serve no purpose. (See II, 173.)

Ever the eclectic epigrapher, the young Gautier quotes here from Byron's *Manfred* (1817), Act II, scene i, when the overreaching hero, punished for stealing the fruits from the tree of knowledge, proclaims his confidence in eventual vindication. Gautier will have occasion to evoke Manfred again, as well as other Byronic heroes. (See note 15, to "Study in Hands, II. Lacenaire," and note 31, to "Contralto," both from *Emaux et Camées*, above, and the unnumbered note to "Imitation of Byron," below.)

7. See note 8, to "The Blue Eyes of the Mountain," from *España*, above.

"Dream"

See unnumbered headnote to "Maiden Fair," above.

The forty-fifth rondeau of Marot, "De celluy, qui ne pense qu'en s'Amye" (see unnumbered headnote to "Sonnet II," above), from which these lines are taken, is generally quoted and presented somewhat differently:

> Toutes les nuicts je ne pense qu'en celle
> Qui ha le corps plus gent qu'une pucelle
> De quatorze ans . . .

(See my *Lyrics of the French Renaissance*, 38–39.)

"Autumn Thoughts"

Paying tribute to the Romantics' taste for the Provençal troubadours (see unnumbered headnote to "Sonnet II," above), Gautier cites four lines of the six-line first stanza of the "Son hivernous" (Winter Song)—not, incidentally, "Son autounous" (Autumn Song) as he erroneously states. The original is found in "Les Saisons," in Antoine Fabre d'Olivet's *Poésies occitaniques du XIIIe siècle* (Paris: Henrichs, an XI [1803]).

See unnumbered headnote to "Maiden Fair," above.

"Falseheartedness"

(Jean-)Antoine de Baïf (1532–1589), arguably the most erudite of the Pléiade poets, was steeped in classical learning and vast Renaissance culture, thanks in large part to the influence of his scholar-father Lazare de Baïf (1496–1547). Though best known for his attempt to reform French versification on the quantitative models of Latin and Greek, as well as suggested spelling reforms—neither of which innovations bore lasting fruit—he also produced much incidental poetry and several plays. The cited line is from his *Traduction complète des poésies de Catulle* (Paris: Crapelet, An XI [1805]), 2:98), suggesting that turnabout is fair play in sentimental infidelities:

> La volonté de l'ingrate est changée;
>   Change la tienne aussi;
> Comme de toy elle s'est étrangée,
>   Fay de l'étrange ainsi:
>   Après sa fuite

Ne fay poursuite:
S'elle ne t'ayme,
Fay-lui de mesme,
Sans vivre plus langoureux et transi.

"*To My Friend Auguste M*****"

See unnumbered headnote to "Maiden Fair," above.

Gautier quotes from the third of the forty quatrains of the sentimental ballad "The Hermit" by Oliver Goldsmith (1728–1774) but offers no explanation of its relevance to his friend Maquet. The ballad also appears in chapter 8 of Goldsmith's novel *The Vicar of Wakefield* (1766).

Whether intentionally or not, Gautier has succeeded in concealing the source of his lengthy quotation from *Le Vagabond*, which I translate nonetheless. Its moral tone hints at a second Goldsmith epigraph, and the text's French spelling indicates the eighteenth century. Even the title suggests Goldsmith's work *The Traveller* (1764). The only problem is that the latter is a poem, which, if it were the source—and it's not—Gautier would have cited in its original English verse and not troubled to translate into somewhat archaic French prose. Perhaps he felt that the passage was too well known to his readers to require identification. Unless, perhaps, he took pleasure in its obscurity.

"*Sonnet III*"

The "memento mori" topos is taken from the first quatrain of a sonnet entitled "Sur l'homme," by one Paul Du May, Seigneur de Saint-Aubin (1585–1645), quoted in Frédéric Lachèvre, *Voltaire mourant: enquête faite en 1778 sur les circonstances de sa dernière maladie, suivie de Le Catéchisme des libertins du XVIIe siècle: Les Quatrains du Déiste ou l'Anti-Bigot* (Paris: Honoré Champion, 1908), 176:

L'homme n'est rien qu'un mort, qui traîne sa carcasse,
L'homme n'est rien qu'un ver, qui de la terre naît,
L'homme n'est rien qu'un vent, qui soufflé un petit trait,
L'homme n'est rien en soy, qu'un songe qui se passé.

One assumes that Gautier had reasons for choosing this rather arcane quotation over many better known and more distinguished.

The Latin epigraph, translated literally as "put no faith in the face" (that is, don't judge a book by its cover), is taken from the *Satires* (II, vol. 8) of Juvenal, first and second centuries CE.

"*Imitation of Byron*"

See unnumbered headnote to "The Captive Bird," above. Given his Spanish predilections, one is not surprised at Gautier's choice of *Don Juan* (1817) for a Byronic imitation. His poem is loosely modeled after Canto I, 122–27, some stanzas—like the first—echoing the original more closely than others:

> We'll talk of that anon.—'Tis sweet to hear
>> At midnight on the blue and moonlit deep
> The song and oar of Adria's gondolier,
>> By distance mellow'd, o'er the waters sweep;
> 'Tis sweet to see the evening star appear;
>> 'Tis sweet to listen as the night-winds creep
> From leaf to leaf; 'tis sweet to view on high
> The rainbow, based on ocean, span the sky.

"*Sunset*"

The pithy epigraph is from the eighth of the thirty-two stanzas of Victor Hugo's "Le Pas d'armes du roi Jean," ballade number 12 in his *Odes et ballades* (1828):

> Notre-Dame!
> Que c'est beau!
> Sur mon âme
> De corbeau,
> Voudrais être
> Clerc ou prêtre
> Pour y mettre
> Mon tombeau!

Various stanzas of the ballad have been set to music by Emmanuel Chabrier (1841–1894) and Camille Saint-Saëns (1835–1921).

8. A bridge has spanned the Seine by Notre Dame since 1370, when a

wooden structure was erected between the Quai Saint-Bernard and the Ile Saint-Louis. When that bridge was destroyed by flood, it was replaced in 1620 by another, which lasted only a few years. The first "Pont de la Tournelle" was built in 1656 and is the one that Gautier would have known. It remained standing until, damaged by flood in 1910, it was eventually torn down. The present bridge of that name was built between 1924 and 1928.

9. The "vieille cité" refers to the Ile de la Cité, the larger of the two natural islands in the middle of the Seine. It has been the spiritual and judicial center of the capital since Julius Caesar conquered its early Celtic inhabitants, the Parisii, in 52 BCE. The boat-like shape of the island, frequently noted for centuries, explains Gautier's water imagery at the end of the poem.

"Avowal"

This poem and the three following were published in a group of twenty dated 1829–1832 added to the original collection *Poésies*, preceding "Albertus" (see unnumbered note introducing *Premières Poésies*, above), and included in Jasinski (*Poésies complètes*, 1:81–126).

Perhaps with a certain proprietary pride, Gautier chose to introduce his love poem with a passage from a baroque poet whom he is said to have rediscovered. François Scalion de Virbluneau (1560?–1640?) was the author of the *Loyales et pudiques amours* of 1599. As for the Madame de Boufflers to whom his poem is dedicated, my attempts to identify her specifically have been fruitless. The most I can say is that she must certainly have been at least a collateral ancestor of a number of prominent eighteenth-century ladies of that name, among them the celebrated beauty and woman of many talents Marie Françoise Catherine de Beauvau-Craon, marquise de Boufflers (1711–1787), as well as many others.

"Sonnet VII"

The cynicism and disillusion with the broken promises of the July Monarchy (1824–1830) that Gautier voices in his poem are evident as well in the metaphor by Nerval (see note 133, to "The Castle of Memory," from *Emaux et Camées*, above) that serves as an epigraph. It is from the last stanza of "En avant marche" of 1831, one of Nerval's youthful Napoleonic "Elégies nationales et satires politiques," bitter and antiroyalist in the extreme:

> Oh! Vers de grands combats, de nobles entreprises,
>   Quand pourront les vents l'emporter,
> Ce drapeau conquérant, qui s'ennuie à flotter
>   Sur des palais et des églises!
> Liberté, l'air des camps aurait bientôt reteint
>   Ta robe, qui fut rouge et bleue . . .
> Liberté de juillet! Femme au buste divin,
>   Et dont le corps finit en queue!

(See *Œuvres complètes de Gérard de Nerval* [Paris: Calmann Lévy, 1877], 4:174.) It is not insignificant that Gautier wrote a brief preface in praise of his friend's "âme pure et patriotique" in undertaking a subject as vast as "la France malheureuse et trahie," despite his tender years. Nerval was only sixteen when he began writing these verses, so unlike the often abstruse Symbolism of his maturity.

The quotation from Canto III of Dante's *Inferno* is from lines 46–48, describing the damned "who have no hope of death, but who, so debased, are envious of every other lot":

> Questi non hanno speranza di morte,
> e la lor cieca vita è tanto bassa
> che 'nvidiosi son d'ogne altra sorte.

10. Gautier avoids falling into a common mistranslation by abbreviating in French the medieval Tuscan inscription over the gates of hell, *Lasciate ogne speranza, voi ch'intrate*—"Abandon all hope, ye who enter here," often mistranslated in English as "Abandon hope, all ye . . ."

11. The restored prestige of the Church under the reign of Charles X, the last of the Bourbons, was characteristic of the July Monarchy, and was looked upon with suspicion by the bourgeoisie. That obvious antireligious, antiroyalist antipathy caused this poem to be suppressed in 1845. (See Jasinski, *Les années romantiques*, 80–81.)

"*Debauch*"

The Huguenot poet Guillaume de Salluste Du Bartas (1544–1590), of essentially religious inspiration, is known especially for his epic, *La Sepmaine; ou, Creation du monde* (1578), an influential history of mankind in verse. Translated into many languages, it is said to have inspired Milton's *Paradise Lost*. The line cited by Gautier is from "Les Trophées," in Du Bartas' *Œuvres Poétiques*, posthumous edition (Rouen: Pierre Calles, 1610), 480:

> O Sepulchre blanchi (dit le sacré Nathan)
> Tu as Dieu dans la bouche, & dans le cœur Satan,
> Tu blasmes en autruy le vice où tu t'enfonces,
> Lasche, sans y penser contre toy tu prononces.

The "whited sepulcher" metaphor, referring to the Pharisees, is from Matthew 23:27.

"*The Bengali*"

The bird in question is a type of beautiful African finch belonging to the Ploceidae, often referred to as a "weaverbird" because of its elaborate nests. As its name implies, it was originally thought to come from Bengal. I keep Gautier's title intact to preserve his exotic intent.

The bengali is only one of the many exotica—flora and fauna—intentionally cited by Jacques-Henri Bernardin de Saint-Pierre (1737–1814) in his immensely popular and influential Rousseau-inspired novel *Paul et Virginie* (1787), set in the "natural" climes of the Indian Ocean, as proof of the basic goodness of man untrammeled by civilization.

According to Jasinski (*Poésies complètes*, 1:xxxiv), the four-line epigraph is taken from the poetry of Louise Arbey, a Creole poet of Gautier's acquaintance, who also inspired his poem "Ce monde-ci et l'autre," of 1833, from his *Poésies diverses*. (See F. W. Leakey, *Baudelaire and Nature* [Manchester: The University Press, 1969], 42.) Jasinski (*Les années romantiques*, 99) vouches for the existence of the lady—though with a slightly different spelling: "Il plaint la jeune créole, oiseau dépaysé sous nos cieux incléments: la jeune créole a existé. Elle s'appelait Louise Arbé, et elle était poète. Des vers s'échangeront encore avant que l'élégiaque et frileux *bengali* ne retourne aux pays du soleil."